A
Life Worth
Living

A LIFE WORTH LIVING

The Autobiography of Lady Colin Campbell

LITTLE, BROWN AND COMPANY

A *Little, Brown* Book

First published in Great Britain in 1997
by Little, Brown and Company

Copyright © 1997 by Lady Colin Campbell

The moral right of the author has been asserted.

A CIP catalogue record for this book
is available from the British Library.

ISBN 0 316 87850 2

Typeset by M Rules in Palatino
Printed and bound in Great Britain by
Clays Ltd, St Ives, plc.

Little, Brown and Company (UK)
Brettenham House
Lancaster Place
London WC2E 7EN

This book is dedicated to my beloved sons,
Dima and Mischa

Acknowledgements

By the very nature of this work being an auto-biography, many of the people to whom I am indebted for the love, thoughtfulness, kindness and consideration they have shown me over the years, are mentioned in the forthcoming pages. To them, and to those whose names have not been mentioned for one reason or another, I wish to say a massive thank you.

To Sara Fisher, my agent at A M Heath & Co Ltd., and to Barbara Boote, my editor at Little, Brown, who do not appear by name, I also would like to express my appreciation for their support and encouragement.

1

When I was growing up, I could not understand why people always described my family as exotic. To me, they seemed perfectly ordinary. It was only when I was well into my thirties, and had a wide cross-section of people to use as a point of comparison, that I finally saw how truly unusual my antecedents were.

The family into which I was born, in St Andrew, Jamaica, in 1949, was one of Lebanon's better-known Christian families. Phoenician in origin, Christian since the sixth century AD, until the eighteenth century the Ziadies were Maronites, the only branch of the Catholic Church which owes it devotion to a national saint and celebrates the Mass in Christ's native tongue: Aramaic. The family's exoticism is inextricably tied up with its roots. Being Arabic, even the name itself has six different but equally correct Romance spellings, depending upon which transcription you prefer. Originally, we came from Kesselwan. Many of my relatives still live there, or in nearby Jounieh, including the present head, Camille, the Christian senator for East Beirut.

Towards the end of the eighteenth century, an ancestor left Kesselwan and moved to Choueifat. In those days, that town, which is now part of Ras (greater) Beirut, and which became

famous during the Civil War as the site from which the
Muslims bombarded Beirut Airport, was an important centre
for the Silk Route. Between the eighteenth and early twenti-
eth centuries, Choueifat was of greater significance than
Beirut, which became Lebanon's capital only after the
Ottoman Empire collapsed at the end of the First World War.

The key to why my-many-times-great-grandfather moved
to Choueifat lies in the history of the town. Commerce was
only one of the reasons for its ascendancy. The centre of the
Greek and Russian Orthodox Churches in a country where
religion and politics were inextricable, Choueifat was the
place from which Imperial Russia attempted to acquire an
outlet to the Mediterranean. This the Russians hoped to
accomplish by strengthening links with the Orthodox community, the long-term objective being to supplant the
Ottomans and turn Lebanon, or at least a part of it, into a
Russian territory. So deeply entrenched did Russian influence in the area become that it eventually resulted in the
Crimean War of 1854–58, in which Britain and France joined
the Ottoman Empire to block Russian ambitions.

Politics and religion played their part in my family's prosperity and ultimately in their exile. It was when my
great-etc.-grandfather moved to Choueifat that our branch of
the Ziadie family broke with the Maronites. Family legend
has it that he and the brother who moved with him were
compelled to do so because of involvement in a blood feud,
but I believe that something much less glamorous was
responsible: ambition. By that time the Ottomans had
embarked upon a policy of stamping out the culture and
language of the Lebanese, of which the Maronites were perceived as the guardians, and any Maronite who wished to
enjoy the many benefits of life under the Ottomans would
surely have realised that he stood a better chance of doing so
by moving away from a bastion of Lebanese heritage such as
Kesselwan to somewhere like Choueifat. Here, Muslims and
Orthodox Christians mixed more freely; religion, though
important, took a back seat to commerce; Turkish authority
was not so openly challenged; and there were even

Lebanese, such as the princely house of Arslan, who were loyal to the Ottoman cause. Whatever the reason for the Ziadie brothers' move from Kesselwan, they flourished. Soon they were well established, with comfortable houses and landed estates surrounding Choueifat. The change in religion proved useful, too, for one of their sons, the paterfamilias of the Ziadies of Choueifat, was created a Count of the Russian Empire by the Czar.

The family's escape from the effects of religious unpopularity proved temporary, however. As the nineteenth century wore on and the European powers sought to lay down areas of influence within the Middle East, the Ottomans tightened the vice against those they regarded as traitors to their cause. Primary among these were the Christians, my family included. Nationalism was now a geopolitical fact of life. Both the Ottoman and Austro– Hungarian empires were involved in a literal fight to the death to keep the various nationalities under their mantles. Whenever the Ottomans wished to raise money or merely assert their authority, they would level punitive taxes against the subjugated nationalities such as the Lebanese. Christian and Muslim alike were beginning to suffer, and a level of co-operation grew up between all the religions. In each Ziadie house in Choueifat there was a large storage room for food beneath the kitchen. Beyond that was a secret room big enough to hide young men evading conscription into the Ottoman army, or wanted for crimes such as the desire to practise Christianity without fear of recrimination.

Between 1860 and 1890, the situation worsened to such an extent that my grandfather, George Ferris Ziadie, and his four brothers decided they would have to leave. This was a momentous and painful decision: not only would they be abandoning a prosperous life – my grandfather, for instance, was an architect with a substantial practice that took him to the far corners of the Ottoman Empire – but also one of the most beautiful countries on earth (the Garden of Eden was reputedly situated in Lebanon). Combining rugged mountains with the splendour of a dramatic Mediterranean coastline, in the winter it is one of the few places where it is possible to swim in the sea an hour after walking in three feet of snow in the Lebanese mountains, home of the biblical cedars. Moreover, the brothers would be leaving behind all the sisters, aunts, uncles and cousins who form such an integral part of Mediterranean family life.

The first to depart was Tewfik, who, according to family legend, was bound for America, but grew bored after making his way across Europe and over the Atlantic and decided to break his journey in Jamaica, only a few days' journey away from his destination. Jamaica was, in many ways, an inspired choice. It is more or less the same size as Lebanon, has a similar climate (albeit with no winter), and a geographical echo of his homeland in the lush Caribbean coastline and the magnificent Blue Mountains which divide the island in two. Exultant to have found a safe country so reminiscent of his own, Tewfik sent word to his brothers, George, Isaac, Adeeb and Alfred, who followed him there.

Life cannot have been easy for the emigrés. They spoke very little English and now had to eke out their living. But flowing in their veins was the blood of the Phoenicians, the creators of the concept of trade and the founders of the first alphabet and mathematics. Resourcefully looking around them, Grandpa Ziadie and his brothers saw a gap in the market. No one in business was catering for the average Jamaican black person: all trade was being conducted, largely by the Jewish community, for the white oligarchy or for the agricultural sector, the plantocracy. My grandfather and his brothers set themselves up as dry-goods merchants, opening shops in the capital, Kingston, which served the black people exclusively. Success was immediate, even if large profits were not – they operated on small margins. But the market was large enough to comfortably accommodate the Ziadies and the other Lebanese families who fled to Jamaica at around the same time, some from Choueifat itself. By the time I was born, in 1949, virtually every shop and manufacturing enterprise in the country was owned by members of the Lebanese community. They were the single richest group in the country, and were perceived by the man in the street as wealthy beyond the dreams of avarice.

This was a fallacy. Although wealthy by ordinary standards, we were hardly rich by the criteria of the truly rich, people like the Rockefellers or the Mellons. None of us, for instance, had a yacht that could sleep twenty, even if some of the family did have ocean-going boats and private planes that could seat up to four. What we did have was a comfortable way of life: ambassadorial-style houses, immaculate grounds, servants, tennis or badminton courts, swimming pools, racehorses. My father, his brothers, and most of their first cousins owned enough racehorses to make us the premier racing family in the land. Several of the cousins had branched out into training as well, so no race meeting ever took place without several Ziadie horses running. This, together with the ever-present family name above the shops, gave us a high profile.

Six feet tall, with raven-black hair, hazel eyes and the pale skin of his Russian grandmother, my father, Michael George Ferris Ziadie, was devastatingly attractive to women. Handsome in the Cary Grant mould, he was also passionate, honourable and ostensibly easy-going. Beneath that veneer, however, lay a volatile and sensitive perfectionist who was a soft touch for any hard-luck story. He stuttered badly, with the result that he was a man of few words, but he was an omnivorous reader and highly intelligent, and whatever he did say was worth hearing. Perhaps his most striking attribute was his complete naturalness. Like many gentlemen of the old school, he treated princes and paupers with absolute uniformity, and was impressed by nothing but character.

When my father was twenty-six, he met my mother. Gloria Dey Smedmore was fifteen at the time of that first meeting. Sixty-two years later, he reminisced, 'I fell in love with your mother the first time I saw her. Her uncle, John Burke, introduced us. She was young, but she was no little girl. She was a beautiful young woman, and very, very entertaining. She captivated me totally with her personality. I loved her then, and I love her now.' Red-haired and brown-eyed, Gloria was one of those lucky girls who had long, slim legs and a slender build crowned with a full bosom.

My mother was related to four of Jamaica's oldest families, and to say merely that she was out of the top drawer would not convey the quality of her breeding. Her father was Lucius Dey Smedmore, a gentleman of such fine social sensibilities that the word snob would not begin to describe the niceties by which he lived. I loved my grandfather and his brothers and sisters, but I must confess I could never understand why they were generally acknowledged as social eminents. The whole scenario struck me as typical English hogwash: assert that you're great for long enough, and everyone will believe it. It seemed to me as if they had never had anything to recommend them except for impeccable manners and an outstanding belief in their own superiority. They had never had a huge amount of money, even before my great-grandfather somehow allowed a solicitor to fleece him of what he did have. They owned no large estates, had no great titles, occupied no significant political positions. They did own a magnificent townhouse in Kingston, which was built, Roman-style, around a courtyard garden – the dining room alone was about forty feet long, and stuffed full of the finest antique furniture – but their most outstanding feature, aside from their niceness, was their position in society.

My maternal grandmother, May Burke, on the other hand, came from a genuinely aristocratic background, which even her disparaging grandchildren acknowledged. On her father's side she was descended from the earls of Mayo, an Anglo-Irish family which gave India its first viceroy. On her mother's side, Grandma was a member of two of the western world's most eminent Sephardic families: the De Passes and the Lindos. (It was at the house of a distant cousin of mine, Commander Robert de Pass, that the Prince of Wales met the adult Lady Diana Spencer, who was a good friend of his son Philip.) The Jews were the true aristocrats of Jamaica, for they were the first settlers, having been induced by the

Inquisition to leave Spain and Portugal – in the early six-
teenth century, Jews were given three options: convert,
emigrate, or burn. Only in the West Indies were they free to
practise their religion, with the result that Jamaica has the
oldest colony of Jews in the western world. Moreover, the
Jewish community has remained consistently prosperous
throughout the centuries, and they are so highly regarded
that anti-Semitism is not an intelligible concept to Jamaicans.

After three years' courtship, my father asked my grandfather for my mother's hand in marriage. Although
Grandpa gave his consent, he was disappointed that
Mummy wanted to marry 'a Syrian', and incited his brother
Julian to snub Daddy when the engagement was
announced. Rather than shake his hand, Uncle Julian turned
on his heels and walked away. To his credit, Daddy never let
such pettiness bother him, nor did he hold it against either
brother. My grandmother, however, had no misgivings
about the match. As she was partly Jewish herself, and had
a healthy respect for 'a handsome devil' and a good bank
balance, she willingly gave her consent with the words she
would never live down: 'If you wanted to marry a horse's
head, that would be fine by me, as long as you loved him.'

Religion now became an issue. Since the move to Jamaica,
where there was no Greek or Russian Orthodox Church, the
Ziadies had reverted to their original religion, Catholicism,
and would sooner have died than gone against any of the
Church's teachings (adultery, fornication and gambling
excepted). The Smedmores, meanwhile, were one of the
staunchest Anglican families in the land, and my grandfather was the latest in a long line of Smedmores to sit on the
governing body of the nation's established Church. It would
have been as unthinkable for Mummy to convert as for
Daddy to marry outside the faith, so a compromise was
reached. They married in the Roman Catholic Cathedral,
Mummy having signed a document undertaking to bring
up all their children as Catholics.

Within fifteen months, my brother, Michael Anthony
Ziadie, was born. A year and nine months later, what should

have been a bundle of joy, but turned out instead to be a load of trouble, arrived on the scene.

To say that my birth was a mixed blessing would be to stretch the truth to breaking point. I was a sickly baby who hovered between this and the afterlife for several months. But that was the least of the problems, for I was born with a cosmetic malformation which led to me being registered as a boy, and given the names George William. The reason why I was not registered as a girl is simple. No one knew I was one, because I was born with fused labiae and a deformed clitoris. As anyone who is familiar with infants knows, the genitalia of newborn babies are out of proportion to the rest of their bodies. This phenomenon is, presumably, nature's way of hitting you in the face with the sex of your child. But nature is not an exact science, and mistakes do occur.

In 1949 there were no such things as chromosome or ketosteroid tests. Guesswork and good intentions were all anyone had to go by. The doctors' normal procedure when presented with children with genital disabilities was to endow the infant with the masculine gender. This made sense for several reasons. There was the general acceptance that boys counted for more than girls; there was also a belief among the medical profession that gender was not an absolute determined at conception, but a social role in which an individual could be conditioned to perform. Most importantly, however, the surgical advances which enabled doctors to correct nature's mistakes still lay in the future. So there was no way of adequately correcting nature's mistakes. By declaring such a child to be a boy, you were at least stacking the odds in its favour.

This was especially true in a family such as ours. Although none of the men of my father's generation would have regarded himself as a male chauvinist, they did inhabit a world where a man's role had greater scope than a woman's. Men could more or less do as they pleased, as long as they showed respect for their wives, sisters and parents by being discreet. Women, on the other hand, were governed by a whole different set of rules. Indeed, until my father's generation, wives ceased to be known by their own names when they married. As a result, Granny was known as Aunt George rather than Aunt Esmine to her nieces and nephews, and to this day I do not know the name of my Great-Uncle Adeeb's wife, for she was always Aunt Deeb to us. So it is easy to see how I became saddled with the wrong gender. It is futile to regret the circumstances of one's birth, or try to apportion blame, and I am pleased that that is one trap I have never been tempted to fall into. Although my teenage years would prove to be anything but a picnic, my childhood was, to all intents and purposes, magical.

Like most Mediterraneans, my family loved children and were good with them. For the Ziadies and the Burkes, and to a lesser extent the Smedmores, life's boundaries were determined by the vast network of brothers, sisters, aunts, uncles, cousins and in-laws who comprised the family. As my father was one of ten children, and my mother, though one of only two, was the granddaughter of families of nine and fifteen respectively, they could easily have gone for months, if they chose, without seeing anyone else. However, they were all highly sociable, so in fact they had an army of friends. Mummy in particular was a dedicated socialite. She was always shooting from party to party, reception to reception, game of chance to game of chance. She was known for her beauty and glamour, and was invariably magnificently dressed in the latest couture creations, as were all self-respecting ladies in the 1950s. She had a vivacious personality, and was articulate and talkative, a perfect foil to Daddy's inability to speak without stammering. Because she was witty and had an irreverent sense of humour, people found her entertaining. Her best friend was Vida MacMillan, whose husband Dudley owned the State Theatre and frequently brought over artists of the calibre of Arthur Rubenstein, Richard Tauber and Nat 'King' Cole. Another great friend was the Countess Violetta de Barovier-Riel, a society columnist who constantly featured Mummy in her newspaper column. So my parents' social life was lived out against a background of household names, which meant that we children grew up undaunted by fame or fortune. Indeed, in my earliest memories life was one long party, frequently conducted at my parents' house, but adjourned, from time to time, to the houses of my Aunts Marjorie Juliette, and Doris, Uncle Salman (called Solomon in Jamaica) and his daughter, my adored god-mother, Cissy, cousins Millard and Helen Ziadie, and such family friends such as the MacMillans, Desnoes (of Desnoes & Geddes Red Stripe beer fame) and Seagas, who would later give Jamaica its pro-American prime minister, Edward Seaga. Whenever the adults grew tired of being in the house, the party transferred to the swimming pool, the beach, tennis or badminton court, or to one of the cays which lie off the southern shore of the island.

About the only activity from which we children were barred were the games of chance. The Ziadies and the Seagas, their firmest friends, were all assiduous gamblers, and several times a week there would be poker and other card games. I used to love it when the games were held at our house. The air was invariably charged with excitement, and just listening to the adults spending the evening in good-natured banter was a pleasure, even though it some-times deteriorated into something less agreeable. Then there would be scenes the like of which I have only ever seen else-where on a stage. Decks of cards and chips would fly with the invective across the front verandah before some relation or friend stormed out, vowing never to speak again to the person with whom he had rowed. Needless to say, no one ever took such arguments seriously, and by the following day all would be forgotten.

If the adults were allowed to grandstand, we children were expected to be well behaved at all times. Although we were usually in evidence, it was on the strict understanding that we conducted ourselves like intelligent and civilised human beings. We were never allowed to get away with any nonsense, and childish antics were promptly punished with banishment. The result was that we were self-possessed from an early age, and could be taken to places where other children seldom went, such as the races. I remember being taken to race meetings at Knutsford Park Racecourse from the age of four, and by the time I was twelve, I was leading in Daddy's horse Samson when it won.

From the age of around six, we were allowed to ride our bicycles far afield, for there were no such things as crimes against children, and the murders which would become an all-too-frequent occurrence in the 1960s were still unthinkable. We spent our summers on the north coast in a beach house, and throughout the rest of the year, my brother Mickey, sisters Sharman (born 1951) and Margaret (born 1955) and I accompanied our parents most weekends on picnics to the beach or to Morgan's Harbour, an exclusive beach club owned by the English baronet Sir Anthony Jenkinson. I took for granted the whiteness of the sand, the clarity of the sea, the deep green of the foliage, the depth of the forests, the splendour of the mountains, and the rich and varied colours of the omnipresent flowers. Never once did it occur to me that I was privileged to be a part of this enchanted environment, and that we were enjoying a beauty which was denied to a great many people.

Idyllic though it was, our lifestyle did lead to some tragedies, notably the murder of my cousin Tony. A tall, handsome rugby fanatic, Tony had a girlfriend who was trapped in Cuba by the Castro Revolution of 1959. His father used his influence and money to buy her out of the country via the good offices of the Swiss, and the Cuban firecracker finally came to Jamaica in 1962. Everyone was so happy for her and Tony.

But within weeks Tony, still in his mid-twenties, was dead. At first everyone thought he had died of natural causes. It was only when a priest to whom the girl had confessed to murder broke the anonymity of the confessional and told his father that we discovered what had really happened. Carmencita, Teresita, Isabelita, or whatever she called herself, had opened up the capsules which Tony had to take for his inflamed rugger knee, poured out the contents and replaced them with ground glass. It did not take her very long to feed him sufficient capsules to lacerate his entire insides. He haemorrhaged to death in days.

No one in the family could understand why she had killed him. It turned out that when she arrived in Jamaica, she had discovered that he had been seeing another girl while she had been trapped in Cuba, but now, over thirty years later, I still find her actions as inexplicable as I did then. One might have understood it if he had intended to dump her, but he had prevailed upon his father to do what was virtually impossible in those days, and have Castro sanction her release. The priest, too, had found her conduct both unbelievable and frightening. He was terrified she might turn her murderous instincts to the other members of Tony's family, which was why he had broken her confidence.

My great-uncle, respecting the delicacy of the priest's position put the murderer on the next plane out of Jamaica with the warning that he would turn her over to the police if she ever set foot in Jamaica again. She never did.

There were others, too, who got away with murder. The most notorious case involved a socialite who was born with one of the most famous names in the country and married another. She made the fatal mistake of blowing out her lover's brains while his head was in her lap. The bullet penetrated her own hip, exposing the incredulity of her claim that they had been shot by a thief. Her poor husband, who was one of the nicest men you could meet, had to pay a fortune to keep the mother of his children away from the courts – and the gallows, for capital crimes carry a mandatory death sentence in Jamaica.

Exposure to all sides of life from such an early age gave me a quality I would sorely need later on: equanimity. It also gave me an understanding of how important it is to keep things in proportion, and how vital compassion is. Before independence, in the days when Jamaica was undoubtedly run for the convenience of the establishment, it was plain to anyone who wished to see it that it is much easier to get people to behave well if they have to accept the consequences of their actions. Although there was only one law, it must be said that there were two applications: one for the haves and the other for the have-nots. The result was that the masses seldom kicked over the traces the way some of the haves did.

Indeed, Jamaica in the 1950s was as close to paradise on earth as you could get – for those who had the means to enjoy it. A British colony, it was secure and relatively crime-free, warm and sunny. Regarded then as one of the most glamorous places in the world, the large network of resident families which formed the establishment (numbering a few thousand at least), were augmented by several resident expatriates such as Noël Coward, Ian Fleming and Errol Flynn, and a plethora of American multimillionaires and European aristocrats – Bill Paley of CBS, the Duke of Marlborough, Baron Heini Thyssen-Bornemisza, for example – who wintered there every year in the houses they owned. Between January and March of any year, the Jamaican beaches like Round Hill or Tryall were dotted with the world's richest, grandest and most successful people.

Few Jamaican-born socialites felt disadvantaged by the influx of famous foreign visitors. Drawing rooms are level playing fields, and Jamaicans, moreover, had enough money and history to hold their own anywhere. Prior to the abolition of slavery in 1834, the island had been the most important colony in the British Empire and had laid the foundations for many of the great British fortunes, such as the house of Lascelles (whose head is the present Earl of Harewood, grandson of King George V and first cousin of the Queen). So rich was eighteenth-century Jamaica that the description of mad Mrs Rochester in *Jane Eyre* – 'Jamaican heiress' – conjured up an image that 'Greek shipping heiress' or 'computer heiress' would evoke in us today. So if Jamaicans were proud of their country and their heritage, they had reason to be. What no one saw at the time, however, was how very near the edge of the abyss the country actually was. So stable did it seem, especially in comparison to postwar Britain, that renowned businessmen such as the taipan of Jardine Matheson, Sir Jock Buchanan-Jardine, rushed to invest in Jamaica. But the halcyon days were rapidly drawing to a close; indeed, they would barely outlive the decade.

The weather and ideal environment aside, what made Jamaica such a pleasure to live in was the availability of labour. Everyone had an army of servants. In our household alone there were eight. Even if all the ladies perpetually complained about how difficult it was to get good service, and in most households the turnover of staff was high, it was the servants who made possible the graciousness which was a feature of everyday life. For us children, they were also a source of continuous warmth, care and affection.

Most black Jamaicans are superb with children. Even if this housemaid or that undergardener was hopeless at his or her job, they were usually delightful to us. George, our chauffeur, was my great favourite, because he allowed me to 'drive' the car sitting on his lap. We always had two nannies, but I have no recollection of any of the many individuals who trooped in and out, for that position above all was in a constant state of flux. What I do remember, though, is the wrench each time we lost a servant of whom we had grown fond, and how one always resolved not to grow as fond of her replacement in case she went as well. Of course, we inevitably warmed to the newcomer as time wore on, and, equally inevitably, she too would depart. At least we learned at an early age how transient life can be.

Despite my happiness I was of course aware from an early age that the gender I had been assigned was incorrect. But I was brought up to believe that the grown-ups knew best, and, trusting them as I did, I did not question my predicament; I simply accepted it. Faith is a great comfort, and a wonderful preservative against anguish, and while it did not protect me from moments of discomfort when I had to dress in a manner that I found discomfiting, it did help me to sail through life with a minimum of questioning. And as luck would have it, I could not have chosen a better place to live with my disadvantage. In a tropical country both boys

and girls dress in shorts for much of the time and this uniformity diminished, rather than heightened, the differences
between the genders. Something else that helped was the
way the average Jamaican spoke. A peculiarity of their
dialect, which must stem from their African antecedents,
was that they invariably used the masculine gender when
referring to either sex. While this was not true of the better-
educated Jamaicans, so much of my time was spent around
the servants that for long periods I was spoken to like other
girls, which reduced my discomfort.

Nor could I have chosen a better family. My mother in
particular handled the situation with noteworthy élan.
Mummy took the view that I should be allowed to develop
naturally, so when I displayed an interest in dolls at about
two or three, I was given them. This allowed a talent to
emerge: by the age of four, I was hand-stitching the most
elaborate ballgowns for my dolls, despite never having been
taught to sew, or indeed to cut out dresses. Daddy's cousin
J.W. Ziadie's wife Eily took me in hand and let me use her
sewing machine. Thereafter, some of my happiest days were
spent with Aunt Eily, busily pumping away on her Singer.

By contrast, my younger sister Sharman was a tomboy
who was always climbing trees with our brother Mickey, or
competing in bicycle races with him and our neighbours,
Michael and Peter Lopez, while I used to love throwing
dolls' tea parties, and had one doll that got married so many
times she was renamed Zsa-Zsa. No one restrained Sharman
any more than they inhibited me.

Because gender is of less interest when one is a child than
it will ever be throughout the rest of one's life, and because
my mother allowed me to express my true gender, I grew
into the sort of person nature intended. This would prove
crucial, and I have always been grateful that this one tree
was left alone to sprout its branches and leaves, rather than
twisted into a shape which would thereafter have been disfiguring to my personality.

Yet I remained sufficiently aware that something profound was lacking to wonder why the grown-ups said that

childhood was the best time of your life. I knew that could not be true, and I could not wait to leave the years of dependency behind. Had I known what anguish lay in store for me, I have no doubt I would not have had the will to survive. The future, however, remained mercifully unseen.

2

Puberty, with all its attendant uncertainties and perplexities, is a difficult time for any adolescent, but without exaggeration, mine was like a glimpse into the bowels of hell. I can remember, as if it were a minute ago, the very moment when the harsh light of reality hit what had been a dark and unseen pit. My brother Mickey, who was fourteen years old, planned to bring a friend by the name of David Boxer home for tea after school the following afternoon. 'I do hope you'll try to act as if you're normal,' he said. 'When you were younger your girlishness was cute. But frankly, Georgie, now it's nothing but an embarrassment.'

To say that I was shocked doesn't begin to convey the way I felt. In a split second, Mickey had brought the great unspoken out into the open, a part of my own personal landscape which had remained unexplored for the twelve years of my life. I made no comment, but that night I went to bed and prayed, as I had never prayed before, for God to rescue me. I could not understand how I, a girl, had been trapped in a boy's identity, and while I knew there had to be a good reason for it, that only made matters worse, for I was afraid of bringing up the subject with my parents lest it seemed that I was questioning their authority.

The next afternoon, when Mickey and David arrived home for tea, I made myself scarce. Always quick to take a hint, and sensitive to others' comfort as well as my own, I had no desire to impose myself on anyone. But the fact that my only brother found me an embarrassment was a stiff truth to absorb.

What Mickey did not know was that I was already an embarrassment to myself. From my very first day at St George's College, the Jesuit seminary which was my father's alma mater and to which I was sent as a day student at the age of eleven, I had been subjected to a barrage of verbal abuse by a vociferous section of the less well-off students. The finest Catholic boys' school in the country, St George's was a grant-aided school with a majority of have-nots and a few very Catholic haves. In 1961, the gulf between them and us was so great as to be unbridgeable, and envy doubtless increased the bullies' enjoyment of the abuse they hurled. Yet unquestionably, had I been a poor black instead of a member of a well-known white family, I would have been given an even harder time, probably being beaten black and blue on a regular basis. But the unwritten rule of society, that the have-nots never, ever touched the haves, not even in gratitude or supplication, was understood by one and all.

Nevertheless I lived in fear. Each day, as shouts of 'Gal', 'White gal', 'Pussy', 'Boy-gal' and other primitive offerings rained down upon me as I walked from the gate where Daddy dropped me off to my classroom, I wondered if the taboo of untouchability was strong enough to hold. I was only too aware that it would take only one idiot to stray into forbidden territory for the verbal assaults to turn physical. And thirty or forty years ago, children who were bullied were expected to put up with it, for the sin of squealing was far greater than that of bullying. Children who 'told' on others would be branded 'sneaks' and have double the abuse meted out to them once the dust had settled. Nor was there any question that a bully would be expelled for anything short of killing a child, or disfiguring it for life.

I had already had a taste of bullying at my first school, run by the Misses Livingston, at the hands of Edgar Munn, whose father owned all the yellow cabs in Jamaica. During breaks he would sneak up on me from nowhere, hit or pinch me, and disappear, laughing gleefully. There was a gully adjoining the grounds, and if ever I made the mistake of going too close to it, he would bolt across the grass and push me in. As I was delicately built, and he had the trunk of a rhinoceros and the hide of an ox, it was no contest. With hindsight, I can see that an added inducement to Edgar Munn was the fact that I never fought back. Had I done so, he would have had a harder time getting away with it, if only because Miss Doris or Miss Elsie Livingston would have found out and punished us both for fighting. And experience has taught me subsequently that no bully likes taking his own medicine. As it was, I finally adopted the only defence open to me: I hid from him.

Edgar Munn aside, I was never mistreated by anyone until I went to St George's. And I always had friends at school, all but two of whom came from the same social set as me. The first exception was John Thompson, a black boy whose father was a civil servant and solidly middle class. My parents were not colour prejudiced in the slightest, unlike many other Jamaicans of their vintage, and they approved of the friendship on the grounds that John was a very nice person from a respectable family. That friendship fizzled out when we were sent to different forms at the end of our first year. My relationship with Audley, a Chinese boy, was frowned upon from the outset, however. His parents owned a grocery store in a poor area of Kingston, and they lived above the shop, although they were in the process of moving uptown to one of the housing developments for the emerging middle classes. This cut no ice with my Smedmore grandfather when I asked Mummy for permission to bring him home for tea. 'Everyone may be nice, but not everyone is your social equal,' Grandpa said. 'You must always be kind to people, but you cannot associate with everyone.' When I argued that I saw no reason why Audley should be forbidden to visit when John was not, I received my first lesson in the class differences that were so embedded in the British Empire. There was a world of difference between the emergent and established members of the middle classes, and while the *ancien regime* like the Smedmores found the former acceptable, they were not prepared to tolerate the latter.

My friendship with Audley also petered out once we were put in separate forms, but not before he became the unwitting catalyst in the breakdown of my relationship with my father. The brightest boy in the school, Audley invariably came first while I came second, much to my father's fury. Daddy had always come first, and took pride in the fact that I was living up to the family reputation for brains. He expected me to fulfil what he saw as my potential, and took it into his head that I was not studying hard enough. It never occurred to him that Audley just might be brighter than me. Every afternoon he would come home from work and ask me if I had done my homework yet. If I said I had, he would reply, 'Go and do it again. You haven't studied enough.' And if I said 'No,' he would forbid me to visit my friends until I'd done it. As during term-time I was only allowed out in the afternoon, never in the evening, I was effectively being grounded. My resentment of this injustice spawned an antagonism that would eventually break out into open hostility and last for many years.

My father was a man of fixed ideas and habits. He rose at the same time every morning, left the house at the same time every day, and returned home at the same time every afternoon. Once an idea took root, it exerted a firmer grip upon his mind than the 3,000-year-old cedars of Lebanon had upon his ancestral soil. So once he had decided that I was not pulling my weight academically, no amount of evidence to the contrary would change his mind – not even when, in my second year at St George's, once Audley was in another form, I romped home first with a ridiculously high average. I was the only student in the school to achieve, and maintain a 100 per cent average in English composition. Yet Daddy refused to give me the present he had promised me if

I came first, whereas Sharman got hers for accomplishing the same feat. 'But Daddy,' I remember saying at dinner that evening, 'my average is higher than hers.'

'But it wasn't as high as it would've been if you'd studied harder.'

The very fact that I can remember this exchange verbatim thirty-four years later shows how deep an impression it made upon me. To me, it was patently unreasonable that I should thrash my guts out to come first with a 96 per cent average when I could achieve something like 88 or 92 per cent without effort. I thought his insistence on me being the best, instead of merely good (which is all I've ever wished to be) was preposterous, and my opinion has never altered. After that incident, I never sought my father's approval for my academic performance, though I did look around for an explanation for his intractability. This was provided shortly afterwards by the outburst from Mickey that precipitated my anguish. Embarrassment, I decided, was at the root of Daddy's attitude. Knowing what a conservative man he was, I became convinced that he was ashamed of me.

Being only twelve, I did not of course see the fuller picture I see now, and I'm afraid I blamed Daddy for more than he deserved. Later, I did come to understand that he loved all his children, myself included. I am sure that he was embarrassed by me, but that was not the whole story. I now believe his speech impediment was the main reason why he seemed so distant and unbending. He was reserved because he found communication difficult; I mistook that for lack of love, and wrongly took too much personally.

What I did understand then was that the solution to my problem rested with my parents. And when I stood back and took a long, hard look at what was going on in our household, I was not confident that my father would come to my aid. Daddy was so excessively resistant to any alteration to his habits that one might have thought the whole world would collapse if everything did not remain exactly as it was. This made life rather trying for my mother. She was a great traveller, and naturally enough wanted her husband to accompany her sometimes. So far, however, she had been unable to get Daddy even to leave Jamaica. Time and time again she would talk him into going away with her; time and time again he would find some excuse at the last minute not to go. She tried every tactic from beguilement to revilement to persuade him, but the outcome was always the same: either she went away on her own or remained at home in thwarted resignation.

Although I was only a child, I was not stupid. I could see how difficult it would be to get Daddy to co-operate in something as momentous as altering my gender if Mummy couldn't even get him to board a wretched plane to Miami. I was also aware, I now realise, that it would be futile to try to get Mummy to persuade him – if she could not influence him in so trivial a matter, what chance did she have with such a big step?

I cannot describe how isolated I felt when I dawned on me that I needed help, but that the two people who were in a position to help me were unable to do so. Time, moreover, has a whole different meaning to children, and as the hours dragged into days, and the days into weeks, the weeks into months, and the months into a year, I felt as if I had been left to rely on myself in a way that would be frightening even for adults. For the first time in my life, I was aware of how alone a human being can be. It was as if I had been thrown into a prison without knowing when my release date would be. To say that I was daunted would be an understatement.

Meanwhile, Jamaica was entering a tumultuous phase of its own. In August 1962, a week and a half before my thirteenth birthday, the country was granted its independence from Britain after 307 years as a colony. Grandpa took us children to the National Stadium to witness the hand-over of power by Princess Margaret. The man in the street was jubilant, having been led by the politicians to believe that great things would come from this change in status, but the established families were full of foreboding. Many were firmly against independence on the grounds that we were too small a nation to rule ourselves. Others felt that we could make our way in the world without the protection of the British, but were nevertheless dubious about what independence would bring. There was an acceptance that the days of stability were over, or at least endangered, for the politicians, in an attempt to capture votes, had made extravagant promises to the people. There was widespread fear about what the general populace would do once they realised that their 'liberation' did not involve an immediate improvement in living conditions. Norman Washington Manley, who had been the last premier of Jamaica under the British (and whose son, Michael Manley, was to be prime minister three times), had been especially keen to point out to his followers that the black man had been oppressed by the white man for too long. His cousin and political opponent, Sir Alexander Bustamante, had traded less on the colour and monetary divisions, and more on the promise of financial betterment for all. 'Busta', as he was affectionately known, was voted into power, became Jamaica's first prime minister and presided over a period of burgeoning prosperity.

In the months after independence, much was made of how well the country was doing economically, due to the bauxite and tourist industries. This enraged the more naïve members of the population, who genuinely expected the government to translate their election promises directly into tangible pounds, shillings and pence. Within a year, there was an explosion of crime such as the country had not seen since the days of the slave rebellions of old. Many were copycat versions of crimes seen on television – the Jamaica Broadcasting Corporation, the country's first television station, arrived with independence and broadcast a diet of American and British cop shows. Every time a novel crime was shown, Mummy took to saying, 'If you want to hold your breath and see how long it takes the criminals to copy this, you won't die.'

Previously Jamaicans had been relatively law-abiding. True, servants often pilfered food from the houses where they worked to feed the members of their extended families who were out of work, but in the circumstances compassionate employers turned a blind eye to this unless it got out of hand. And one was obliged to give away 'old' clothes that one might still want before they went 'walkies' of their own accord. These practices, however, were not viewed as breaches of the law or of the moral code. They were regarded as the needy merely taking without asking, and I know of nobody who ever tried to have an employee jailed for dishonesty. In fact the reverse was often true: when, for example, the police discovered, during routine investigations into an unrelated matter, that one of our gardeners had some of our property and charged him with theft, Mummy went to court and asked the judge to let him off.

Now you could not pick up the *Gleaner* or the *Star*, the two daily newspapers, without reading about crimes against the property and person. Thefts, burglaries, muggings and stabbings seemed to be becoming an everyday feature of Jamaican life. Although some of the burglaries took place in the smarter residential areas, the majority of crime was limited to the rougher parts of town. Murders of the haves by the have-nots were still unheard of, and although murders among the have-nots had increased, they were relatively uncommon. So the haves remained assured, for the escalating violence had not yet reached too threatening a point.

I can remember the moment the established families were shaken out of their reverie. It was a Sunday morning, 19 May 1963. The event that carried the ugly wave of crime on to their shores was the first of many subsequent killings perpetrated by the small but venomous criminal class. The man murdered was my mother's father, Lucius Dey Smedmore.

By rights, Grandpa should not have been killed, for there was no money in the house – indeed, he had none himself. The thief, however, thought otherwise. At 8.15 p.m. on Saturday 18 May, he entered an open door into the drawing room of my Aunt Marjorie's house, where Grandpa was sitting in an armchair reading his Bible and listening to Stainer's *Crucifixion*. The robber demanded money, and when none was forthcoming, he battered Grandpa with a plank stuck with nails and chopped at him repeatedly with a machete. Although he was sixty-three and suffering from osteoporosis, Grandpa was basically strong, and fought for his life with such vigour that he was able to push the fiend outside and close the drawing-room door. In the confusion of the moment, however, he neglected to lock it.

While Clifton Eccleston was outside hunting for a weapon to kill him with, Grandpa, who was always fastidious, went into his bathroom, washed his face and hands, and took off his shirt, leaving it on his bed. He then went to the tele-phone to call the police, unaware that Eccleston had re-entered the house. As he was dialling, Eccleston crushed his skull with a large terracotta flowerpot from the garden. Grandpa died instantly.

Eccleston then moved Grandpa's body back to the chair where he had disturbed him initially, stripped off his watch, and stole the five-shilling note that was in his wallet. For everyone in the family, it was forever afterwards a source of great consternation that the life of a good and loving man, who had done so much unsung good for many poor people, as well as for those he would have called his social equals (snobbishness being his only real failing), should have been sacrificed for so little. To his credit, during his trial Eccleston did stop my grandmother on her way back from the witness box and say to her, 'Mrs Smedmore, me hear your 'usband was a good man. Me truly sorry me kill him, ma'am, but me come into this world like a wild beast, and me going leave like one.'

Grandpa's murder caused a media sensation. Being the first of its kind, it had novelty value, but it also featured other elements the newspapers like. The family was known and liked, and the death had been gruesome. Later, when the details were publicised during Eccleston's trial, they were reported with unsparing exactitude.

And I had better reason than most to know how accurate the reports were. On the day after the discovery of Grandpa's body, I had opted to go to school rather than stay at home suffering from grief and boredom. Daddy took me, stopping at Aunt Marjorie's house on the way. Intrigued by all the snippets I had gleaned from the radio, television and the adults' conversations, I disobeyed Daddy, who had said I must stay in the car, and went inside. The first thing that struck me was the sight of Grandpa's brains, which had oozed out of the back of his head, down the back of the chair and on to the floor. Looking around, I noticed that one wall of the dining room was sprayed with blood. The peculiar thing was that some of it had reached the ceiling. I had never imagined that anyone's blood could spurt so far. Almost transfixed, I walked past the spot where the thief had dealt the final blow, which was oddly devoid of any trace of abnormality, to the bedroom. Sure enough, there was blood on the bed where Grandpa had taken off his shirt and thrown it down. The basin in the bathroom was drenched bright red. Having seen all there was to see, I quickly returned to the car before Daddy discovered me.

Later that day, the horror of what I had seen hit me like a punch in the gut. From nowhere, a wave of nausea overcame me, and I was sure I would throw up on my desk. Retching, I started to tremble from the shock, and had to be excused and go home.

The funeral was held the following day. Never before, nor since, have I seen so many people, except for the crowds for the Prince of Wales' wedding. Kingston Parish Church was filled to bursting with friends, relations, dignitaries, acquaintances and staff of the family enterprises. Outside, the large central square was so packed with spectators that the police outriders assigned to accompany the cortège to the graveyard had a job clearing a path for the cars. Having heard that the police were working on the theory that Grandpa's death might not be a failed robbery but an assassination plot, I should have been terrified that one of the faces in the crowd might pick us off. But I was not. Indeed, when a black bystander pushed her hand into the car and stroked my cheek, saying, 'Don't cry, darling. Not all black people are like that murderer,' I felt that she had expressed a compassion most of the onlookers seemed to feel.

When the excitement of the funeral was over, the family was left with nothing but the awful aftermath. Fortunately one British habit the Jamaicans have never acquired is leaving the grief-stricken to cope on their own in the misguided belief that they will prefer privacy to companionship. There was a steady stream of visitors, though even their presence could not prevent the terrible reality of what had happened from sinking in. Aside from the grief, which was worse for my mother and Aunt Marjorie than for anyone else, there was the insecurity of not knowing who the murderer was, and whether we would be next. I refused to sleep alone, so my Great-Aunt Cissy Burke came to stay, sleeping with me and the machete which I insisted was kept within easy reach. I fully intended to defend myself before anyone had a chance to kill me.

Although my grandmother had been divorced from my grandfather since 1956, they had remained good friends and had even had lunch together on the day of his murder. She had been the first person in the family to see the body, for she had been the first on the scene and had pushed aside the hand of the policeman who had tried to prevent her from entering the house. Upon seeing Grandpa, she immediately lost her memory and remained bedridden for a month in a state of amnesic shock.

Only when Clifton Eccleston was caught did the terror that any one of us could be the next subside. It never disappeared completely, for the long line of such killings in Jamaica has not stopped to this day. The rest of my teenage years were marred by insomnia. The sounds of the night, which had hitherto been so reassuring, now became potential warnings. Did that bush rustle because a wildcat was running past it, or was it a thief, and prospective murderer, lurking in the grounds? Did the wild dogs that so proliferate in the West Indies, roaming from one house to another searching the dustbins for food, bark or give chase because they saw another dog, or a man?

Even when my grandmother recovered and my mother and aunt had come to terms with their grief, my father remained excessively vigilant about our safety. All four of us children were now banned from leaving the grounds of the house without his, or Mummy's, permission. As I was the only child not at boarding school, I was the only one who had to live with this restriction all year round. But if there is one quality I have never lacked it is resourcefulness, and I took to sneaking out until Daddy was due back home. I had finally found a reason to appreciate his rigid punctuality.

After Grandpa's murder things were never the same for any of us again. The solid texture of our family life began unravelling in unforseen ways. Some were trivial. For instance, the murderer had decided to rob Aunt Marjorie's house after reading in the *Gleaner*'s social column that she and Uncle Ric were away in Mexico. Daddy and Mummy therefore took the sensible precaution of forbidding Violetta Riel, the social columnist, to report any of our movements, especially our future plans. We children were also discouraged from ever revealing information about Daddy and Mummy's activities to anyone at all, with the result that discretion became second nature to us. The more profound effects on the family were rather sadder. Uncle Ric's health deteriorated dramatically and he died of a heart attack four years later, aged forty-three. Mummy was never quite the same carefree person she had been before. Daddy, who had had to identify his father-in-law's brutalised body, was so traumatised that he became even more anxiety-ridden. And I lost the one person whom I felt could help me out of the jam I was in.

Throughout the previous year, I had thrashed about looking for someone who could intercede with Daddy and Mummy. Instinctively, I knew it could not be a friend. The taboo of taking one's problems outside the family – washing your dirty linen in public – was too great. That narrowed down my options to the most appropriate people within the family. And it seemed to me that only Mummy's father had the degree of leverage required.

It took me several months to screw up the nerve to speak to Grandpa. On several occasions, I nearly got it out. Each time, however, I would back off. He knew I had something on my mind, but sensibly, he did not force the issue. The night before his murder, Grandpa took Mickey, my best friend Suzy Surridge and me to the movies. Afterwards, he dropped Mickey off at a party, took Suzy home and then me. 'Grandpa,' I piped up as he attempted to turn the car round (he was an appalling driver, and I, who had been taught to drive by Mummy when I was eight, often had to reverse his car for him).

'Yes, dearie,' he said, struggling manfully to avoid hitting the culvert.

Once more, I went quiet. After sitting there in the dark for several minutes trying to find the right worlds, I said, 'It's OK, Grandpa. I'll tell you some other time.' But by now I sensed I would soon have the strength to jump over the parapet. Although Grandpa's death removed his ability to intercede, it did not dissipate the strength I had been garnering. But I was back to square one in the matter of finding someone who could intercede. It so happened that Mummy had recently had surgery, and, hearing how highly she spoke of her gynaecologist, I decided to go to him. If I had to go outside the family, a doctor, I now realised, would be more appropriate than a friend. I knew instinctively that a picture is worth a thousand words, and a living one provides a greater explanation than anything one can say. I made an appointment to see the gynaecologist in the name of Betty Brompton. I wanted to conceal my identity in case the visit went wrong.

When the morning of the appointment came, I listened out for Daddy's departure, got up, had breakfast quickly, then returned to my bedroom. I knew that I could leave the house undetected as long as I dressed quietly and escaped stealthily. Mummy was not an early riser, and the other children were in bed. I quickly applied the make-up I had bought, donned a wig to cover my short hair, hauled on the dress I had made especially in the previous weeks and slipped on the stockings and high-heeled shoes I had removed from the shoe department of Daddy's shop downtown. Checking my appearance in the mirror, I was surprised to discover that I looked better than I had expected.

This moment was momentous in that it was the first time that I, a girl, had seen myself dressed as one. But the matter was far too important for me to get bogged down with trivialities such as whether or not I was an attractive one. That was not the issue. Even if I had been ugly as sin, I would still have needed to find my true identity. Moreover, having been brought up not to fancy myself, I dismissed the encouraging reflection as a subjective opinion, opened my bedroom door carefully and tiptoed down the passage, through the family dining room into the kitchen, out of the back passage, past the family dining room into the kitchen, out of the back passage, past the servants' quarters and out to the driveway. Walking quickly lest anyone should see me, I made it to the street undetected, walked to the nearest main road, Hope Road, and hailed one of Edgar Munn's father's yellow cabs.

I was a jangle of nerves. As I waited to be called by the doctor's receptionist, I was in such a state of agitation that I was amazed I could sit still. Not for one second, though, was I tempted to turn tail. This, I knew, had to be faced, and I just hoped it would mark the beginning of the end of an acutely painful year.

The moment I walked into the doctor's office and started speaking to him, I realised why Mummy liked him. He was humane. From the word go, he treated me with a combination of focused professionalism and quiet compassion. I could tell from the questions he was asking, and the respectful way he listened to my responses, that he viewed me as a living, breathing individual worthy of being listened to, not as some child who should be dismissed until she is old enough to be permitted to have a voice. He then asked me to strip, examined me and made an appointment for one week hence. I had told him who I was, and we agreed that neither of us would tell my parents about this visit until after the next appointment, as he wanted to make medical inquiries.

At the time, I had no way of knowing that my condition

was rare: most doctors would not encounter such a case in their whole professional lives. But it was not unheard of, for medical science had progressed significantly in the thirteen years since my birth. Although experts in the field still did not know enough about sex and sexual identity to agree upon exact definitions, they had recently formulated tests to determine chromosomes and the hormonal levels. They therefore knew how to identify two of the most basic scientific differences between the sexes.

Any responsible gynaecologist, confronted with a case like mine, would have had to locate and read up on some fairly inaccessible research before he could handle it with any confidence. Experts in sex and gender were few and far between then, as it was an area of expertise not even a decade old, and such research as existed was seldom trumpeted. Moreover, there was little interest in a group of patients whose problems were viewed as acute embarrassments. Remember that, prior to the mid-1960s, the whole subject of sex – whether it was sexual activity (or indeed sexual inactivity), sexual identity, sexual orientation, sexual preference or sexual problems – was simply not discussed openly. It would take Helen Gurley Brown's *Sex and the Single Girl* in America, and the Profumo scandal and the Argyll divorce in Britain, to put sex on the front pages of the newspapers and the tips of our tongues. Only then did what we now know as the Sexual Revolution begin, and even then, it took a good few years to get the ball rolling.

So the gynaecologist used the week between my first and second visits to gather as much information as he could. The plan was that I would go to his office, he would contact my parents, they would come and see him, and we would have a calm and constructive airing of the problem. I was very clear about what I wanted, and the doctor was in agreement. I should cease functioning in the masculine gender, and begin functioning as the female I really was.

Luck, however, was not on my side. When I sneaked out of the house for that second appointment, our cook saw me leave. Terrified at what might happen to her if she did not report me, she did. Owen, our head gardener, was sent to fetch me back. For a split second, I thought of disregarding the instruction to return home, but, being obedient, I turned around and took my first steps into the hell I had glimpsed at the onset of puberty.

Now that the subject was out in the open, and my parents realised that I was distressed by my predicament, they attempted to find the best help available. Daddy took over the management of the whole problem, proving to me that my grandfather had been right when he used to say, 'The way to hell is paved with good intentions.' To Daddy, the gynaecologist, who would have been the best person to handle the matter, was too untried to deal with such an important issue. So he personally took me to our family doctor, who was an old friend of both my parents. As the doctor and Daddy discussed the question of my gender over my head, making a wealth of inaccurate assumptions which I was not allowed to challenge – every time I tried to do so I was informed that I was only a child and had no say in such a crucial matter – I began to get the strong feeling that things would never go my way if no one even wanted to listen to what I had to say.

Sure enough, in the ensuing days and weeks, things went any way but mine. Daddy adjudged me too young to merit being provided with even the most rudimentary scraps of information about what steps were being taken to help me. The contrast between the way he and the gynaecologist dealt with me was so great that I sensed the true reason for the secrecy was that plans were being laid to treat me in a way in which I did not wish to be treated. Anxious to the point of collapse, I asked to be restored to the care of the gynaecologist, only to be told the family doctor was arranging for me to receive the best treatment available.

In the event, my case was turned over to a German husband-and-wife team. He was an internist, she a psychiatrist. Neither knew the slightest thing about the field into which they were now delving as if they were experts. That did not stop them from confidently putting forth opinions which impressed my father no end. The wife was especially capable of bedazzling my intelligent but authoritarian father. Highly articulate, and blessed with the plausibility that used to be the speciality of Freudian psychiatrists, she asserted that gender was not an absolute to which you either belonged or did not (a claim now disproven by recent findings concerning the differing size of gender zones in males and female brains). She told him that it was a series of habits and learned responses. The reason why I wanted to live as a female was not because I was female, but because I was rebellious. She supported this breathtaking claptrap with the contention that the tussles which Daddy and I had been having over my scholastic performance for the previous three years were manifestations of the same rebelliousness.

Adding insult to injury, she claimed that rebelliousness was a symptom of maladjustment, and that I was obviously maladjusted, otherwise I would not wish to swap the gender I was being raised as. People who wanted to exchange one gender for another, she advised, were invariably ill. My dissatisfaction was understandable, she explained. Someone who was expected to function in the masculine gender should look the role, which I did not. Two weeks short of my fourteenth birthday, such evidence as there was of puberty was not masculine. My voice was high-pitched; I was smooth of face and body; I had budding nipples. I was also thin, being five foot four and weighing only eighty-four pounds, although I had a good appetite. Her recommendation was that Daddy should permit her to hospitalise me, allow her husband to shoot me full of male hormones for the month I was out of circulation, and begin the process of masculinisation which would give me a body I could be proud of. Meanwhile, she would administer daily and intensive psychiatric treatment to break down my resistance and restructure my personality to be better adjusted and less rebellious – that is, more accepting of the masculine gender. When I was released from hospital, the process would continue, with the help of medication from her husband, therapy from her, and visits to the gym so that I could build up my muscles. Although I would need to be on male hormones for the rest of my life, she had no doubt that this was the best course of treatment – infinitely preferable to altering my gender. That would involve extreme awkwardness. Not only would I be the centre of unwelcome attention, but I would have to familiarise myself with an entirely new role. And what would happen if I could not cope with the pressure, or disliked my new gender?

The insanity of what she was advising might be apparent now, but in 1963, when the medical profession knew less about gender, and when psychiatry, especially Freudian psychiatry, enjoyed a better reputation than it does today; when the surgical skills for dealing with genital malformations were still in their infancy and when scandal was a horror most people would do anything to avoid, it was reassuring and plausible. But in truth her recommendation amounted to the essential destruction and reconstruction of my personality against my will. No human being with empathy or compassion could have devised such a stupendously cruel approach to a medical problem, and sure enough, within minutes of meeting her, I took a definite dislike to this sadist even though I had no idea what she had in store for me. She was a caricature of German womanhood, with a manner better suited to the role of guard in a Nazi concentration camp than to encouraging people to trust her with their most personal considerations. When she informed me at the end of our meeting that I should prepare myself to be hospitalised the following day, I asked her if she was aware that day after that was my fourteenth birthday. 'I know that from my notes,' she responded coldly.

'But surely I could go in the day afterwards,' I said. 'I'm supposed to be having a party.'

'There are other priorities now,' she told me, leaving me with the impression – accurate, as events proved – that she had deliberately chosen the date to show me who was boss. It was the first sign I received of her cruelty, and it put me on my guard.

Forewarned is forearmed, and I was full of foreboding as

Mummy drove me home. Every fibre of my being screamed out that something awful was going to happen, and though I hoped against hope that I was wrong, I knew in my bones that I wasn't.

The following day, Mummy drove me to the hospital, which was run by nuns. It was loaded with significance for me. It was where Aunt Flower, Daddy's sister, was taken for shock treatment every time she 'went off her head'. She was not really mad, but prone to depressions which were a result of having been prevented by the family from marrying the man of her choice. As she was no great beauty (hence the nickname pretty as a flower), no one else had ever wanted to marry her, and over the years the loneliness and frustration had taken their toll.

So began the most terrifying three weeks of my life. Much of that time is lost to me, for the psychiatrist's methods were unorthodox, to say the least. Not once did she conduct a session without first knocking me out with sodium pentathol. Although I did not know that her aim was to brainwash me into accepting a role I did not want, I was sufficiently sensible to know that she was doing something I did not wish her to do, otherwise she would not have had to resort to such subterfuge. She also put me out every time her husband 'treated' me. Your guess is as good as mine as to what his treatment involved, for they never did any of the tests, such as chromosomal or ketosteroid tests, which were appropriate to my problem. The result was that I was unconscious for much of every day, Saturday and Sunday excluded, and hovered between being hung over and depressed or apathetic when I was awake. As I was normally high-spirited and enthusiastic at the worst of times, this was a new and unwelcome experience. I did not like it in the least, and, from that day to this, I have hated not being in possession of my faculties, hence my distaste for any form of intoxication.

In the late afternoons and early evenings, I usually had a lot of adult company. Mummy invariably came; Daddy often dropped in on his way home from work, and various aunts, uncles, and good family friends such as the Countesses Kobylanska and Potworowska all visited, bringing white grapes and commenting on the quantity of flowers in the room. My brother, sisters and friends were banned, however, and nights were lonely after everyone had left for dinner, as there was no television or radio. I was therefore reliant on books to an even greater extent than usual, but they offered no relief from boredom or loneliness, I can tell you, especially when I'd been so shot full of drugs that I could barely concentrate or feel anything but the numbness which the psychiatrist had induced.

One morning Mummy dropped in unexpectedly just as the nurse was about to administer the knock-out injection for yet another brainwashing session. Caught off my guard, when she asked me how I was, I burst into tears and asked her if she couldn't get the doctor to stop doing whatever it was she was doing to me. She tried her best to soothe me, then said she must leave before the psychiatrist came for her morning session.

Unbeknown to Mummy or to me, the doctor had overheard most of our conversation from the passage. She waited until Mummy had left my room before accosting her and banning her from visiting again. She was encouraging my rebelliousness, the psychiatrist said, and the treatment would fail unless her harmful influence was neutralised. This was her big mistake. Although she did succeed in keeping Mummy away, she had sown the seeds of her own eventual destruction by gaining a well-placed opponent. In the short term, however, I still had to withstand what had now become overt sadism. 'You are a spoiled brat,' she told me. 'But you don't have your Mummy's skirts to hide under any longer. You will learn your lessons. The first one will be tomorrow morning, when you will have your first shock treatment. And you will keep having them until you learn that resistance is pointless.'

Terrified as I was, I retorted, 'And you are nothing but a stinking bully. I hate you, I hate you, I hate.'

The following morning, the doctor appeared bright and

early, brandishing a syringe filled with liquid. This in itself was unusual, for my private nurse always administered the injections. 'Good morning, George,' she said pointedly.

'My name is Georgie,' I replied quietly.

'No, it is not. It is George from now on.'

'You don't have the right to name me. You are only a doctor.'

She turned puce, pulled up a chair to the right-hand side of the bed, sat down, and said, 'Please present your right hand.' Present? For God's sake, I thought, you really are quaint, and I started to laugh. She grabbed my arm, and as she tied a rubber tube above the elbow, she said, 'You think you're so superior, don't you? You smug, spoiled little brat. Vell, before I'm through with you, I'll vipe that smile off your face.' She took my fingers, doubled them into a fist, pointed the needle at the upturned part of my hand and stabbed at it. Whether her failure to find a vein was due to incompetence, anger or because she was deliberately trying to hurt me I cannot be sure, but she stabbed at those veins seventeen times after I started counting – and I didn't begin until about the third or fourth attempt, when it dawned on me that it might be intentional. I was left with the distinct impression that her message was: 'You had better watch how you challenge me, for I have an armoury of weapons for bringing you to heel.'

The rest of my stay in hospital is a haze of drugs and abuse. Unless you have been through it yourself, it must be hard to imagine what it is like to feel your true self being battered down by brainwashing, drugs and shock treatment. Certainly I was frightened; certainly I wanted a way out. But what was the way? I was not going to give in and say I wanted to live my life as a male, because that was palpably wrong, and would have been a betrayal of myself. Having been brought up to have integrity and the courage of my convictions, I did not see why I should now go against my parents' upbringing as well as my own identity just to satisfy the doctor.

Meanwhile, the husband's 'treatments' were having the

desired effect. My voice started moving down the scale from soprano to contralto. My neck developed two small lumps. Blonde down appeared above my top lip. And my nipples shrank. I can remember the second I realised that they were altering me physically. That terrified me in a way that all the mind games did not, for what would become of me if they altered my appearance so that I stopped looking feminine, and started seeming to be masculine?

The time had come to get out of the hospital; to grow up, to learn the lesson these medical sadists were unwittingly teaching me, which was that life is not ideal, that people can be terrible, and that the way to beat them at their own game is not necessarily to show your true colours, but to play the game by their rules, and beat the bastards by playing better than they can. So I began greeting the psychiatrist pleas- antly, speaking to her before she put me under for my shock treatments or brainwashing sessions. I would tell her I had come to realise she was right, that it would be much better for me to remain in the role assigned to me, and that I was now prepared to give things a go. The fact that the blithering fool fell for such a rapid and total *volte face* only goes to prove that she never once used those sessions to probe my psyche. Otherwise, under the influence of sodium pentathol, I would have revealed how deceptive I was being.

Confident that she had made the breakthrough, the psy- chiatrist allowed me home after three weeks in hospital. She instructed me to take daily the tablets her husband had pre- scribed, but, now knowing that they were male hormones, I agreed meekly to her face and then flushed them down the loo as soon as her back was turned. She even summoned up a smile as she said that she and her husband would see me for my appointment the following week. It was intended to be the first of many appointments – more than one a week, every week, for the foreseeable future.

The best-laid plans can come a cropper, and hers unrav- elled before Mummy got me home. En route, I told Mummy point blank that nothing would induce me to see that woman ever again. 'Take it up with your father,' she said, and I did so that very evening. 'She was awful,' I said, 'and *I will not go back to her.*' I did not threaten or scream or plead. My tone was pure steel, and sensing my determination – and knowing that Mummy would not back him up after the ignominy of having been declared a bad influence upon her own child – Daddy backed off, saying something like, 'Well, it's your life.' I never did see the psychiatrist again, and years later, Mummy informed me that she had died of cancer. 'I hope it was as painful as the pain she subjected me to,' I said. Mummy scolded me about wishing the dead ill, but I stood by every word then, as I do now, and even she had to concede that the woman was a monster.

The only pity is that she was not unique. I have subsequently heard of many other psychiatrists, psychologists and psychotherapists practising torture and calling it medicine. For reasons which should be obvious to any thinking person, the profession attracts a fair share of sadists who prey upon the vulnerable while hiding behind theoretical dogma. Of course, there are also humane therapists, and it was later my luck to meet one.

But if I had won that battle, I had lost the war. I now found myself in limbo. I did not have my rightful gender, nor did I see any way of achieving it. Before this debacle, I had at least nurtured the hope that once my parents knew how distressed I was, they would help me. But, due to a complete lack of communication on this subject, they were still as ignorant about the depth of my suffering, and all hope had gone.

As if that were not enough, I was left with the residual effects of the abuse to which my system had been subjected. No one can undergo a regimen of mind-altering drugs, insulin, sedatives and narcotics for a period of nearly a month and not be 'hung over' for some considerable time thereafter. For months I felt as if I was wrapped in cotton wool. The vibrancy which was a major part of my personality remained beyond my reach, and I was physically as well as mentally depressed. Benumbed, as opposed to merely numb, would be the most accurate word to use. I can only say that it was a most disagreeable sensation to have to endure.

Life, however, had to continue, and, terrified that I might be put into the hospital again, I kept my head well down. I assumed that my father, who had seemed a staunch admirer of the psychiatrist, was as much to blame as she was. I had no idea that he was a victim just as I was, and with each passing day, as I struggled out of bed in the morning to face a day of hell at school, only to return home to boredom and dead possibilities, I grew ever more antipathetic towards him. For his part, he did not appreciate the way I felt. Our relationship had never extended beyond the most rudimentary of exchanges, and we were further apart than ever. He seemed to think that the treatment had taken to the point where I was prepared to live out my life in twilight.

But my brother Mickey was about to accidentally change my life for the better. Now sixteen, with an ever-expanding circle of friends, he was a student at Jamaica College, the premier Anglican school in the land (following my mother and grandfather, he had opted to be an Anglican). One afternoon, he brought home two friends for tea. I had intended to keep out of the way, but I was forced to return home from Suzy Surridge's house before the friends left because I heard Daddy's car arriving. So it was that I met Bindley Sangster and Gilbert Ward.

Bindley's parents owned a chain of bookshops and his uncle, Donald Sangster, was the prime minister of Jamaica. Gilbert's father was dead, but his mother was married to the eminent jurist Sir Gerald Cash, who later became governor-general of the Bahamas. Good manners alone required me to spend a few minutes talking to Bindley and Gerald, but I made my exit as soon as I could, for I did not want to embarrass Mickey with my presence. I was stunned when Mickey came into the study after they had left and said, 'Bindley really liked you. He thought you were very amusing.'

In the ensuing weeks and months to come, Bindley became as much my friend as Mickey's. Gilbert, too, became a close friend, but Bindley and I had a special bond. An only child, Bindley was spoiled rotten. He had his own car, a generous allowance and lots of freedom. He was also great fun, and we used to have the most wonderful time. It put a whole different perspective on Mickey's feelings about me. Once he realised that his friends would not necessarily mock either of us because of the way I was, I became persona grata once again. I needed that fillip as much as Mickey did. Although school was as bleak and lonelier than ever, I now had a good social life, for Bindley, Gilbert, Mickey, Suzy, Sharman and I went everywhere together – to nightclubs, to restaurants, to the beach (where I always had to swim fully clothed to cover up the budding breasts which caused such merriment at school), to the movies, to friends' houses.

Life took another turn for the better when Tony Shalom, a childhood friend and neighbour, broke his leg and was laid up for three months. Every afternoon after school Suzy and I would climb over her back fence and visit him. Before long, just about every one of our contemporaries was dropping in at Tony's after school. On a daily basis there must have been between ten and twenty teenagers there, all from what our parents deemed suitable backgrounds. Jamaica was not the most egalitarian of places in those days, and considerations like that counted for a lot.

When Tony's leg mended, the party was transferred to the Ziadie swimming pool. Daddy and Mummy did not mind how many friends we entertained during the holidays, so then Mickey, Sharman and I played host to anything from ten to thirty friends every day, all of whom had to be fed lunch and given drinks. On Sundays we always went to Morgan's Harbour, if we were not on the north coast at Ocho Rios.

Teenagers often do not know when to stop, and we were no exception. Towards the end of the summer of 1965, Mummy said, 'I don't want to spoil your fun, but you children have been taking advantage of the servants. You simply cannot have them running up and down between the kitchen and the poolhouse all day, every day. They have feelings too. I want you to give them a few days' rest. Tell your friends not to come.' Being as indulged as we were, it had never occurred to us that the servants were not hot and cold running taps. The lesson was not well received, and we were back to our old tricks when the few days' embargo had passed.

Despite the fun I was having, I was only too mindful that I was living a life behind glass. I used to say, 'I feel as if I'm watching a banquet, yet whenever I reach out to satisfy my hunger, my hand hits the invisible glass separating me from everyone else, and I have to sit on the sidelines, hungry.' Like teenagers anywhere, we were preoccupied with love. It was the only topic of conversation, except for the inevitable sports discussions among the boys. At the time, truth books were all the craze. On each page of an exercise book, there would be a question. On the same line of each page, one would answer the question truthfully. I never saw a book which didn't ask 'Who is the best kisser?' and 'Are you still a virgin?' At first, I used to avoid writing in the books, because I did not want to lie or to reveal too much about myself. Later on, I did play the game, but so enigmatically that few people could make head or tail of my answers.

It was only too obvious to all my friends that the masculine gender and I were incompatible. Because our circle was largely from a privileged background, we were all rather sophisticated for our ages. Many people thought I was going to change sex, and although this was erroneous, they completely accepted the idea. I refused to even acknowledge that the subject of my gender existed to anyone but Suzy, much less impart any information about it. However, I was careful never to wear masculine clothes. Always short white shorts, baggy, rather feminine shirts and leather thongs.

All that changed when I was sixteen and fell in love with Michael Silvera. Michael was 'the' boy whom all the girls wanted. He was mature, fun, exciting, handsome and stylish. By now he was also my brother Mickey's best friend. Michael was the first person, apart from Suzy, in whom I confided. Gradually, he also realised that I was in love with him, something he handled with a delicacy and consideration that still astounds me, for he managed to make me feel feminine and desirable without actually stepping over the line of friendship. His girlfriend, Suzanne Chin, who was one of my closest friends, also handled the situation with grace and kindness, encouraging Michael to set time aside for me, with the result that he visited me regularly and frequently.

But all the kindness in the world couldn't make the gruesome reality go away. Once love and sexual feelings were introduced into the equation, my gender became of overriding importance. Without my correct gender, I could not have boyfriends. I could not lose the virginity that everyone else maintained they were clinging on to while they were having it off in the back seats of their or their parents' cars at the drive-in cinemas at Harbour View and Washington Boulevard. I could not dance, or kiss, or do any of the things that everyone else was doing. There were times when I felt as if I would burst, and sometimes I was so keyed up that I would lie on my bed and kick the air in silent futility.

By the summer of 1965, I could not stand watching life pass me by any longer. Terrified as I was of a repetition of the hospital episode, I had to reopen the subject. I spoke to Mummy, with whom I at least had channels of communication, who spoke to Daddy, with whom I had none. Once more Daddy was advised that a psychiatrist should be called in. This time, however, it was not some Freudian crackpot, but a sensible practitioner. He visited me twice, on Saturday mornings, up at the pool (it would not have done for me to have seen him at his office, lest word got out). After the second visit, he advised my father that my problem was not psychiatric, and that therefore the solution did not lie with psychiatry. He then withdrew from the case, but not before I managed to use his presence to my own advantage, to be allowed to smoke. Thereafter I was the envy of all my friends, none of whom was permitted to smoke in front of adults. With such trivia did one console oneself.

I half expected Daddy to tell me that he had made an appointment with another doctor, but, as the days became weeks, I got the drift. Nothing was going to happen. This time, my response was open rebellion. I don't think the poor man ever got over what hit him. 'You were certainly troublesome,' he reminisced to me a few years ago.

Sex and pop music were the latest rage, and I now used them to challenge him. I became an open advocate of sexual freedom, something which was anathema to my religious father, who still believed that all nice girls went to the altar virgins. I grew my hair as long as I could, wearing it *très* Audrey Hepburn, which resulted in a bitter confrontation every few weeks when he wanted me to cut it and I refused to do so. I took advantage of the new styles in both male and female clothing to wear trouser suits or outfits with shorts which could not be termed anything but feminine. Except when Daddy asked me what I was wearing. 'It's the very latest. It's Carnaby Street. The Beatles wear things like this.' Depending on his mood, he would either look dubious and retreat into his bedroom, or appeal to me to try to look more masculine, saying that I was pursuing a path that was bound to open me up to a great deal of prejudice. 'You have no idea how cruel people can be. It's my duty as your father to protect you,' he often said.

'You can't protect me from life,' I would reply.

As for school, I now made absolutely no effort, and took secret delight in coming third, then fourth. My father freaked out, but when he realised that I had genuinely ceased to care, he launched into the first of many subsequent appeals. 'I'm not always going to be here to take care of you, Georgie. Your education is the most important thing in your life. No one can take knowledge away from you.'

'Spoken like the true son of refugees,' I retorted. 'Well, this is Jamaica 1965' – or 1966, or 1967 – 'not Lebanon 1899, so why don't you just get off my back? I'm not a horse and you're not a jockey.' Poor Daddy, lost for words at the best of times, was no match for me verbally. He used to walk out of my room shaking his head.

As in so many situations, both parties are right, but the channels of communication were so silted up that nothing positive could get through. For two years we were at daggers drawn. Daddy and I had found ourselves marooned on separate islands of hostility, recrimination and misunderstanding, and neither of us had the wherewithal to get off them. Never once did it occur to me that I could express my concerns in words. People in our circumstances at that time simply did not behave like that.

With hindsight, I can see that Daddy was trying to bridge the gap. Occasionally, he would come into my bedroom and try to talk. Sometimes it was about nothing; other times he would touch upon the question of my gender. 'I know you think I don't love you, but I'm only doing what I think is best for you.' One of Daddy's traits was that he would have conversations that were exact replicas of previous conversations. This could be quite funny, and led to us children mimicking him wickedly from time to time.

'You're only worried about the scandal that will attach itself to your precious name. You can't fool me. You're as transparent as glass and I can see right through you.' Faced with my barrage, he would leave the room, looking stricken.

After two years, during which my health began to suffer – I had severe headaches and developed allergies – I could finally take no more. Yet again I went to Mummy, who took the message to Daddy. This time I insisted that I was taken to a doctor who knew something about the subject. These doctor's visits were becoming something of a ritual. Again, Daddy arranged for the latest 'best' doctor to see me. This time, the man was a racing crony of his, which filled me with misgivings, but at least he knew about things like chromosome and ketosteriod tests. When they came back with an unacceptably feminine result, however, he confirmed my earlier reservations by announcing that such tests were unreliable and therefore inconclusive. I could hardly believe my ears. Here I was, now seventeen years old, eighteen in a few months, and I was being told yet again that I could not have my proper gender.

As luck would have it, I had read only a few weeks before in *Time* magazine about something called the gender identification clinic at Johns Hopkins Hospital in Baltimore. I knew if I could just get my case referred there, this ridiculous pussyfooting would have to come to an end. Banging my open hand down on the doctor's desk, I shrieked, 'I'm sick and tired of being messed around. Everyone else has their sex. I want mine. I will not be brushed aside like a dead fly. I demand that you send me to Johns Hopkins. They have a gender identification clinic there, and since you all seem to be having so much difficulty in taking me down the only road open to me, maybe they'll have the guts you lack.'

If you could have seen the looks on the faces of the doctor and Daddy you would have laughed. Neither of them had heard of the clinic, of course, but the doctor promised to make the necessary arrangements. A few weeks later, I took off for Grand Cayman with Aunt Marjorie, Uncle Ric, Sharman, Margaret and Suzy Surridge. I was due to go to school in New York that September, and the arrangement was that Mummy would take me to Baltimore first. The relief I felt was overwhelming. Although life had taught me never to count my chickens until they were hatched, at last I had real hope.

Quite what went wrong, I will never know. I have heard several versions of the same story, none of which makes sense. My own opinion is that Daddy had already made up his mind to leave the ultimate responsibility to me once I turned twenty-one. He realised that Johns Hopkins would force his hand, and as a delaying tactic, he had to fob me off with an excuse. Whatever the truth, I was informed when we returned to Jamaica that the visit was off. Having come so close, I was in despair.

As so often happens, in the midst of this drama, something even more awful happened. Uncle Ric, plagued by ill health since Grandpa's murder, died of a heart attack, in front of Auntie, who found herself widowed at forty-one. Uncle Ric was a great favourite of everyone in the family, and we all felt his death acutely. Mickey, Sharman, Margaret and I took it in turns to go up to Auntie's house and sleep with her. It was there that I resolved to do something to make Daddy take action.

I went into Liguanea Pharmacy, where I was on cordial terms with the staff, and found out what the safest maximum dosage of valium was. In Jamaica in those days, you could buy any drug you wanted over the counter. Valium, amphetamines – you name it, it was yours for the asking. Armed with as many valium tablets as I could take without actually killing myself, I went home and chose my moment carefully. To be on the safe side, I waited for an evening when everyone was at home and there was no chance of me not being found. I went into the kitchen, poured a glass of water, swallowed the tablets and went into the study to wait for them to take effect. I had naïvely imagined that I would pass out within moments, but when several minutes had elapsed and I was still as alert as ever, I walked up to the pool, where Michael Silvera and Mickey were chatting on the verandah of the poolhouse. By this time, I was half convinced that the pharmacist had misinformed me and I had taken too mild a dose, but, to avoid frightening them in case the tablets did start to work, I told them what I had done. Like a typical elder brother, Mickey said, 'Don't chat rubbish. You haven't done any such thing,' and asked me to drop him up at Auntie's.

On the way back from her house, the tablets took effect. God knows how I drove home, for I have no recollection of doing so. Nor of parking the car in the garage. Mummy told me afterwards that it took her a half an hour to get it out, so I must have jammed it in. I staggered into the house and collapsed in the family dining room in full view of everyone who was watching television on the adjoining back verandah. Had I planned it I could not have come up with a more dramatic scene.

Mummy quickly realised what was happening when she smelled no alcohol on my breath. She telephoned the family doctor, who was there within five minutes.

In Jamaica in 1967, anyone who was taken to a hospital with a drug overdose had to be treated as a potential suicide. Because killing yourself was a criminal offence, the hospital was obliged to call in the police, which could result in criminal charges and, in instances involving a well-known name, embarrassing publicity. Daddy and the doctor therefore decided to treat me at home. Instead of pumping my stomach, he gave me salted water to induce vomiting, followed by strong black coffee as a stimulating antidote to the tranquillisers. For the next several hours he and Mummy walked me round and round and round the dining and drawing rooms, until he adjudged it safe for me to be allowed to sleep.

I remember nothing of this, but my cry for help certainly caught my parents' attention. Neither of them had any idea that I had stage-managed the whole episode, so the question of my gender was back on the agenda in a big way. Daddy even went as far as asking the family doctor to arrange for me to be seen by a famous hospital in New York the following month, when Mummy was due to accompany me there to school. 'What I want to know is, does that hospital have as much expertise in coping with cases like mine as Johns Hopkins does?' I inquired of my father.

'Yes.'

'Then why doesn't it have the same reputation as Johns Hopkins?'

'It's as g–g–g–good a hospital,' Daddy stuttered. 'Ju–ju–ju–st because you ha–ha–haven't heard of it, it d–d–doesn't mean it's no good.'

By this time, I was too world-weary to be satisfied by any reassuring noises. The question I wanted answered was simple: was this a step in the right direction, or had Daddy found another way of fobbing off both me and his conscience with medical help that was really nothing but hindrance?

3

New York represented liberty. I loved the city even before I laid eyes on it. This was just as well, for in this particular race, I was one filly who would prove far stronger at finishing than at starting.

The Fashion Institute of Technology, where I was to be a student, was then, as now, the finest design school in the world. A college of the State University of New York, its academic requirements were stringent. No student could graduate without the requisite credits in subjects such as chemistry, biology, and English literature, which had to be pursued along with the technical disciplines complementary to one's artistic major. Mine was apparel design, for my ambition was to become a dress-designer.

This ambition did not last past the first semester, when I made the Dean's honour list. I was as pleased as Daddy to have my talent quantified, but no amount of success could conceal the fact that I had chosen a career which already bored me. There was much about apparel design that appealed. I enjoyed the creativity of draping garments and sketching designs, and could happily do that for hours. The precision and attention to detail required drove some people mad, but I found it absorbing. My problem was more fundamental. I simply could not summon up enthusiasm for a profession which was not intellectually challenging in any way. I needed a profession where new ideas were continually required, not one where they entered into the equation in the beginning, when one was sketching and selecting designs for a collection, but thereafter became statics which had to be translated from paper into cloth and could not be changed.

I was still registered as a boy. The embarrassment of just getting through each day was so acute that that alone made life unbearable right from the start. Each instructor looked at the list of students, saw my name and the gender ascribed, looked at me, and delivered a variation on the same theme: 'There must be a mistake here. It says you're male and you're obviously not.' Although I had long since learned how to maintain my dignity by deflecting embarrassing questions with enigmatic retorts, each time something like this happened I wished I could simply disappear. Naïvely, I had expected to blend in, because FIT was a fashion institution whose students and instructors covered the sexual spectrum so comprehensively that it was sometimes hard to tell whether you were in a college of queens, city of straights, mid-town Manhattan or on the isle of Lesbos. Yet instinctively, people picked up, as they had at St George's, that I was not a gay boy. Whereas the earthiness and lack of sophistication of native Jamaicans had led them to trust their instincts and call me a girl, here, in America, where people thought more and trusted their observations less, they were in a dilemma. If I wasn't a gay boy, what was I? This question seemed to so perturb one or two busybodies that I was hassled on more than one occasion by the school authorities. Once an instructor asked me in front of the whole class if I could try to look less like a girl, to which I replied, 'I'll try if you can make an equal attempt to look less like a swine.' To her embarrassment, the class erupted into laughter, and it was she, not I, who was left looking like a jerk.

As people got used to me, the novelty of my appearance wore off. Thereafter, everything was fine until the beginning of the next semester, when the school psychologist called me into his office and told me there were concerns about me. He offered to help me define my sexuality, whatever that meant.

'And how do you propose to start?' I asked naturally, having learned the art of giving people enough rope to hang themselves with.

'Maybe we can start with you not wearing nail polish,' he replied.

'I don't,' I said, looking him straight in the eye.

He actually had the temerity to grab my hand to check my nails before saying, 'Well, even if you don't wear nail polish, you wear lipstick, and it offends people.'

I informed him that I did not wear lipstick either, and that I could hardly be blamed if my diet was so healthy I had lips with colour in them.

The encounter with the psychologist was the final straw. I went to see Dean Brandriss, told her I wished to withdraw from her school, and left. Knowing that Daddy would not approve, I did not tell my parents until afterwards.

What to do now? Whatever career I chose, I intended to start living in my true gender full time from now on. Money was not an immediate issue, as I had enough to last me for the remainder of the school year. But I would have to work to support myself in the longer term, and quite possibly to pay for whatever medical treatment I was going to need. In the meantime, the basics were taken care of: I had an apartment in London Terrace Gardens on West Twenty-Third between Ninth and Tenth – a beautiful, prewar complex with its own swimming pool, hairdresser and just about everything else.

My father was also covering my medical bills, which as far as I was concerned were a massive waste of money. Twice a week, every week, I had to take the subway up to the Columbia Presbyterian Hospital, where I was under a psychiatrist. There was absolutely no need for this, for my problem was not psychiatric, as the Jamaican psychiatrist had rightly stated.

It had become apparent to me within ten minutes of my first visit to Columbia Presbyterian with Mummy that they did not have the facilities or expertise for coping with a medical condition like mine. They had no specific department as Johns Hopkins did. There was a wealth of discussion between various doctors about whether I should be turned over to an internist, an endocrinologist or a psychiatrist. Finally, they settled upon the psychiatrist, using my overdose as a rationale and stating that the most appropriate course to follow would be to have the psychiatrist confirm my mental health before any other course of treatment were considered.

I complained to Mummy as soon as we were alone. 'I want to go to Johns Hopkins. They're only a few hours away from New York and they won't have to embark upon a long debate as to which department I should be treated in. They have their *own* department for treating people like me. It's the gender identification clinic.'

'This hospital had been recommended to Daddy as the finest in New York. He won't consider anything but the best for you.'

Knowing from bitter experience that it was impossible to change Daddy's mind once an idea took root, I resolved to co-operate and try to enlist the help of the psychiatrist, who, I hoped, would refer me to Johns Hopkins when he had given me a clean bill of health. So twice a week, every week, I boarded the 'A' train and headed uptown for visits which the psychiatrist later told me were a pleasure.

In the meantime I thought I would try my hand at writing. I had always loved everything literary, and with writing, even the most tedious subject has intellectual challenge built into it. This choice of career also had the merit of being suitably blue-stockinged for my father, who gave his assent. In those days, one did not go to university to learn to become a writer. One got a typewriter, chose a subject and got started. One evening, on the *David Susskind Show* on television, I saw a group of male models being interviewed. I decided that would make a fitting subject for an article. It was glamorous and unusual without being too quirky or uncommercial. I hoped to place my piece with one of the women's magazines such as *McCall's* or *Cosmopolitan*. Instead, I opened up a whole new world for myself.

The Paul Wagner Agency, where I interviewed the model Nick Cortlandt, had both a male and a female section. When I had finished the interview, Zolie, who ran the agency, asked me if I had ever thought of modelling myself.

'No,' I replied truthfully.

'If ever you do, give us a call. We could do something with you. You're a beautiful girl, but more than that, you look like yourself. Most girls look like someone else, which is great for catalogue models, but you have the potential to be another Jean Shrimpton or Twiggy or Penelope Tree. Just look at that nose! I've never seen a straighter nose. Look at those eyes. Look at that skin,' he rhapsodised to his colleagues. 'And you're so thin. How much do you weigh? Ninety-eight pounds? A hundred?'

I actually weighed 104lb. I'd spent all my teenage years trying to put on weight. I used to order various fattening-up formula foods advertised in American magazines, and I ate like a horse. But I gained maybe a pound every six months (ah, for those days now). Yet here I was being compared to the quintessence of contemporary beauty, and for the first time in my life, I was pleased that God had made me as thin as he had.

I embarked upon my modelling career with relish. The first step was to get a book of test shots together. These were obtained by traipsing around from photographer to photographer asking them if they would like to take free photographs of you. If they agreed, and the pictures turned out well, you had more shots to add to your portfolio and so did they. Models' portfolios had to be comprehensive, covering the range of your possibilities, for you were hired partly on the basis of how your 'book' showed you. If you had the versatility to go from infinitely grand to charmingly rustic, you did better than girls who could not carry off conflicting 'looks'. The result was that most models 'tested', even after years in the profession.

At first I found the whole business great fun. For someone who had not even realised that she was passably attractive until recently, it was a treat to be praised by photographers for the beauty of my nose/eyes/mouth/neck/ shoulders/hands/legs/forehead/hairline/skin/shape of face. Zolie decided that I would be best suited for 'head-and-shoulders' and legs-and-hands work, as I was on the short side, being a quarter-inch under the absolute minimum of five feet seven. Soon, however, it emerged that I photographed tall because I had long limbs, a long neck and a head that was small in proportion to my body. 'Fashion', where the majority of the work, if not the money, lay, now beckoned as a possibility.

Within two months, however, the gilt was off the lily. The work was one long, dreadful slog. Looking glamorous in front of the camera required you to be little more than a baggage attendant behind it. Because they had to be prepared for any eventuality, models always carried huge bags containing several pairs of shoes, changes of underwear, differently coloured tights, various outfits, wigs and hairpieces, a full range of make-up and hairspray, false nails and bottles of nail polish in all the fashionable colours. All this had to be dragged around the pavements of New York City, along with one's 'book', which was a large black leather photograph album measuring about two by three feet. We all used to joke that the reason why models had such long arms and graceful carriage was not that we had good proportions, but that the book and the bag had lengthened our arms and strengthened our spines.

Modelling could be fun when you were not called upon to twist yourself into poses that would have challenged a gymnast, or asked to hold a pose beyond endurance, both frequent occurrences. Contrary to what people may think, it did involve a certain amount of inventiveness and creativity, for you had to project moods and messages. What I found less appealing was having to go home and practise a whole range of poses and emotions in the mirror. I understood that this would help me to deliver the goods the photographer wanted quickly and effectively, but I became self-conscious whenever I did it. Moreover, one's judgement was liable to be influenced by mood, with the result that an angle that looked acceptable one day seemed doubtful the next. This, I discovered, was a common problem among the girls.

Another difficulty was a genuine ambivalence about one's own looks. Few of the models I knew, or the beautiful women I have known since, for that matter, liked their faces unconditionally. Not only did they realise that different tastes mean that no one is universally beautiful to everyone, but they were also aware of their faults. This tendency towards extreme self-criticism was compounded by the professionals one encountered on a daily basis. Some of the photographers were nothing but sadistic jerks who delighted in crushing the girls' confidence, telling someone with a perfect nose that she should have it 'done', for example. Female solidarity was also often in painfully short supply, as some of the models did their level best to undermine anyone they perceived as competition. And the bookers, who were arguably the most powerful people in the agencies, were a law unto themselves. Many of them were lesbians, and woe betide any model who did not butter them up and deflect the advances they frequently made with charm and tact. They were quite capable of damaging the careers of models they did not like, and I was warned at the very outset to be gracious to one and all, but to keep my distance.

It was now 1968, and the Sexual Revolution was at its peak. So, too, were the penises of just about every other photographer a girl went to see. In their vernacular, few were fussy whether they 'got laid' or you gave them good 'head'. At first, I was frankly offended and disgusted when man after man unzipped his trousers and displayed an erect penis without so much as a word of warning or an iota of encouragement. What, I asked myself, was I doing wrong? Why did so many men behave like that with me? I soon discovered that I, as a person, had nothing to do with it. Far from doing anything wrong, I was doing everything right. They liked what they saw, and 'scoring' was the name of the game. They never gave a thought to whether their attentions might be unwelcome. The sad truth is that many girls played along. I made up my mind that I would not be so stupid as to prostitute myself on the off-chance that some creep might employ me. No photographer ever got even the chastest of chaste kisses from me, much less a 'blow job' (penetration was in any case out of the question until my labiae were surgically unsealed). If they did not want to use me, that was fine by me. No job was worth giving favours to men one would not otherwise even spit upon.

Whether I would ever have achieved the ambitions Zolie had for me will never be known, for, just as my career was about to be launched properly, my father found out about it. Having finally conquered his antipathy towards leaving Jamaica a couple of years previously, he boarded a plane and flew up to New York with Mummy to take me back home. That's what he thinks, I said to myself, and refused to see him until we met at my psychiatrist's office.

The doctor had always been sympathetic to my plight but, more than that, he admired the way I had coped. 'You should be insane or a suicide,' he had observed two months previously when he asked me to co-operate in a televised study of my case for medical research and teaching. 'Instead, your personality is intact and you display good ego strength. You are without doubt an unusual person. I'd go as far as to say that you've discovered life's most profound secret, which is how to remain cheerful and positive regardless of your circumstances. As you know, there is very little data on cases like yours. You can advance the cause of medical science, and help other people who are in positions like yours but have less developed coping skills.'

This was all very well, I thought, but my first duty was to myself. I was worried that my co-operation might result in the violation of my privacy. Sensational publicity was my great horror, as it was my father's, and I did not want to be turned into a spectacle. I had had quite enough of that, thank you very much. All I wanted now was a normal life. The psychiatrist, however, assured me that no one would ever know my identity. The camera would be behind me, and the technicians could distort my voice so that it would be unrecognisable even to myself. It was not a chance I was prepared to take, and I felt I had no choice but to decline. I had no idea how important my refusal would prove. The psychiatrist, who was only about thirty-five, had high hopes of using me to enhance his career, and, without my co-operation, he had no incentive to fight for me to stay in New York.

I went to the meeting with my father full of confidence. As soon as we were shown into the office, Daddy launched into a diatribe. 'You have to return home. I can't allow you to live in New York modelling. What happens if you're a success? Sooner or later someone is going to find out that your papers say you're male. What then? Do you realise you can be arrested for dressing in clothes that are not of the sex on your papers? I can't allow you to put yourself in such danger. You must come back home.' Not for the first time, I noticed how his stammer improved when his blood pressure rose.

'I've taken the precaution of modelling under a pseudonym,' I countered, proud of my perspicacity.

'You are so naïve,' he said. 'You're begging for trouble, and you'll get it. You have to come back home, where you'll be safe.'

'I can't and I won't.' I looked at the psychiatrist for support. 'Tell him how awful it is for me. He has no idea.'

'It has been acutely painful,' he agreed rather more sheepishly than I expected. I knew that Daddy was an energetic man with a powerful aura, but I had certainly not anticipated my all-powerful psychiatrist, with whom I had established such trust over the previous nine or so months, to crumble so quickly.

'Tell him I can't take any more,' I said to the psychiatrist, as he shifted in his chair, obviously feeling he had already fulfilled his obligations to me.

'If you don't come back home willing, I'll force you to,'
Daddy interjected. 'When I get home, I'll get in touch with
the American ambassador and arrange to have you
deported.'

'You wouldn't dare.'

'Try me.'

'You're bluffing. It would cause a scandal, and you don't
want your precious name sullied.'

'It will not cause a scandal, because no one will find out
about it.'

'Can't you make him see what he's doing to me?' I
pleaded with the psychiatrist.

'It's between you and your father,' said Pontius Pilate.

I was not going down without a fight, though, so I
changed tactic. 'Columbia Presbyterian is not the medical
centre for me. They don't even have a specialist department
for cases like mine. Send me to Johns Hopkins and I promise
I'll give up modelling.'

'You will never model again, and you're going nowhere
until you're twenty-one,' Daddy said. It was my first clue to
the solution he had arrived at.

'Twenty-one?' I screamed. '*Twenty-one*? That's over two
years away! What the hell do you think this is, a goddamned
picnic? Do you seriously expect me to go back to Jamaica
and become a neuter gender, when I can stay in New York
and have a nice life?'

'I'm your father and I know what's best for you,' came the
old refrain. 'If I didn't have your best interests at heart, I
wouldn't mind you running amok.'

'Your love has been nothing but an intolerable burden,' I
said as pointedly as I could. 'I wish you'd just leave me alone
or drop dead.'

Daddy had it all figured out. Harking back to the first
psychiatrist's analysis, he decided to treat the matter as an
episode of rebelliousness. He left Mummy behind with me
to close down my apartment and donate my clothes to the
poor. I was absolutely broken-hearted. Life had been bad
enough before I knew what it was like to have my own

gender, but to have enjoyed it and then be deprived of it
was cruel indeed. I knew only too well the kind of humilia-
tions that lay in store for me in Jamaica, but not even I could
foresee how completely dreadful the experience would be.

Daddy had a regime ready and waiting for me. According
to his line of reasoning, I was a spoiled brat who had not
appreciated being sent to college in New York and had dis-
graced my family. I was therefore to be made aware of the
luck I had squandered by working for him. My brother, my
sister Sharman and I had had experience of this throughout
our teenage in the run-up to Easter and Christmas. 'You children need to know that money doesn't grow on trees,' he
would say. But I would almost have preferred to clean
sewers rather than work for Daddy, because he was such a
hard taskmaster. He believed that we, as Ziadies, had to set
a good example to our employees. That meant we were on
our feet from 8 a.m. to 4 p.m., with exactly thirty minutes for
lunch. During that time, we were not allowed to sit down, to
lean against chairs, walls, pillars, counters or any other edi-
fice, to joke or gossip with the staff or the customers – and
woe betide anyone who did not adhere to every injunction.
His philosophy was that the customer was always right, that
he or she should always leave having purchased something,
otherwise the failure was ours; that the staff were there to
cater for them willingly and happily, with a minimum of
distractions, and he brooked absolutely no complaints or
excuses for underperformance.

Now I can sympathise with his point of view. I've been to
too many shops, in Britain especially, where the staff behave
as if they're doing the customer a favour, or as if his or her
presence is an inconvenience to them. Running a business in
a laid-back place like Jamaica cannot have been fun, either.
Daddy constantly had to 'inspire' people to perform effi-
ciently, and I dare say the years of doing so took their toll,
until he was incapable of differentiating between a
moment's respite and the first signs of laxity. But then, we
children found working for him akin to punishment.

Not only did I have to work for Daddy from Monday to

Saturday once he dragged me back to Jamaica, but I was forbidden to go out without his permission – and it was frequently withheld, just so that I would see who was in charge. I was paid the princely sum of £8 a week, of which £5 was deducted for my board and lodging at home. That did not leave me enough even to buy cigarettes, much less go out to the movies with friends on the few occasions I was freed from what I now saw as my 'prison'. But I found a way around that problem. I simply helped myself to whatever money I needed from the shop, taking secret delight in out-manoeuvring dear Daddy.

Of course, I was only too aware that I had to be careful. Daddy had already threatened to put me back into the care of the first psychiatrist and her husband unless I played by his rules. I did not seriously believe that he was capable of allowing them to masculinise me against my will a second time, but I was taking no chances, so I kept my head down and placed my nose squarely on the grindstone. There were times, though, when I loathed him so completely that I wondered if he would not dissolve beneath my furious glower. If he noticed, he never let on.

It took me only two weeks to figure out my escape route. I waited another two weeks, went to Mummy, and told her how much of a mistake it had been to leave the Fashion Institute. She encouraged me to reapply for admission, which I did. Having been a honours student, I was reaccepted for the coming semester.

September 1968 could not come quickly enough. As I was packing to leave, Mummy restored my faith in humanity somewhat by handing over all the money that Daddy had deducted from my wages for board and lodging. She also added something on top, warning me not to breathe a word to a living soul, which I never did until now.

My Jamaican sojourn had jolted me profoundly. I have always been fortunate in having wonderful friends, and they helped me to cope. Chief among them is Frances Bacal, a family friend who was my guardian in New York and without whom I could not have survived this period of my life. I often went to her apartment for weekends or to stay the night, just to bask in her warmth and understanding and to soak up some of the compassion which fuelled me through this ghastly time. The degradation of having to toe the line and turn up at FIT every day in what passed for boy's clothes was torture. I felt a total fraud. Not even the fact that everyone perceived me as female until they were told otherwise was much compensation.

My three closest friends at FIT, Carolyn Kelton, Jill Sprinczellis and Jennifer McFarlane, now knew the truth about my predicament. Each was kindness itself, offering support without pity, for the one thing I did not want was pity. As far as I was concerned, there was nothing wrong with me as a person. I was not suffering from a serious or incurable disease, merely the failure of anyone to rescue me from a cosmetic malformation which had dictated my future. I tried to keep a sense of proportion and humour about it all.

How to cope with attending classes was a problem I faced squarely. Although I loathed the conditions under which I had rejoined, and was bored with the work, I knew that the school was my passport to a vastly improved quality of life. Half a life here was better than none at all in Jamaica. One had to zero in on the positive, and protect it, which entailed doing well enough to please Daddy and the school. However, I was fully resolved not to do more than I had to. I attended the barest minimum of classes and devoted the barest minimum of energy to my work, reserving the rest for my real life outside school, where I was acknowledged as the person I was.

Quite what my future held was now even more of a taboo than ever. There was no longer any attempt to placate me with 'treatment' from doctors whom Daddy paid to delay a solution rather than provide one. For Daddy this was the most comfortable position to be in. As long as he did not have to confront the issue, he could play ostrich (something which he had always done superbly, and would continue to excel at for the remainder of his life). To him, my problem no longer existed. Within the family, I still occupied the position of 'child' and was therefore not accorded the privilege of contributing to discussions about either my gender or my future. Such serious issues were the preserve of adults, while the 'child' was left to flounder in a sea of mystery and supposition. I was therefore no wiser as to how the anomaly would be resolved. I could only search for clues, which, with someone as reserved as my father, meant staring into an unlit pit without the benefit of a torch.

In the meantime, here I was, stranded at the height of the Sexual Revolution. No man would accept a relationship with a woman that did not include full, penetrative sex, and until my lips were opened up, I was effectively prevented from having a full relationship. That, of course, was not something I could ever broach with my father, who would have dismissed me as 'immoral' and a 'whore'.

I was also under the impression that my papers could not be changed until the genital defect had been corrected, and wrongly supposed that I would have to live in legal as well as sexual limbo until such time as I could come up with the money for corrective surgery. The prospect looked bleak. Unless I was prepared to take the risk of being butchered, and of being deprived of ever being able to enjoy normal sexual relations, the surgeon who rectified nature's error would have to be skilled. That, I discovered within a month of returning to New York, from an obstetrician and gynaecologist who also specialised in the field of sexual malformations, meant I would have to come up with something like $5,000. It was a great deal of money in 1968, especially to a student.

I had been boxed in without any realistic chance of making the money I needed to solve my problem. Unless my papers were changed, Daddy could have me deported if I worked in the US. I started to sell my designs as a freelance to chic boutiques like She on First Avenue and Abracadabra on East Fifty-Sixth Street, but it was going to be impossible for me to churn out enough outfits at profit margins of $30 to $65 to accumulate the money quickly enough. So unless I could convince my father, who had the money readily available, to pay for the necessary surgery, I was condemned to years of waiting, working and frustration. And, having already endured six years of this, I did not possess the inclination or the stamina to put up with much more.

The great irony is that I used to 'run' sums of cash in US dollars every time I flew from Jamaica to New York. This money, which was far more than my operation would have cost, I brought for friends of my parents who were in business and needed to settle bills in the city. Had Daddy given me his own cash, I have no doubt that I'd have made off with it and put it to what I regarded as the best use, but because it was not Ziadie money, I never once even considered misappropriating it. It was only when I was well into my thirties that I realised how frequently I had had the money I needed right on my person, and that Daddy, being honourable, would have made good my misdeed. It is a testament to the honest manner in which I was brought up that the thought did not even occur to me.

This period of my New York life was not all doom and gloom. Outside of the Fashion Institute, I lived as the girl I was. My looks were fashionable at the time, and the approbation I received was like rainfall in the Sahara. I scarcely went to a party where I wasn't swamped by admirers, all of whom competed with the most extravagant compliments about my desirability. Even walking down the street in those prefeminist days, some presentable man would usually try to pick me up. On several occasions chauffeur-driven stretch limousines even screeched to a halt and the occupants (invariably middle-aged and unattractive to a young girl) would ask for my telephone number with a line like, 'You're one of the most beautiful girls I've ever seen. Can I call you?' Although I did not consider meetings that did not result from 'proper' introductions worthy of a follow-up, I must admit that it all appealed to my vanity.

Those really were the Big Apple's glory days. The city was rich and clean, and full of prosperous people and high-powered socialites who threw the most amazing parties.

Everyone dressed smartly, and glamour was as much a part of life as air. To compensate for my misery, I immersed myself in as much pleasure as I could. On my return from Jamaica, as soon as I had found an apartment and bought some clothes to replace those that had been given to charity, I telephoned some of the people I had met before I left. I had some propitious contacts, including New York's leading PR, Colonel Serge Obolensky, a Russian prince and former husband of Czar Alexander II's morganatic daughter. He was instrumental in organising many of New York's main social events, and he was always on the look-out for pretty and well-bred girls as window-dressing for his parties. Within days I was back in the social whirl in an even bigger way than I had been during my modelling days. Then, I had had to get my sleep, to look rested in front of the camera; now I could stay up as late as I liked. If I had to go to school the next day, I could drag myself there and remain half asleep throughout my classes. I perfected the art of sleeping sitting up, with my hands cupping my chin and my eyes hidden behind large tinted prescription glasses.

I soon met the other public-relations czar who ruled New York's social scene. Bob Taplinger's speciality was showbiz parties – and what parties they were. Held mostly at his brownstone on the Upper East Side, they were jammed with just about every star of the screen, stage or social world. Among the many luminaries I met there were Cary Grant, Joan Fontaine, Rosalind Russell and Gloria Vanderbilt. There were few large parties among the old-guard set, the new-money set or the showbiz set to which I was not asked. Then there were the fixtures of the social calendar, such as the opening of the opera season at the Met or the innumerable charity balls held at the St Regis, Pierre and Plaza hotels. Sometimes I had to pinch myself to believe that all this magic was really happening to me. But it was, and I relished it. It was heady stuff for a nineteen-year-old.

I especially remember the Diamond Ball at the Plaza in 1969. Teddy Kennedy, who was the guest of honour, zeroed in on me to such an extent that I felt compelled to escape his attentions before a photographer captured us for my father's delectation. I found him attractive, but I was not about to jeopardise my liberty, so I fled downstairs to the nightclub on the ground floor. I often came here with various beaux, so the maitre d' knew me well. He could not have been kinder when I explained my plight (even in those days Mr Kennedy was known for his roving eye), and he gave me a glass of champagne and a ringside table all to myself from which I could watch John Davidson's show. Only when I was confident that Mr Kennedy would have forgotten all about me did I return upstairs, where, sure, enough, he was otherwise engaged.

The events that were the most fun were the parties held in nightclubs. At the opening of Numero Uno – a members-only discotheque owned by the Cassini brothers, Igor and Oleg, which rivalled Le Club, New York's most chic nightspot, for a year or two – I met Aristotle Onassis for the first time. He was vastly entertaining and, although he was ugly as sin, he was still ruggedly attractive, even to a nice young girl whom he treated with all the decorum and respect an older man ought to show. His laughter started deep in his belly, and he exuded such warmth and energy that he would have been irresistible to any woman he focused upon.

Numero Uno was where I met Norton Simon, the multi-millionaire philanthropist and art-collector. At the time, he was a distinguished older gentleman impeccably turned out by what must have been an artist of a tailor. I can no longer remember who introduced us, but I do remember liking him and his girlfriend, who was a ravishingly beautiful top model in her early twenties with dark hair and blue eyes. When he offered to drop me home I thought nothing of it; nor were my suspicions aroused when he suggested that we stopped by his apartment so that he could show his girlfriend and me something connected with whatever topic had been under discussion. Although 'swinging' was at its height, I had never met anyone who wanted to 'swing', so I walked right into the trap. No sooner were we in the apartment than dear old oversexed Norton manoeuvred us into the bedroom. While I was in the loo, he got his girlfriend to strip. They were ready and waiting for me when I came out. I had never been so offended in my life. 'How dare you expose me to such decadence without a by-your-leave from me?' I snapped. 'It's one thing to swing if everyone wants to do it, but quite another to presume that every girl you meet will go along with your perverted tastes just because you're rich. All the money in the world couldn't convince me to even touch you, you dirty old man!' I sailed out in high dudgeon with my nose in the air.

The Norton Simon incident aside, Numero Uno was one of my favourite haunts, along with Le Directoire on East Forty-Eighth Street. I first went there when the club was taken over for a huge party in honour of the Duke and Duchess of Bedford. Ron Galella, the photographer who professionally stalked Jackie Kennedy Onassis until she took him to court and got him banned from approaching her, seemed transfixed by me. He spent the whole evening trying to photograph me, while I did my level best to avoid him. When I realised that I had failed, I walked straight up to him and said, 'You're wasting your time on me. I'm nobody of consequence.'

'There's always room for a beautiful girl in the papers,' he replied, sending a chill down my spine.

I begged him not to use any shots of me, explaining that my father would not approve, and he agreed that he would not provided that I went out with him. He was not my cup of tea, but I kept my word and attended the premiere of *The Shoes of the Fisherman* with him. David Janssen was one of the stars, and when I was introduced to him, I thought he was one of the most attractive men I had ever met. Mr Galella I found rather less appealing, and when he tried to kiss me at the end of the evening, he nearly induced an attack of vomiting. Fortunately that discouraged him from pressing his attentions further.

It was at the premiere party for *Midnight Cowboy* that my

life changed for both the better and the worse. It was held at Wednesday's, a trendy discotheque on East Eighty-Sixth Street. I was chatting to a group of friends when a stunningly handsome tall, blond hunk joined the group. He was introduced to me as Tucker Fredrickson, a name which meant nothing to me but was known to just about everyone else in the United States. He was the quarterback for the New York Giants, and one America's leading athletes. Never having read a sports page in my life, I was clueless about his celebrity: even when he mentioned what he did, I did not appreciate the significance of it. What I did appreciate, however, was the Nordic splendour of this ultimate specimen of masculinity, so when he asked me out the following evening, I said yes.

Tucker turned out to be a great guy. As well as devastatingly handsome, he was warm and friendly, elegant and intelligent, and very hospitable. At his apartment on Sixty-Fifth and First, he played host to a large circle of friends, many of whom were from the athletic and modelling worlds.

Sadly, we were fated never to be anything but friends (one night of passion excluded, but more of that later). On that first date, Tucker took me to Swain's, a nightclub above Kenny's Steak House on East Fifty-First between Third and Lexington avenues. There, he introduced me to his best friend.

Bill Swain was even bigger than Tucker and a dead ringer for Clark Kent. I was powerfully drawn to Bill, a linebacker for the New York Giants who operated the club in the off season. Twenty-eight years old, married and divorced twice, with raven-black hair and blue eyes which he hid behind thick black-rimmed glasses, he was not as handsome as Tucker, but he exuded sexual attractiveness. He had a taciturn manner and a droll sense of humour, and was almost as quiet and reserved as my father – of course, it did not take a psychiatrist to see the connection there. Undoubtedly, what I viewed as my father's 'rejection' not only influenced my taste in men, but also cast a huge shadow over my life until he and I excised the black spot. But I would have found Bill attractive in any circumstances. Tucker immediately saw how well Bill and I were getting along, and, being the gentleman he was, he graciously stepped aside and let us get on with it.

In those days, every girl had a major dilemma: when should you go to bed with a man? The customs governing such behaviour were changing, so we were all in the dark. Some believed that you could be forthcoming on the first date without suffering the consequences; others disagreed. Although my own personal situation curtailed full intimacy, it did not prevent anything but, although I avoided the practices of Indian virgins, who went to the altar with only one orifice unexplored. I had concluded that the most sensible course of action was to let the guy wait a bit, but not so long that you lost him or frustrated yourself needlessly. So I declined Bill's initial invitation to go to his place for 'coffee', though I did agree to have dinner with him the following evening.

Some time between walking into Swain's and leaving with Bill later that following evening, I fell in love with him. This was not an unmitigated joy, but, if it caused me emotional turmoil – he was never in love with me, though he did like me and we got along well – it also introduced me to the splendours of passion. Bill had a body hewn out of rock. Not even Michelangelo could have carved a more perfect representation of the male form. From the tips of his large but well-shaped fingers, past the immensity of his wrists and calves, through the magnificence of his thighs and chest, to his infinitely succulent neck, he was an artist's dream come true. Where he transcended artistry and bordered on divinity was in the generosity and perfection of his most masculine of attributes. Looking as he did like Clark Kent when clothed, it was difficult not to extend the analogy to that fictional figure's other persona when he was divested of clothing.

Bill's physical perfection was only one of his qualities. Fastidious to an exaggerated degree, he introduced me to the seductive delights of natural scent. Just smelling him was a pleasure in itself, exceeded only by the pleasure of tasting him. I could have happily feasted upon him for hours on end. I had not expected to fall in love, and of course it exacerbated my impatience to have my gender problem solved, especially since Bill did not love me as I loved him and continued seeing other girls. I blamed my inability to deliver the ultimate goods, though I can see now, looking back, that that was at best a marginal factor.

I did not know whether I should confide in Bill, or just let him continue thinking that I was an old-fashioned girl. I decided that I had better examine the issue carefully, as it was one I might have to address again. As I saw it, I did not owe anyone any explanation unless the relationship were heading towards the altar. At that point, my history would become material – not every man would necessarily want a wife who had spent her childhood in boys' clothes. Besides, I could not envisage a marriage without genuine solidarity, which obviously meant that my husband-to-be would have to understand the circumstances that had shaped me. Regrettably, Bill and I seemed in no danger of getting married, much as I would have liked it, so I decided to keep my own counsel.

Nevertheless, I continued to see as much of Bill as I could. Despite being caught up in the maelstrom of passion and emotion that only unrequited love brings, I still led a full and energetic social life with my smart friends. Often, I would go on to Bill's club, or we'd go together to Billy Gallaher's all-night drinking club on First Avenue and Sixty-First Street after one of Serge Obolensky's balls or Bob Taplinger's parties. At first, eyebrows in those clubs would raise when I arrived in some exotic creation or ballgown, but only too soon I was a regular fixture whose presence required neither comment nor explanation except to newcomers. Indeed, when Bill was in a jocular mood, he would rib me gently. 'Come on, tell the girls what the Duchess of Windsor is like,' he urged after I had been to Raffles with the Duke and Duchess. I told them that she was small, sparrow-like, stylishly dressed, chic, and quintessentially American in an early twentieth-century way (accent, powerful but charming manner, gracious to the point of largesse), while he was tiny, mild, almost Transatlantic at times (in speech and manner), but had a quiet dignity.

In America, where wealth and celebrity are more openly acknowledged than in Britain, I was intrigued to see that there were residues of the old European imperial class structures. Society was then regarded as being 'above' celebrity, so, while Bill and his friends were established professionals with the status and salaries to match, and I was merely a well-bred young girl who got asked to nice parties, I was perceived by his friends and employees as 'ranking' above them. This perturbed me, for Bill maintained that our relationship could never work as anything more than an affair because we were 'from two different worlds'.

You might imagine that, loving Bill as I did, I would remain faithful to him. But I was about to discover some interesting facts about myself, not the least of which was that love frequently has little or nothing to do with passion. All my life I had heard how passionate the Ziadie and Burke families were. Certainly, those who did not prostrate themselves before the altar of religion had fine track records in the horizontal stakes, but it had never occurred to me that my blood would be as hot as theirs, or that that hot blood would lead me to commit passionate acts that I now look back upon as mere silliness.

At the start of the 1969–70 football season, Bill was traded to the Detroit Lions. This was good news and bad news, for, though I missed him, it forced me to face the fact that my love was hopeless, and that I would be better off replacing him. When I returned to New York from the summer training camp at Bloomfield Hills, Detroit, where I went to administer my own brand of encouragement, I promptly got in touch with Tucker, who asked me to a party he was having. In the interests of banishing Bill, from my mind, I was far more flirtatious with Tucker that night than I had ever been. Although I did not succeed in plucking Bill out of my affections, I did end up in bed with Tucker.

Beautiful as Tucker was when his clothes were off and the lights were dimmed, with his blond hair and smooth, firm, rugged muscles, I still only liked him. So I transferred my attentions to Ernie Koy, another member of the team. Sadly, the electricity wasn't there either, although it was with Marlin McIver, who played for the Dallas Cowboys, I think. He was a powerhouse of pure, unadulterated passion. The pity was, he didn't live in New York. If he had done, he might have accomplished the trick and weaned me off Bill. The next thing I knew, another Giant, Fred Dryer, who, with his room-mate Ray Hickle, was a platonic friend of mine, was warning me to be careful. Apparently, just about every member of the Giants team was exchanging stories about their amorous adventures with me. That astonished me – even guys I hadn't met were saying what a great 'lay' I was. If only they'd known the full story. 'You don't want Bill to hear,' Fred said, but I wasn't so sure; maybe it would make him jealous. 'And maybe not,' Fred concluded, neatly encapsulating my options.

So I took my attentions elsewhere, to the scions of Fifth and Park Avenue, none of whom would ever know Bill (or so I thought, until I turned up at a party at Dr Scholl's heir Don Scholle's East Seventy-Second Street penthouse and saw the object of my love leaning against the wall drinking Scotch). But despite my best efforts, I had been spoiled by those athletic paragons of masculinity. Money did not buy a beautiful body, at least not in those days, and on more than one occasion I committed the unpardonable faux pas of backing out when the guy's clothes were off. One man even accused me of being a ball-breaking bitch, which I regarded as perfectly understandable, considering the appalling way I had behaved.

By now the Vietnam War was at its height, and every now and then colleagues of mine at FIT would invite me to join protest marches. To be truthful, I had no inclination for any form of protest. My own life was bogged down in quite enough involuntary protest as it was. Even so, it was just one of the many effects of my upbringing which kept me apart from my peers. I also had a strong antipathy towards drugs at a time when you could not visit friends or attend parties without being offered 'stuff'. This was partly an after-effect of the period I had spent in hospital in a drug-induced state, but another factor was the strong influence of my Lebanese heritage: the culture does not lend itself to substance use, much less abuse.

Teenagers, however, like to fit in, and I was no exception. I therefore tried pot (and so hated feeling out of command of all my faculties that I swore never to touch it again); amyl nitrate, the climax-enhancer which many a jock wanted to push up *your* nose when *he* was coming (I got such a ripping headache, I would have preferred being hit on the head by a baseball bat); cocaine (which was wasted on me, as I was already confident and outgoing by nature, and rather than talking more, I needed to talk less). I knew only too well that my mind was my salvation, and that without it, my life would not be worth living. So the idea of dabbling with psychedelic drugs like LSD filled me with horror. I could do very well without seeing colours more vividly or taking a 'trip' that 'blew' my mind. What would happen to me if I went on a 'bad trip', or worse, permanently blew my mind?

As I look back on that period, I can hear my father's voice ringing in my ears, stressing the value of clear thought; of doing what was right and not what everyone else was doing (Mummy was big on that one, too); of being a credit to God, family and self; of not allowing people to lead you down futile paths. Even though I sometimes mocked him for being a 'stiff' and a 'square', I was enough my father's daughter to have listened and learned. So I developed a reputation for being a clean-living, virtuous girl (the Giants football team excepted) who loved a good party and indulged in nothing more than a bit of heavy petting. And, unlike many relicts of the sixties, I can actually remember what I did. And with whom.

4

In February 1970, I graduated from the Fashion Institute of Technology. A measure of how much that accomplishment meant to me can be gleaned from where I spent the graduation ceremony: at the Waldorf Astoria Hotel attending the Viennese Opera Ball.

With my graduation, the official reason for my presence in New York ceased. I was not unduly nervous, however, for I had finally learned how to 'play' my father. I told him that I was staying in New York to get work experience as a designer. He wasn't happy about me being so far away with no person or institution to 'protect' me, but I had made up my mind that I could not endure his 'protection' in Jamaica in the run-up to being twenty-one. There was just no way I was going to spend another six months shorn of my identity.

Daddy was obviously still waiting until I was old enough to sign the papers for my surgery myself, and whether he would foot the bill was still a moot point. So when he telephoned me from Florida, where he was staying for the races at Hialeah, to ask me to come back home for two weeks – ' I want to see for myself that you're OK' – I resisted the temptation to ask him why he should think I wasn't, when he had just seen me over the Christmas holidays. Instead I agreed to go home as long as he gave me his word of honour that I would be allowed to return when the fortnight was up, which he did.

Making sure I left my apartment in New York up and running, so that I had a reason to return quickly, I flew back to Jamaica a few days after Daddy and Mummy. It was now seven years since Grandpa's murder, and during that time, Daddy had overcome his fear of change enough to actually travel quite regularly with Mummy. Whether he could go that extra mile, and commit himself to an even more profound journey, was something I feared finding out. Mummy obviously felt the same way, for no sooner had I made sounds about going back to New York than she asked me to stay. 'He's so worried in case things go wrong. Can't you remain here and show him how wrong he is?' No one needed to explain to me the intolerable emotional burden Daddy and his concern could place upon his loved ones. Reluctant as I was to stay, I did not wish Mummy to bear the brunt of it, so I agreed. I was there for six months.

Preparations for Sharman's wedding, which were gathering momentum, helped to keep me occupied. Mummy had not acquired a reputation as a formidable organiser of social events (personal as well as charitable) for nothing. I found myself cast in the role of assistant, running here to arrange for flowers to be put into cold storage, there to proof the invitations with the printers, and elsewhere doing the myriad things that make the difference between a superb occasion and an ordinary one. In the process, I acquired invaluable experience which I was later able to use for the benefit of various charities.

On the surface, I seemed to be coping well. My mood remained cheerful, my attitude positive. I was often out, usually with my Azan cousins Ken, Abe, Richard, Charles, Lorraine, Beverley and Thelma, and Thelma's fiancé (and first cousin), Milade. I adored them all. They were warm, kind, generous, hospitable and protective. They made it clear to me, and to everyone who asked – and those who didn't, for that matter – that they were behind me 1,000 per cent. They included me in virtually everything they did, from hunting at night for crabs by the seashore, to going to dances, parties, the racetrack and the cinema. Yet underneath my coping mechanism was finally failing. I had had too much pressure and, without even realising what was happening, I stopped eating. My future brother-in-law, Ken, who is a doctor, spotted what was happening. 'You're developing something called anorexia,' he said. 'It's very serious and it can kill you.'

'But I feel fine,' I protested.

'Are you aware that you've eaten practically nothing for the last few weeks?'

'Haven't I?' I asked, surprised.

'Georgie, anorexia is life-threatening.'

'Don't be so dramatic, Ken. I'm fine. I promise. I just don't understand how I could've stopped eating without noticing.'

'Well, you have. And if you lose any more weight, no reputable surgeon will touch you,' he warned me shrewdly.

And indeed, I was displaying symptoms of anorexia, but I was not a classic anorexic. I did not possess the delusions of self-image which lead thin girls to consider themselves fat; on the contrary, I had always considered myself too thin. Nevertheless, I was suffering from a stress-induced form of the condition, so Ken prescribed Peryactin, an anti-histamine which made me sleep virtually around the clock. I would fall asleep literally in the middle of a sentence, something which his brother Richard, who often sat with me to keep me company, found as funny as I did. What was no joke was eating. My throat constricted every time I tried to get any food down, and if I forced myself, I gagged. If I did not force myself, I became so ravenous that I felt like fainting – until I tried to eat.

This was a whole new nightmare, but Ken handled it sensibly. 'Don't worry about nutritional value. Just eat anything that will go down,' he advised. So I lived on chocolate ice cream.

When Ken married Sharman, they moved to Canada. I

was now the only 'child' at home. My little sister Margaret was at boarding school and my brother Mickey was a barrister in England. Cousin Abe stepped into the breach to protect me against further stress. In many ways, he was an ideal protector. He was Daddy's favourite nephew, closer to Daddy than his own son. Mickey, for instance, loved classical music while Daddy and Abe loved horses. They would chatter away happily for hours about the form or breeding of this horse or that, whereas Mickey had never had a common interest with Daddy as a basis for easy conversation. 'I'm sure Daddy wishes Abe had been his son instead of me,' Mickey said on many occasions, and, while I regretted the poignancy of the situation, I was now glad of it. Abe stood up to Daddy when he tried to get me to stop wearing discreet make-up. He danced with me when we went to parties. He took me to the races, to the movies, to the country to see his parents. Had it been anyone but Abe, there might have been trouble. As it was, Daddy only said, 'You'd better be careful, Abe, or people will think you're Georgie's boyfriend.' Daddy and I were both speechless when he replied, 'And what of it if they do, Uncle Mike?'

Between June and August, I had my gynaecologist in New York check out who had the reputation as the finest surgeon in the United States. For once I was going to take a leaf out of Daddy's book and opt for the best. Word came back that he was a plastic surgeon in New York whose speciality was vaginal reconstruction, and that he had extensive experience both with malformed females and with males who wished to change sex. Good, I thought, I won't be a guinea pig.

On 17 August 1970 I turned twenty-one. Ten days later, Frances Bacal picked me up at Kennedy Airport and took me back to her New York apartment. At my initial appointment with the plastic surgeon, he explained that he could not be sure exactly what the operation would involve until he opened me up, but he expected it to be reasonably straightforward – cleaning up my clitoris, parting my labia and thereby opening up my vagina. He said there seemed to be no reason why I could not have a full sex life, with complete gratification. He even advised an interesting postoperative pastime: masturbation. He said it was his observation that patients with genital abnormalities profited psychologically as well as physically from playing with themselves once their problems had been straightened out, because so few of them had touched themselves beforehand. Having been brought up in a prudish atmosphere, I nearly fell off my chair at what I felt was a recommendation of vaguely immoral conduct, but I was careful not to let the doctor see how shocked I was. It was just as well, for then he brought up the question of my weight. 'I've always been thin,' I said, my stomach sinking somewhere down by my ankles. 'My father is skinny and my mother slender. It's genetic.' That seemed to convince him, and I breathed a sigh of relief when he suggested that I checked into his favoured private hospital on the 2 September.

No one ever faced the knife more eagerly than I. You would have thought I was going on a wonderful cruise – which, in a way, I suppose I was. Finally, after twenty-one long years, I was taking the first irrevocable step – the second would be when my identity was ratified legally with a change of papers – towards acquiring a birthright everyone else had from infancy and took for granted thereafter.

I did not expect people to understand the torture I had had to endure for so long. Bitter experience had taught me that the world was divided into two kinds of people: those who recognised suffering and had compassion for it, and those who did everything in their power to distance themselves from anything disagreeable. All I wanted was to be allowed to lead as normal a life as possible. Although it later emerged that I could not have children, the operation turned out to be even more straightforward than the surgeon had hoped. This I found out when a sixty-four-year-old transsexual, who was operated on on the same day, came into my room and said, 'I'm Hester. I went to the theatre after you. My surgery was an hour early. But you're a girl!'

'Of course I'm a girl,' I snapped.

Hester turned out to be sweet and generous. She could not have been happier that I was having a chance to lead a life she never could. She and an actress who was in for a facelift often came to see me during the four days I was there.

The doctor was pleased with the way I was healing and confirmed that my vagina had required less work than expected. But he was concerned about my inability to eat, which he now recognised as anorexia, and refused to discharge me from the hospital except into the care of my mother. To his credit, he did not remonstrate with me for minimising the problem, but he did say that my body weight was perilously low, and that he could not accept responsibility for my welfare. So Frances Bacal took me back to her apartment, and Mummy flew in from Jamaica.

If I was in danger of fading away, I nevertheless retained a sense of humour. One evening Frances made me a cream cheese and smoked salmon bagel, which was one of the foods I usually loved. But one look at it was all it took for my face to contort with revulsion.

'Georgie honey, you've gotta eat. You've just gotta. You'll die if you don't. You're nothing but skin and bones. You look awful – just like Greta Garbo in *Camille*.'

I burst out laughing. 'Frances,' I said, 'everybody should look as awful as Greta Garbo in *Camille*.'

Poor Frances had a terrible time getting me to eat. Mummy was very sporting about leaving her own life and coming to New York to be with me, but the lion's share of the cajoling was done by Frances. She gave up trying to appeal to my vanity when even the TV repairman tried to pick me up, much to the horror of her sister Belle. 'You can't ask her out,' she said, shocked. 'She's a society girl.' Yet for all the trouble I was having with food, I had never been happier or more at peace. The sense of relief I had experienced when I opened my eyes in that hospital and realised that no one could ever get me to live as a boy again was beyond profound. My mind could not help wandering back to the truly remarkable life I had just left behind. Now that I was free of it, a part of me viewed it with incredulity. Had I really lived through all that?

It was a healthy affirmation that the past was past. So, too, was my unnerving habit of breaking without warning into floods of tears for minutes on end. The first time it happened was the day after I was released from hospital. I was alone at Frances's apartment, Mummy and Belle having gone to the diamond district. I was completely surprised. It was as if the tears were flowing from a stranger. I did not feel sad, nor was I upset. For a split second I wondered what they could mean. Then I realised that it was merely my psyche releasing all the years of pent-up emotion. For I had been steadfast in avoiding self-pity, and never cried, not even once, throughout the whole of my ordeal. I did not anticipate another release, but when it came, I knew what it was, and explained it to Mummy, Frances and Belle. The only difficulty was, I never knew if a cloudburst would strike when we were out. Sure enough, more than once it did. 'I'm only crying because something wonderful just happened to me,' I said to a dubious-looking waiter. After a few weeks, the downpours stopped as suddenly as they had started.

Although I was recuperating, I was fortunate in having inherited the constitution of an ox from both sides of the family. Moreover, I was eager to be out and leading a normal life as quickly as I could. So much of my time had been wasted that I had a heightened awareness of how precious the here and now is. Mummy and I used the two weeks we were together in New York to hit the high spots with Frances and Belle, and then we flew to Canada to stay with Sharman and Ken, who had settled in London, Ontario. Mummy returned to Jamaica from there, and I stayed on for another week. In Canada, food ceased to be a problem. This was another relief, for there are few more dreadful sensations than dying of hunger and not being able to eat.

In November 1970, I had to face my second irrevocable step. Unless my papers were legally changed, I did not possess the rights of a woman. I could not marry, and, should I ever have a problem with the law, I would be sent to a male prison. As an original birth certificate is a historic record, it could not be pulled out and replaced, but the British law allowed it to be amended upon presentation of a statutory declaration from two sources to reflect that a mistake had been made in 1949 and rectified two decades later. I played no part in the process at all. The surgeon who performed the corrective surgery provided the first document; my parents the second. They needed to swear the statutory declaration in front of a justice of the peace, so they chose someone who was the soul of discretion: their old friend Mitry Seaga. Thereafter, it was up to the registrar of births, deaths and marriages in Jamaica to implement the correction.

Anxious though I was to have my status confirmed, I did not necessarily have to return to Jamaica now or at any time in the future for that to be done. In fact, there were strong reasons for never going back at all. As long as I stayed away, there was less chance of precipitating the sensational newspaper publicity that Daddy, and now I, so dreaded. Now that the papers could prove that I was living as the female I had always been, the media had the material for a dramatic story.

The protocol in the world I came from was that pretty much anything goes, as long as it does not receive an airing in the press, so I was fairly confident that I would be able to enjoy a normal life as long as the newspapers kept their claws out of me.

But Jamaica was my home. Was I really going to be so cowardly as to allow myself to be frightened off for the rest of my life? What had I done, beyond having the misfortune to be born with a birth defect which had been rectified rather later than it should have been? Unless I faced this problem now, I would never be able to return home openly; I would be like some convicted criminal on the run from prison. No, I had done nothing wrong, and I was not going to behave as if I had. It takes as much courage to face the consequences of a cowardly act as it does to face those of a courageous one. I was going to confront squarely a possibility I dreaded.

Maybe I would be lucky and the papers would leave me alone. If they didn't, I would sue them if they published even one word that was a lie, or distorted the facts.

That flight back to Jamaica was the most nerve-racking I have ever made. Not knowing how the press works, I half expected photographers to be waiting for me at the airport, and for my proper life to be over before it had had a chance to get underway. In the event, I arrived to nothing more than a reception committee consisting of my mother and the various Azan cousins. Later, I was to learn that in fact the newspapers had been alerted to my story, but that Theodore Sealy, who was the editor of the *Gleaner*, had said, 'Gloria Ziadie has done so much for charity that we can't repay her by destroying her daughter.' It was the first time, and the last, I ever heard a journalist who was not a personal friend advocate a decent or compassionate policy. So thanks to Mr Sealy, my future was free and clear. I breathed a sigh of relief; so did Daddy.

I had spent so long loathing my father, and blaming him for the lack of help, and I was so tired of the years of silent hostility punctuated by vociferous arguments, I decided to wipe the slate clean. After all, he was the only father I had. I never regretted this decision. All things considered, he was a good and well-intentioned man. With the passage of time, I became fond of him, and consoled myself with the fact that what was done to me was done out of love.

There was only one thing left to do to bring the whole episode to a conclusion. To spare Daddy and Mummy the embarrassment, I took their statutory declaration and the surgeon's document to the registrar of births, deaths and marriages in Spanish Town, the old Jamaican capital, where I could not have been treated with greater consideration. Appreciating the need for privacy, the registrar decreed that the statutory declaration be placed under lock and key. While the birth certificate itself was a public record, she issued me with a second which made no mention of the sex I was assigned at birth. 'It's usually given to adopted children, to save them from everyone knowing their business,'

she explained. 'It will work equally well for you. It doesn't
have your parents' name on it, and it doesn't have any of the
information before the amendment, but it has everything
you'll ever need. Name: Georgia Arianna Ziadie. Date of
Birth: 17 August 1949. Sex: Female.'

I was on my way. My day had really come, and it was to
prove every bit as glorious as I had ever dared to hope.

5

In 1971, the values and morés that would change society so radically were not yet widespread. Women's lib was a new-fangled concept being aired on the pages of the more avant-garde publications. Between the sheets, girls adhered to the current philosophy of free love, usually in the hope of hooking as nice a guy as they could find. Marriage was the priority of every female, and we all spent most of our time and energy perfecting our man-snaring skills.

It is now difficult to credit not only how different my generation was from young people today, but also how idealistic, indeed arrogant, we were. We firmly believed that our parents had botched life totally. We disparaged, as contemptible pragmatism, the realistic adjustments they made in order to accommodate the imperfections all human beings are prey to. We sneered at the conventions the vast majority of our elders held dear, branding them hypocritical and dishonest, and vowed to lead our lives in a purer, more honest way. We didn't need money, or security, or any of the authoritarian hedges which society had erected over the centuries. We certainly didn't need governments that fought wars against foreign states and called them strategies to prevent the spread of communism. We had love for our fellow humans, we wanted peace in Vietnam (if only to keep the youth of America safe for marital consumption), and we were intent on fashioning a world of tolerance and understanding. To many of us, the slogans 'Peace and Love' and 'Make Love, Not War' were a living philosophy, and while I never had the slightest tendency towards hippydom, I was as infected with the spirit of the age as any of my peers.

In Jamaica especially, my generation had the scope to indulge their quest for personal development. With girls, this excluded, if possible, anything as mundane as work, for careers had not yet come into their own as a required accessory for the politically correct, and people only worked if they needed to make some 'bread'. The result was that we all dabbled without commitment, without this having much of an effect upon our 'real' lives. And, of course, there were the ever-present servants in the background to pave the way for a gracious standard of living.

'Authority' was a dirty word, and only shepherds followed the flock, so everyone was assiduously individualistic, avoiding conformity or uniformity as being representative of the old order. Grass was as common in the drawing room as it was on the lawn, so no one thought of it as a drug. Jamaica, of course, was the 'ganja' capital of the western world. The older generation were dismayed by their children's interest in something they saw as the preserve of Rastafarians and ne'er-do-wells. My own parents had few worries on that score. Not one of their four children was at all druggy. My brother Mickey did try smoking pot once or twice, but neither of us enjoyed the effect. As for my two younger sisters, one was still in school (and schools were not yet targeted by pushers) and the other safely married and living a pure life in Canada.

My circle regarded themselves as clean-living: a few avoided drugs altogether, but most merely dabbled, smoking pot socially and steering clear of harder drugs. Cocaine was not yet fashionable, heroin was for junkies and LSD was something only the truly reckless experimented with – only people without brains were prepared to blow them. As for the more obscure drugs such as mescalin, they were so rare that I never even heard of them until I married Colin Campbell three years later.

It was astonishing how quickly the world was changing. Everywhere you looked, what had until recently been the custom was now a barely tolerable anachronism. Even five years earlier, most Jamaicans of good families had mixed exclusively within their own peer group. Now we, the younger generation, were not only mingling with people who were patently not our 'class', but we were also declaring our way the better way. Many of my friends' parents were completely horrified by the people we socialised with, and my own grandmother once summoned Mickey and told him, 'I understand you've been seen around Kingston with a black girl. Don't you realise you're going against God's law? How would you feel if you married her and every time she answered the door to a tradesman he asked, "Girl, can I see your mistress?" You are my only grandson, and I want better for you than that.'

But if my grandmother was not in tune with the changes taking place in society, my parents were. In quite a leap from their attitude in our teenage years, they allowed us to be friends with anyone, regardless of background, as long as he or she displayed the decency they regarded as essential. And they themselves lived by their own rules. The servants, however, were less tolerant. On one occasion, I went into the pantry to find Edward, our butler, grumbling under his breath. When I asked him what was wrong, he said, 'Too much peasant coming to the house nowadays. Can you imagine, I ask the man' – 'the man' was one of my parents' closest friends, the attorney-general, Victor Grant, who had risen from humble beginnings – 'what him want to drink, and him tell me sherry *with ice*? Don't him know that you have sherry straight or not at all? I tell you, Miss Georgie, it going end bad. You watch my words. Sherry with ice! What next, is what I want to know.'

Jamaica was changing even more rapidly than countries such as the United States and Britain. And no one could fail

to notice it, given the proximity with which the haves and
the have-nots co-existed. In rural areas, every 'great house'
was near a village where a good proportion of the peasant
houses were little better than shacks. In the capital, the disparity was even more pronounced. Kingston was divided
into a downtown and an uptown. The commercial district,
was downtown, and beyond were vast areas of slum
dwellings which people like us never saw. Uptown, there
were more commercial sites and shopping centres cheek by
jowl with residential areas. Some, such as Mona, were
middle class, while others, like Barbican and Stony Hill,
were smarter. There, you had Beverly Hills-style houses with
large plots of land and beautifully manicured grounds, often
with swimming pools or tennis courts. Yet in whichever
direction you drove, you were only minutes away from a
cluster of shanties where the poor dwelt in grinding poverty.

No compassionate person could fail to be moved by the
plight of the people. Coming from a family where social consciousness was fostered as a spiritual and practical
imperative, it was almost inevitable that I would feel compelled to do something positive. Having only recently come
through a difficult time myself, and having lost my apartment in New York (Frances Bacal had had to close it down
while I was in Jamaica the year before, nursing Daddy
through his prevarications in the run-up to my surgery), I
was in Jamaica on a sabbatical until such time as I decided
what to do with my life and had time to kill. I resolved to fill
it constructively. My first attempt was to volunteer to work
in the paediatrics department of the University Hospital of
the West Indies, but after a long day tending to dying children, I was so upset that I decided to do something less
emotionally taxing.

While I looked around for something suitable, I dabbled
as a freelance designer and model. This was hardly a full-
time occupation, but I earned enough money to buy the
occasional plane ticket to go to New York and get a buzz.
Jamaica, I had already concluded, was not right for me. It
was great to visit for a few weeks, but deadly dull to live in.

The weather was idyllic, the scenery magnificent, and the way of life gracious, but you never did anything for yourself, everyone knew everyone else, and, making a few new friends among newcomers aside, the sad truth was that it was boring to the point of suffocation. Moreover, within a month of returning, I had assessed the husband material and come to the conclusion that there was a real dearth of prospects. This was nothing to do with the problems I'd had. Friends, relatives, acquaintances and even strangers seemed to have fallen into a uniform line of compassionate acceptance. Some people even admired me for having had the courage to risk public censure, while others thought the whole thing ineffably glamorous. Word had spread that I was beautiful, and that I had already been acknowledged as such in fashionable New York circles.

This acceptance was not entirely accidental, however. Friends of mine such as Suzanne Chin, Maxine Walters, Cookie Kinkead and Pam Seaga set the pace among our age group, while the older generations of the Seaga family formed a solid phalanx of support for both me and my parents which spread outwards to the older, more established circles. The result was that everyone else followed suit and I was welcomed with open arms wherever I went. And did I go everywhere. Within days of returning, I had hopped on to the merry-go-round of parties among the old guard and new people. When I wasn't out privately, I was out publicly, and soon, there was no fashionable restaurant or nightclub which did not see my face several times a week. The person who most influenced my life then was Pam Seaga. Through her, I met the very first man who made a play for me in Jamaica. He was the most eligible bachelor of my generation, but I could not have been less interested in him, not because I did not like him – I did – but because for a start I did not fancy him, and secondly, I saw within three minutes of talking to him what a future with him would be like.

To his credit, he did not take no for an answer. He enlisted the help of Pam's cousin by marriage, Madge Seaga, in talking me round. 'He's serious about you, you know,' she said.

'Give yourself a chance.' Madge did not need to spell out the advantages. He was from a good family who owned one of the largest and most beautiful estates in Jamaica. He had money and he was generous. Daddy would have been ecstatic if I had married him: not only would I have fulfilled my duty as a daughter by hooking a succulent fish, but I would also have established my ascendancy over the competition and proven my worth to everyone. As my gender misallocation was still capable of exploding into a fiery problem, despite all appearances to the contrary, he dismissed me as an 'impractical dreamer' when I said I would prefer to wait for someone who moved me more.

As time would prove, Daddy was right, but so too was I. The girl this beau subsequently married indeed leads the life I foresaw: stuck in the country on her own after the first few years, with occasional trips up to the townhouse to run into yet another pretty brown-skinned girl who is the latest 'secretary', 'housekeeper' or 'assistant'. She is always treated with the utmost respect, but hers is the lot of the traditionally well-off wife: pampered, ignored and cheated upon. I might have been a romantic fool, but I wanted more. And it was essential that I fancied my husband. I wasn't a Ziadie for nothing, and all that hot blood precluded me from lying back and thinking of practicality.

For years I had been keen to be rid of my virginity. I was just waiting for the right man to come along. It did not have to be someone I loved (I might have to wait forever for that), merely someone I liked and fancied. It was almost inevitable that Pam Seaga would prove to be the catalyst, and sure enough, she introduced me to my deflowerer at one of her parties. Maurice Shoucair was the thirty-seven-year-old scion of one of Jamaica's wealthiest families and a distant cousin of my father's, and I had known him vaguely for years. Tall, burly and attractive, and a genuinely kind man, he had gained my undying affection by treating me during my teenage years with the decency and respect many others denied me. He was in the process of his third divorce and when he started flirting with me. Pam, Madge and Dawn

Bitter, another childhood friend, and her husband Robert Mendelsohn, took up his cause. 'Go with a nice Lebanese man the first time,' Madge advised. 'They give the best introduction a girl can have.'

Lebanese men have a reputation for making good husbands and excellent lovers, and Maurice knew exactly how to sweep me off my feet. He picked up the telephone and rang Daddy. He told him he was much taken with me and wanted his permission to pay me court. In our culture, this meant that he had 'honourable intentions' and would not be toying with me. I was pleased as punch, and so, I suspect, was Daddy, for the following day he chattered away most uncharacteristically about Maurice's father, and the family connection between the Shoucairs and the Ziadies.

Indeed, no girl could have received a better introduction to the pleasures of the flesh than I did. Maurice was not only attractive but also experienced. Being richly endowed, he needed to take his time, which he did. But I must confess I found losing my virginity a mixed blessing. It was painful, and I was not sorry when it ended, but at the same time I could discern that pleasure lay beneath the discomfort, and I was keen for an action replay once I had had a few days to recover.

Maurice, however, was not fated to play a continuing part in my life. Someone mentioned to my parents that his father had left the lion's share of his money to his elder son, Eddie. (In Lebanese families there is no primogeniture, it is unusual for the eldest son to get everything.) Suddenly, the prospect of me being saddled with a thrice-divorced man did not seem so attractive to my parents. Almost overnight, approval became disapproval. 'He's a married man,' I was told. 'Do you want to be cited as a co-respondent?' Argument proved futile, so Maurice suggested that we met secretly. I decided against this, explaining to my sister in a letter, 'Maurice has a bad heart. Can you imagine how Daddy would rip down the house if he died on top of me after I had sneaked out to meet him?' And indeed, later that year, Maurice did die of a heart attack. Sad though I was that such a nice man had passed away so young, I was also relieved that I had been an obedient daughter, for I was saved the grief I would otherwise have had to have faced.

At twenty-one, a week can be an eternity, and while I was convinced I would wither on the vine before I bagged myself a husband, the reality turned out to be quite different. For a year I went out with Eugene Brown, a charming American who was ideal husband material. The only problem was, I didn't fancy him. As the months passed, Daddy became rather concerned. 'What are you going to do with your life?' he wanted to know. 'It's all very well for you to be footloose and fancy-free now, but what happens when I'm dead? You need someone to take care of you.'

He thought he had found the answer when Max Langner, a German-born shipping magnate who was in love with me, came to Jamaica to see me and brought up the subject of marriage. I had met Max at a ball in New York, and used to have dinner with him about once a week. He could not have been nicer, and I really liked his soul, but I did not like his body, and would not allow any intimacy. To Daddy, however, Max was perfect: he was very well off, he was a gentleman and he was of good character. 'For God's sake, Daddy,' I snapped, 'the man's forty years older than me. I don't want old age creeping all over me, thank you very much.'

'You're a silly girl and you'll live to regret throwing away a good man, mark my words. All you can talk about is love, love, love. You can't eat love. Love doesn't put the clothes on your back or the house under your feet. Do you think love buys the cars you drive or the plane tickets you use? You must be practical, child. Max is a nice man. He will take good care of you. You will grow to love him.'

'Did your sisters?' I shot back at him. Several of Daddy's sisters had had arranged marriages, none of which had proved happy. Indeed, my Aunt Mathilde had so hated her husband that she promptly divorced him when her mother died.

Looking hurt, he said, 'I'm only trying to help you arrive

at the right decision. It's my duty as a father to see you suitably married off.'

'Well then, Daddy, look at it this way. Why should I marry someone I don't love, when you waited until you found someone you did love before you married?'

Marriage, I could see, was shaping up to become the new bone of contention between my father and me. I did not expect it to blow up into a full-scale problem, however, for I was only marginally less impatient than he was for that ring to be slipped on my finger.

Some people might wonder why I didn't escape Daddy's pressure by getting my own apartment. The truth is that in spite of the changing society, girls from good families did not leave home until they were married. To have broken that convention would have sent a clear and erroneous message to the world that I wanted to lead an immoral life. And I was not about to destroy my reputation, especially as it already had one dodgy aspect to it. Besides, I enjoyed living in the lap of luxury. Not only was it comfortable, but there can have been few households with more interesting visitors. As well as my well-placed relations, such as the chief justice Sir Herbert Duffus, there were family friends like the chief of staff of the army, Brigadier Rudolf Greene, and virtually every musician and artist of note who lived in or visited the country – especially after 1972, when Michael Manley's People's National Party gained power and Rita Coore's husband David became foreign minister.

Rita Coore, the most eminent piano teacher in the West Indies, had been my brother Mickey's music teacher and lived for music as much as Mickey did. Music to Mickey was almost as important as the air he breathed. Although he was not allowed to pursue a musical career, he made sure that his work, first as a barrister, then a solicitor, did not stand in the way of his great love. Even in his early twenties his knowledge was immense, and acknowledged by such foremost musicians as the pianist Shura Cherkassky and the flautist Richard Adeney. Through Mickey, I developed a love of music which has enriched my life, and through me, he developed a love of art. I was supposedly a gifted child artist, and though I stopped painting once I came out of hospital after the attempt to masculinise me, I still adored pictures and sculpture, and would later embark upon assembling a collection.

Wanting to be married was one thing; lust, however, was quite another. In May 1971, I walked into the Jonkanoo Lounge, a fashionable nightclub in the Sheraton Hotel in New Kingston, with my cousins Elaine Ziadie and Lorraine Azan and some friends. Suddenly, as if I were a marionette, I felt my head swivel round. My gaze alighted upon this tall, blond god-like figure. 'See that man over there?' I said to my cousins, 'I'm going to have him before the night is through.' This was not a statement of intent, or even of desire. It was an affirmation of something beyond my control.

Lorraine laughed, embarrassed. 'But you don't even know him.'

'I can't think why I said that,' I agreed. 'It's quite, quite ludicrous. I might never even meet him.'

Fate, however, intervened in the form of Billy Young Chin, the companion of this Adonis. Someone in our group knew Billy, the owner of a large carpet factory, and before I had a chance to draw breath, I was being introduced to the object of my desire, Bill Madden, Billy's adviser from Monsanto, the American textile giant. Bill immediately asked me to dance. Never before had I wanted someone the way I wanted him. It was atavistic, compulsive. 'I want you so badly,' he said, as if I needed words to convey what his body was already telling me.

'So do I,' I gasped, short of breath from the passion and excitement of it all.

Bill was staying at the hotel, and within a half hour of meeting, we had slipped out of the nightclub, crossed to his room, and made mad and passionate love.

Never before or since have I been so instantly attracted to someone as I was to Bill. He was physical perfection – six foot three, with the body of a professional athlete and the scent of an angel. I would gladly have stayed in a hovel with him, as long as we could have continued making love the way we just had, but he was due to leave for New York, where he lived, the following day. I cheered up when he told me he'd be returning in a few weeks.

An hour later, Bill and I returned to our friends in the Jonkanoo Lounge. 'We've been looking everywhere for you,' Elaine said.

'I did it,' I said.

'You're lying,' Lorraine hoped.

'No, I'm not. It was absolutely wonderful.'

'But he won't respect you,' Lorraine said.

'I'll worry about that tomorrow,' I replied, still glowing from the encounter.

Bill Madden was the first man I had met since Bill Swain whom I thought of as a serious marital prospect. My criteria, regrettably, were different from my father's. I cared nothing about bank accounts or suitability or indeed good character. All I cared about was love and lust. To me, love started with lust and was consolidated in the bedroom into companionship and a shared life. I had an infinitely flexible attitude and was only too willing to adjust to the ordinary neuroses so many people seemed to display. As for good character, it never occurred to me that anyone would be malevolent or treat me badly.

Bill was undoubtedly interested in me, which was just as well. I had vowed after Bill Swain that I would never again become entangled with someone who did not return my love, a principle to which I have adhered religiously. And in a way, Bill II was suitable. Although he was not rich, he was a good earner with prospects. Well educated and solid to the point of stolidity, (as it turned out), his character and background would have appealed to dear Daddy. Our attitudes, however, were not quite so complementary, for while he was a WASP from a good family, he was much too prissily East Coast 'proper' for my taste.

This disparity reared its head on the first evening we had dinner upon Bill's return to Jamaica. We were having drinks with a bunch of corporate couples he knew. The conversation swung around to airlines. I said in passing that I did not like Pan-Am, as the service was never as good as on other airlines. No sooner were we on our own on the way to the restaurant than he hauled me over the coals for being 'controversial' and 'indiscreet', concluding that I might have 'offended' someone. 'Bill, I didn't tell some woman that her husband was ugly as sin, or vice versa. I merely gave a perfectly innocent opinion. If people take offence at something as stupid as that, surely they're not worth worrying about.' If you could have seen his face, you would have understood why I never became Mrs Wilson Hadley Madden.

If our approach to life was out of kilter away from the bedroom, it certainly wasn't in it. Making love with Bill was like going to heaven alive. So, too, was lying with him afterwards. Within a month of his departure, I was in New York, with Mummy and Daddy's approval, to see if something would come of this new romance.

Unfortunately Bill proved to be as wishy-washy in matters of the heart as he was in conversation. I wanted love and passion and excitement and interest in bed and out, but the only part of Bill which seemed capable of reaching great heights was the one which no one saw when he had his clothes on. Naïvely believing that I might shock him into action, I asked him for dinner early in the summer of 1971. I was staying at a friend's apartment on East Seventy-Third and Park while he was away for the summer. My cousin Elaine Ziadie was visiting me from Chicago, so I made up the numbers with someone attractive I knew from my early New York nightclubbing days. Russell Price had studied for the priesthood, given it up and become the boyfriend of my friend Peggy de Benedictis, and now they had broken up. He'd often flirted with me in the past, so I asked him to make Bill jealous. At some point during the evening, however, my interest in Russell suddenly became more real than illusory. Thereafter I let the two men fight it out among themselves. Bill, of course, was hardly going to win the contest when he couldn't parry and knew about only one type of thrusting. Although I did feel an almighty bitch when Bill realised, at the end of the evening, that he was going and Russell was staying, I cheered myself up with the thought that it served him right. Faint heart never won fair maiden. I only wished I could erase from my memory the crestfallen look on his face.

Russell was a diverting entertainment, in and out of bed, but hardly a prospective husband. Within three months the passion had burned itself out, so I rang Bill, hoping that this time the special relationship which existed between the sheets could bounce out of bed with us.

Despite all the signs to the contrary, I had my priorities straight. Marriage was what I wanted, and marriage was what I would have. However, our second attempt to make things work served only to conform that Bill and I had nothing in common except good sex. Every time I saw him the same thing happened. From the moment we met until we were in bed, I kept on thinking, 'Why doesn't he just shut his mouth and open his trousers?' He was so dull that I always saw him as flat champagne and myself as a syringe trying to inject fizz into it. Much as I wanted to fall in love with him, his personality prevented me from ever getting beyond the infatuation stage. Recognising that this was hardly a good basis for a continuing relationship, I left for Christmas in Jamaica, deciding not to get in touch with him when I returned to New York. Nor did I see him again until the night of my divorce from Colin Campbell.

In theory, finding a husband should have been easy; in practice, it was proving to be rather arduous because I was so picky. Because Jamaica so far proved, against the odds to be such a propitious hunting ground, I decided I would stay on for another extended holiday. This time, I thought, I will occupy myself fully and make use of my interests and talents until the holy grail comes along. Christmas might have been a time of joy for people like us, but for many of the poor, it was a time of want. I devised the idea of getting the relations and friends who owned shops and factories to donate presents which I could distribute among poor children. All day, every day, I canvassed for donations, casting a wide net that reached even companies I did not know, until I had enough presents for several hundred children.

It was at this point that a good idea became sullied by political expediency. I had asked Victor Grant, the attorney-general, for his thoughts on the best way of distributing the presents. He told me he would make some arrangements. On the appointed day, his wife Anna and I were bundled into a car, a large van following behind with the presents, and driven off to villages I had never even dreamed of. It gradually dawned on me that we were being taken all over his constituency, and that the presents were being given to the children of his supporters. I was so angry I could barely speak.

Those, of course, were the days when people still believed you could change society with a pure heart and kind deeds. Viewing Victor as an aberration, I plunged into my next project: raising money for the department of obstetrics and gynaecology of the University Hospital of the West Indies, which needed a machine to monitor the heartbeat of foetuses. I asked the French pianist Andrée Juliette Brun (the Princess Oukhtomskaya in her private life) to give a recital at the State Theatre in aid of the cause. The gala concert couldn't fail, I reasoned, because all the music-lovers would turn out to hear her play, while all the socialites would come to see the princess, and to be seen by their friends seeing her.

Andrée and her boyfriend Jim Anderson, who lived in New York, were refreshingly unopportunistic after Victor. In return for their help, I arranged for BOAC (now British Airways) to fly them out and for the Skyline Hotel to put them up until they came to stay at our country house on the north coast. The event itself was a howling success. Andrée's playing was superb, and the State Theatre was sold out. All my friends and relations advertised in the programme, which raised a small fortune for the hospital. Even the governor-general, who was the guest of honour, turned out to be a game old thing. I had last seen him the previous New Year's Eve, when he had been the guest of my cousin Joe-Joe

Ziadie at a ball, and had been full of life. Now, however, Sir Clifford Campbell fell asleep and began snoring. For all of one second I had a dilemma. Should I wake him, or should I tolerate such interference with an artist's performance? In my scale of values, pandering to governors-general came a long way beneath consideration for a fee-paying audience and an unpaid performer, so I gently poked him with my elbow. When that didn't work, I poked him harder. It did the trick, and he awoke with a start. 'You jab me any time I doze off,' he whispered, giving me a beatific smile. 'At my age, it's a struggle to stay awake unless I'm on my feet.'

I enjoyed charity work, but it was merely a stop-gap until I could embark upon my real vocation: being a wife. Unfortunately, I was about to be derailed by yet another handsome and unsuitable man. Two weeks before Andrée's concert, in Epiphany, the most fashionable discotheque in Jamaica, where I'd been with Michael Silvera and his wife, Suzanne Rees, a tall, strapping stranger had come up to me and asked me to dance. As we had not been properly intro-duced, I was taken aback by his forwardness, but his physical appeal swept aside such considerations.

Nevertheless, while we were dancing, I had misgivings about this handsome stranger, who identified himself as Ron from Wales. Even when he asked me to a party the following day, I still couldn't decide whether I was attracted to him. It was only when we got to the party, where I didn't know a soul – it was all new people and British expatriates – and we started to talk that I realised how highly intelligent Ron was. I've always been a sucker for a good mind in tandem with a good body, and our romance was underway.

To say that Ron and I were ill suited would be an under-statement. An accountant by profession, and thoroughly British in his attitudes and perspective, he had recently come to Jamaica to work for Peat Marwick, a firm whose senior partner was the father of my friend Joanna Thwaites. Ron was my introduction to the extreme destructive preoccupa-tion most British people have with class. Traits that anyone else would marked down to a personal failing or even as the fault of the cat were invariably attributed to class. For instance, Ron could not understand why he could not address my mother by her Christian name. When I explained that she expected my friends to maintain a respectful distance and either call her Aunt Gloria or Mrs Ziadie (depending on the relationship with their parents), he decided that my family thought they were better than everyone else. Thereafter, he gained her undying antipathy by addressing her in an overfamiliar manner as 'my dear,' beginning a set piece which incensed both of them but which I found funny. 'How are you, my dear?' he would ask every time he saw her. 'Very well thank you *without you*,' she would reply, pointedly turning her head away from him.

Daddy did not feel so strongly about Ron, but, knowing that Mummy did, he asked me on several occasions to stop seeing him. I refused, because I genuinely liked him (he was a decent guy, for all his nonsense), and because he was good company, when we weren't rowing about class. Moreover, I enjoyed his friends. The men were all rugby-players, and their girlfriends mostly representative of the new Jamaica, with the exception of Lorraine Drew, who was from a similar background to mine. Lorraine, Opal Groves and I used to spend many a Saturday afternoon huddled in deep gossip while the men were knocking the daylights out of one another on the rugby field. Afterwards, we cooed in all the right places while they relived a game we hadn't even bothered to watch – those were the days when girls played the feminine role to the hilt.

I would be a liar if I claimed that I did not enjoy playing the little woman to Ron's big, strong man, and he undoubtedly expanded my horizons.

But this obsession with class, above all, made me aware that there could be no future with Ron, even if my parents could be talked round to grudging acceptance, so I was keeping my eyes fully open for a husband while he kept my bed warm. Then, on Christmas Day, Ron did something that precipitated the end. After dinner, we dropped in, as is the Jamaican custom, on my relations, ending up at the house of my father's cousin Joe-Joe and his family. Joe-Joe and his wife Dorothy had been wonderfully supportive to me, and his youngest sister, Toni, was one of my closest friends. Ron knew this, but it didn't stop him leaving us chatting in the drawing room while he went into the kitchen to tell the cook, who had been with the family for nearly thirty years, that the Ziadies were exploiters of labour and she was being taken advantage of. She was so incensed by what she saw as Ron's abuse of Joe-Joe's hospitality that she recounted the conversation to Joe-Joe as soon as we left. Joe-Joe, who was the kindest and most benign of men, telephoned my father in an apoplectic rage and left a message for me: I was always welcome, but that troublemaking boyfriend of mine was never to cross his threshold again.

The relationship might have survived had Ron been able to see how misguided his behaviour had been. However, when he was still trying to justify himself weeks later, while I became increasingly vituperative about what I now described as his disloyalty, we admitted that we had come to the parting of the ways. We did remain friends – and I even had a fling with him the following Christmas – but as far as anything else was concerned, there was no way back.

But the path towards marriage was in sight, had I but known it. It was a circuitous route, and had I not met Kari Lai the previous year in the Jockey Club Enclosure (her husband Eddie owned the racetrack), I would never have encountered Colin Campbell. Kari and I had become great friends, and through her, I had met the present Duke of Marlborough's sister, Lady Sarah Spencer-Churchill. Sarah had a beautiful house, Content, in Montego Bay, and was almost a resident, spending half the year on the island. She filled her time organising the most entertaining house parties, and virtually every evening she and Montego Bay's other noted British semi-resident, Dolly Burns (only child of the famous art-dealer Lord Duveen), threw dinner parties. Sometimes the two grande dames attended one another's events, but essentially they were rivals for the crown of premier hostess, and the Montego Bay social set effectively divided into Sarah people and Dolly people. Sarah had a great personality and a wide and varied circle of friends, but Dolly was nothing but a committed socialite who rushed around from party to party booking everyone up two weeks in advance. With the intolerance of youth, I looked down upon her as having 'false' values, and invariably declined her invitations.

Two weeks after breaking up with Ron, I drove down to Content for a long week-end, where Sarah and I were joined by Kari, Eddie and Ian Hamilton. Ian, who was not handsome, but personable and great fun, pulled out all the stops to flirt with me, and gradually I became drawn to him. I did not hop into bed with him, the way I had with Bill Madden; instead, I let him work. Think of yourself as Everest and the man as a mountaineer. Let him hack away with his pickaxe until he reaches the peak. That was my attitude, and I stuck to it until we reached Kingston and were safely ensconced in my brother's pied à terre, where we consummated our romance.

By my parents' criteria, Ian was suitable. Although not rich, he was comfortable. He owned a stud farm in Newbury, England, while his elder brother farmed Caymanas Estate, one of Jamaica's larger sugar estates and the site of the racetrack. The Hamiltons were as racing mad as the Ziadies, so to that extent there was a common interest, although I must say that our greatest bond was horizontal.

When the time came for Ian to return to England, he asked if I would come and see him? I thought I might be able to arrange it. By this time, Daddy had finally learned that nagging was not the best way of getting me to do something. He therefore sensibly kept out of my hair, though he showed his approval of my relationship with Ian by promising me a plane ticket to Greece to cruise on Sarah's and the Onassis yacht in June, stopping off for two weeks on the way to see Ian.

In the intervening couple of months, I spent a great deal of time with Kari and Sarah at Content. *Papillon*, the movie starring Steve McQueen and Dustin Hoffman, was being filmed near Montego Bay, and we became friendly with the cast and crew, especially with Tony Masters, the art director who had won Oscars for *Nicholas and Alexandra* and *2001: A Space Odyssey*. Evening after evening, Sarah established her ascendency over Dolly Burns by having Steve McQueen and Ali MacGraw, Dustin and Anne Hoffman and other visiting actors and actresses for dinner, although her *coup de grâce* was when she was asked to entertain the Shah of Iran's second wife, Princess Soraya. Her fiancé had just been killed in a plane crash, so she was not exactly full of beans, but she was sweet and very, very beautiful.

Steve McQueen was my all-time favourite because he was so straightforward. The first time he came to dinner, he confessed to me as we chatted on the sofa that he had nearly backed out. 'I've never met blue-bloods before. I don't know how to act.'

'You're joking,' I said, thinking he was.

'No, no, no, I really haven't. What do I do?'

I laughed. 'I wouldn't worry if I were you. If you prick the veins of everyone here, you'll find the blood flows red each and every time. Just be yourself. The one thing no one can stand is pretentiousness.'

We separated for dinner, which was served under the stars on the patio. The conversation bubbled along as everyone tucked into a delicious fish soup made by Melvia, the cook. Suddenly, Steve threw back his chair, jumped up, and said as naturally as I had advised him to do, 'Sarah, where's the nearest john? I need to take a piss.' All the other soup spoons were suspended in shock. I quickly looked to check Ali MacGraw's reaction. She was coolly drinking her soup as if nothing untoward had occurred.

After Mr McGrath, as Sarah's sister Lady Caroline Waterhouse kept on calling him, had left, we all decided we liked them both. At the time, they were about the most glamorous couple on earth. Ali was certainly beautiful, dressed all in white with her hair pulled back in a ponytail and not a scrap of make-up, but still so elegant. When they left, we chewed over what she could have meant when she told Mary-Anne Innes Ker that they were a 'different' couple.

At Sarah's, there was almost as quick a turnover of house guests from Britain, the US and the Continent as there were of dinner guests. After her sister Caroline, one of Princess Alexandra's ladies-in-waiting, left, her son Michael flew out with his good friend Mark Shand, who would later achieve fame as an intrepid traveller and as the brother of Camilla Parker Bowles.

Naturally, I placed both Michael and Mark under my marital microscope. Michael was good-looking, with a hairy chest and dreamy eyes, while Mark was hairless of body but hairy of head, with craggy features and an endearing manner. But neither, it must be said, held much appeal for me, though we had huge fun while they were in Jamaica. We went on picnics up the Martha Brae River, swam, went nightclubbing and to dinner parties. Every now and then Mark would do something which made me wonder if he fancied me, but no sooner did I get a glimpse of interest than it would be concealed. The evening before he left, however, he spent about two hours chatting to me in the poolhouse long after everyone else had gone to bed. I wanted to see if I had intuited correctly. Eventually even my vanity could not prop up my eyelids any longer, so I had to draw the encounter to a close before receiving the confirmation I sought.

Months later, when I was in London, I ran into Mark in Annabel's on Berkeley Square. He made a beeline for me and asked me to dance. On the dancefloor I discerned that he was indeed happy to see me. 'I'm so glad to run into you,' he kept saying, as if he were trying to hark back to the non-starter in Jamaica. Although not the most patient of people, I was curious to see how this was going to pan out. So when Mark asked me not to go home with my friends, but to let him drop me off, I agreed.

Mark's conduct in the flat where I was staying at 7 Bina Gardens (he bought a flat beneath it himself a few weeks afterwards), still brings a smile to my face twenty-four years later. I went into the kitchen to get us something to drink, and, when I returned, there was Mark, stark naked from the waist down, with a proud and magnificent erection. 'What do you think you're doing?' I snapped, rather angry that he had jumped the gun in such an unmistakable way. Had I said yes yet? Had I even indicated anything so much as a possible maybe? Such presumption really was insupportable.

'I'm shy. I like you and I didn't know how to tell you.'

'Well, you don't look shy to me. Indeed, you look rather proud,' I retorted. 'Now, please put your trousers back on.'

Mark pulled on his trousers sheepishly, battling for a good minute or two with his steely member before it relaxed enough to be tucked away. Unsurprisingly, poor Mark never tried to get into my knickers again, although he has always been affable whenever I have seen him since.

My encounter with Mark Shand would not have taken place if my relationship with Ian had not come to an end the way it did. Two weeks of the Newbury countryside was enough to kill any interest I had in continuing an intimate relationship with him. While I enjoyed his company and that of his friends – notably Vickie Learmont (Lady Valentine Thynne), Henry, Earl Sondes and Confrey Phillips, the bandleader – and the time we spent in London at places like the Clermont Club, where the Earl of Lucan and Margaret, Duchess of Argyll's first husband, Charlie Sweeny, were regular fixtures, I simply could not abide being buried in rural England. One morning I woke up and simply couldn't face another barren day with Ian puttering in the garden. I reached for the telephone and rang Mary Anne Innes-Ker, a friend from Jamaica, to ask her if I could go and stay with her until I found somewhere else. Sarah was delayed in California, and God knew where Jackie and Ari were, so Greece was on hold.

After a week at Mary Anne's, I moved into the flat at Bina Gardens, sharing with two other girls. One of them, Diana Ballard, became a good friend. I was also fortunate that quite a few friends I knew from Jamaica lived in London. Most of these were well placed, so my introductions were impeccable. Bobby Alexander, for instance, owned a bloodstock agency with offices in Piccadilly where David Cecil, brother of the leading trainer, Henry, worked. His office was staffed with girls from good English families who were my age and became friends. One of them shared a house with Georgina Blunt, who was an object of adoration to Prince Michael of Kent (handsome and unassuming then, before he married the impossibly grand German 'socialite' Marie-Christine von Reibnitz and grew that fluffy beard which I find repellent, but which makes people say that he looks like his grandfather, King George, and the last Czar).

The English, I'm afraid to say, were of no interest to me. Whether they were princes or paupers, they brought out in me an *ennui* which was rooted in my childhood feelings about my Smedmore relations. Although I was happy to become friends with people I liked, my set was more cosmopolitan. And London, it emerged, was an ideal base, for it had a large international community: there were Americans, such as Peter and Brookie van Gerbig, Huntington Hartford and Kurt Newmann, and a plethora of Europeans and Middle Easterners. Moreover, one could live there very well on a modest allowance (England was much cheaper in those days).

To repay hospitality and to occupy myself, I used to have drinks parties for twenty or so friends every week or two. On one occasion Stanley Vaughan asked if he could bring along the actor Terence Stamp, who had a set of chambers at Albany near Stanley's. This was a difficult period for Terry. His career was in the doldrums, and he was virtually a recluse, so I was happy to say yes and contribute to Stanley's attempts to cheer him up. When he arrived, however, he bolted straight into my bedroom, lodged himself between the chest of drawers and the wall, and refused to budge. Nothing Stanley could do would convince him to join the party, and in despair he came into the drawing room and asked me what he should do.

I set my jaw and in we sailed to the bedroom, where Terry was cowering. 'What's wrong, Terry?' I asked.

'I can't face your friends. No one wants to meet a has-been.'

'Nonsense,' I said, marching over to him. 'Everyone is very keen to meet you. They've all seen you in *Billy Budd* and God knows what else.' I took his hand in mine. 'Better to be a has-been than a never-was, Terry.' I yanked him up with a smile.

If you could have seen his face. He looked just like a little boy who had been given an ice cream. I linked arms with him, walked him through to the drawing room, introduced him to everyone, and of course he was a big hit.

Sarah Spencer-Churchill and the Onassises got to Greece around this time, but by now I was in no mood to leave London, because I was having a furiously intense romance with Serge Beddington-Behrens. Serge was the son of Princess Irina Obolensky and Sir Edward Beddington-Behrens, the famous banker who bailed out King George V when Daisy, Countess of Warwick blackmailed the royal family over her love affair with his father King Edward VII. He was well off and had a fabulous art collection featuring Augustus Johns and Picassos left to him by his father. He was tall, blond and slim, not really my physical type – I liked men to be hunky and burly – but the force of his ardour and personality was such that I quickly overcame that reservation. When he proposed marriage after our third date, I was truly thrown off balance. Not only was I becoming increasingly keen on him, but it seemed he wanted what I wanted.

Only too soon, however, it became apparent that Serge and I were hopelessly mismatched. He might have been a tiger in bed, but he had turned his back on the 'smart' way of life and lived almost like a hippy. I did not even own a pair of jeans, an oversight which he rectified promptly, but try as he might, he could not wean me off dressing up and going to smart places with my friends. Nor could he convert me to his vegetarian, macrobiotic diet. I loved meat and fish and all the things he deplored, and while I was prepared to accept him as he was without changing him, he was not prepared to do likewise. By the time we finally parted later that year, we could not be in the same room without shouting at each other – unless, of course, we were making love. That remained as passionate as it had been at the beginning, but my God, was I glad to have some peace and quiet, even if I lost out on the most fantastic lovemaking a girl could have.

But the break-up of my romance with Serge was so bitter that it jolted me to my core, and I really do not know what I would have done without the support of my little sister Margaret, who was at school in England, Mary Anne Innes-Ker and my dear friend Mary Michele Rutherfurd (whose step-grandmother, Lucy Mercer, was President Roosevelt's great love and with him when he died). I decided that I really needed a break from men. Much as I loved them, they could be a thankless task and I wanted time and space to regroup. So what if I didn't get married right now? I was only twenty-four. I could afford to wait. Why not try to have a career that interested me, and which could keep me, if not in the style to which I was accustomed (that I didn't expect – it took too much money), then at least in reasonable grace?

In one respect, Serge had done me a favour. He was as interested in the human condition as I was. While we had radically different ideas and approaches, he had inadvertently shown me that the psychiatrist from the Columbia Presbyterian Hospital in New York had been right: I had somehow picked up the secret of happiness. Looking around, I saw practically everyone else floundering in a morass of uncertainty, needlessly making real hashes of their lives. I will write a book on philosophy, I decided, and plunged straight into it.

All day, every day, my ideas poured out on to the page. In the evenings, I frequently went out with friends to dinner and parties or to Tramp, the discotheque part-owned by Jackie Collins' husband and Johnny Gold. The dancing was better there than at Annabel's, and while I knew fewer of the members, I was most entertained when types like Bianca Jagger and Ryan O'Neal approached me with a view to getting to know me better.

That November, I broke my writing routine to go to a

Thanksgiving luncheon, only because the host, Dulany Howland, another American aristocrat living in London at the time (and now married into the Hunt family), was a dear friend. But when you least expect to meet a man is when you trip over a prince among men. One of Dulany's guests was a tall, blond, attractive American named David Koch, who was visiting England. I had no idea he was one of the richest men in the world, which was just as well. Had I known, I would probably have hung back, for the one thing I cannot stand is people who suck up to the super-rich. As it was, we got along so well that he asked me out to dinner at Parkes, a chic restaurant on Beauchamp Place. So began a truly lovely swansong to the only period of my life that was truly care-free.

Within weeks, London was in the grip of the three-day week. Every day there were power cuts, and, while I could live by candlelight, I was not prepared to freeze to death without central heating. So, early in December, I hopped on a plane to New York to stay with Sarah Spencer-Churchill at her East Seventy-Second Street townhouse prior to returning home for Christmas. While I was there, I got to know David better – a lot better. Although he was a considerate lover, I did not feel the passion for him that I had felt for Serge, but he was such a nice person, with such a sterling character, that I began to doubt the wisdom of my requirement for sexual fireworks. Without exactly categorising him as a marital prospect, I began wondering if I shouldn't add him to my list.

In January David came to Jamaica to spend a weekend with me and edged even closer to the list because of the way he handled me and my brother. Mickey was my chaperone, David had asked Roger Samet and I had invited my childhood friend Judy Ann MacMillan, the celebrated artist, to complete the house party. Mickey, who, by his own admission, had a controlling spirit, obstructed me at every turn, doing everything in his power to become the centre of all activity. I became so furious that I rounded upon him during dinner on the Saturday evening. 'Are you trying to ruin our weekend?' was only one of the more delicate questions I shrieked at him. David's response endeared him to me as nothing else could have. 'Brothers. I know all about them. I've got three.' Years later, two of them, Billy (of Americas Cup fame) and Freddy (the owner of Sutton Place), ended up in very public litigation with David and his eldest brother, so I dare say he knew even more about fraternal strife than I realised.

But for now romance took a back seat to my book on philosophy, which I finished in February 1973. For once, Daddy was encouraging, and even paid for a secretary for the chore of professional presentation. Once it was all typed up, I prepared to leave for New York, where I intended to stay until I found a good agent and/or publisher. I was to be put up by Jeanie Campbell, second wife of Norman Mailer and the daughter of the 11th Duke of Argyll.

As I boarded the flight to New York, my glory days were about to end.

6

At the age of twenty-seven, Lord Colin Campbell was a textbook romantic figure. Tall, dark and handsome, he captured the spirit of the age with just the right mixture of adventurousness and nonconformity. Three-quarters American, and raised in upstate New York for much of his childhood, he had left school at fifteen, and gone to work as a jackeroo in Australia before becoming a deep-sea diver in Fiji. In between, he had worked for a short while as an assistant to Jasper Johns in New York; tried living in London doing nothing but having a good time; and bummed around Australia and New Zealand doing a bit of manual work and having a lot of fun. So international was he that even his accent was firmly planted in the middle of the Atlantic, with the result that he sounded British to the Americans and American to the British. His manner and behaviour certainly owed more to his American than his British heritage, which gave him a robustness few lords shared.

Colin was Jeanie's brother, the younger son of the 11th Duke of Argyll and his second wife, Louise Clews. He had the strongest personality of anyone I had ever met – he simple exuded strength, decisiveness and charm. Within minutes of crossing the threshold of Jeanie's Park Avenue apartment en route to Paris to see his stepmother, he had the guests assembled for his 'homecoming' party in his thrall.

Jeanie had warned me about him in motherly fashion before he arrived. 'Colin is very good-looking and loves beautiful girls. I'm sure he'll be smitten by you. Don't make the mistake of going to bed with him. He'll lose respect for you if you do. He doesn't admire girls of easy virtue.'

'I know the type only too well,' I said. 'My mother always says my father was like that when he was a younger man.'

In fact, upon meeting Colin, I was not at all moved in a personal sense. He certainly wasn't my type. Although he was tall, he was thin as a stick with the aura of a lone and hungry wolf. He gave off none of the 'vibes' that sexual men do, but he had a captivating manner and was undoubtedly entertaining. By the time the other guests had left and he, Jeanie and I set off for P.J. Clarke's to have a hamburger, I liked him enormously.

'It's time I went to bed,' Jeanie declared at about 11.30. 'You two stay and talk. You seem to be getting on so well.'

'My body clock's askew. You will stay up with me, won't you?' the charming Colin said pleadingly.

Two hours later, he said, 'I feel as if I've known you forever.'

'I do too,' I replied truthfully.

'Why don't you come to Paris with me? It would be great. Then I wouldn't be lonely. You have no idea how lonely it gets always being on your own.'

Genuinely touched, I said, 'I would if I could. But my father would freak out if he heard that I'd made off across the Atlantic with someone I'd just met.'

We adjourned to Jeanie's sitting room, where we had a typically seventies young people's conversation. Colin evinced great concern for living life on the 'real' instead of the 'bullshit' level, which led me to believe we had a great deal in common. My book, after all, was titled *The Substance and the Shadow*, and dealt with how false values destroyed people's lives. By this time, I thought he was a great guy, so when he leaned over to kiss me, I let him. Within seconds he was getting all hot and heavy. Pushing him firmly away, I said, 'Colin, the apartment's full of people.'

'No one will come in,' he said.

'They might.'

'They won't, he said, pressing me.

'Colin, no. I really mean it.'

'You're not a virgin, are you?' he asked.

'No,' I laughed. 'But if it will keep you from exerting pressure, then I recommend that you view me as one.'

'You've got principles, haven't you?'

'I hope so.'

'Will you marry me?'

'What did you say?' I was not sure if I'd heard properly.

'Will you marry me? You're the most beautiful girl I've ever seen. I feel as if I've known you all my life. Jeanie says you're from a good family, and you've got character. You're everything I want in a wife. And, before you answer, she can tell you I've always been a confirmed bachelor. I never thought I'd meet anyone I'd want to marry. This may sound spur-of-the-moment, but I've never been surer of anything in my life. You're the girl for me. Please say you'll marry me.'

Stunned. That's what I was. Stunned. Serge Beddington-Behrens had proposed to me on our third date, but that was after three days of constant togetherness and serious nookie. Colin, however, didn't know me at all. Should I respect or be watchful of such decisiveness? I barely knew him; on the other hand, I was captivated by him. I really did feel as if I'd known him all my life.

There seemed to be parallels between the way Colin was starting this relationship and the way Serge had started ours. Maybe this was my opportunity to rectify what had gone wrong with Serge. Perhaps if I had matched Serge's initial commitment, instead of holding back until I was sure, our relationship would have turned out differently.

Maybe Daddy was right. Just before I'd left for New York, he had come into my bedroom after hearing Mickey ribbing

me about David. 'David's so boring,' my brother had said.
'All he can talk about is his oil tankers. I give you another
two months before you replace him with a stud.'

'What's wrong with you, my girl?' Daddy had demanded.
'You discard men other girls would give their eye teeth for.
When are you going to face up to facts and settle down? All
this talk about love is just romantic nonsense. It doesn't last.
It's no basis for a marriage. What are you waiting for? The
perfect man doesn't exist, so there's no point in being too
critical. Just find a kind and decent man who can afford to
give you the necessary luxuries of life, and get your head out
of the clouds.'

Perhaps I *was* too picky. Maybe what I thought was sensible idealism was unrealistic romanticism.

Whatever the uncertainties, I knew one thing. I was smitten by Colin, and I did not want to wreck this relationship
with too much prevarication. I stalled for time gently. 'Colin,
we barely know each other.'

'But you yourself just said that you also feel as if we've
known each other for ever,' he protested.

'I know. But marriage is a very big step.'

'You're not saying no, are you?' he asked, a look of
absolute terror on his face.

'No, of course not. I just think we should wait a bit before
we come to a decision.'

'I have an idea. Why don't we ask Jeanie what she
thinks?'

'That's a good idea,' I said, grateful for the opportunity to
postpone this discussion until the morning. By this time, it
was nearly four o'clock and I was dog-tired.

But without more ado, Colin marched straight into
Jeanie's bedroom and woke her up. Within minutes, he was
back in the living room, grabbing me by the hand and
wheeling me in to see Jeanie. 'She thinks it's marvellous,' he
said, to my consternation.

Once more, I gently counselled waiting, but it was to no
avail. 'Whether any marriage works is the luck of the draw,'
Jeanie opined. 'I've known people who got married a week

after meeting who are still happily married years later, and people who knew each other beforehand for years, only to divorce within a few months.'

'Ian proposed to Iona the first night they met, and they've been happily married for ten years,' Colin said. Ian was his elder brother. Jeanie suggested we phoned him and shared the good news with him.

While the call to Scotland was being placed, I tried to think the whole thing through sensibly. What did I really want? Did I want to get married? The answer to that was a resounding yes. The only problem to date had been the husband. Well, here was a tall, dark, handsome twenty-seven-year-old with a bewitching personality and the same outlook on life as mine. Admittedly, I did not know him, but I did know Jeanie. Rather naïvely, I assumed that her brother would have 'good' values like her own, especially after the in-depth philosophising we had just indulged in on the sofa. Moreover, Jeanie was a robust individualist, rather like me, and Colin seemed to be the same. After men like Bill Madden, that was an attribute not to be underestimated. So, too, were the sparks of excitement that flew from him. He was certainly a far more exciting proposition than David Koch, good character and hundreds of millions of dollars aside. And last, but not least, though I was not yet in love with Colin, I knew myself well enough to know that that process had already started.

Jeanie and Colin made assent easy for me. I never did actually accept the proposal; I only had to allow myself to be swept up the aisle to reach the destination desired by most girls of my age in that era, myself included.

After Colin and Jeanie had spoken to Ian, who seemed as thrilled about the news as his siblings, Colin and I went into the living room to talk some more.

Now that he had my agreement, he was keen for me to appreciate one or two important details about him. The first was that he had a chronic stomach problem. That only triggered off a powerful resonance within me, for my father had had a similar condition throughout my early childhood. It therefore brought me closer to him than he could have realised.

It was also with relief that I heard Colin say, 'I don't want children. You can't marry me if you want children. I never want children – they just ain't my thing.' I did not answer. I wanted children, but, unless medical science progressed astonishingly rapidly while I was still young enough, I would be more likely to win the lottery than to have a baby in the normal manner. This did not seem a suitable time to discuss adoption, however, so I remained silent.

It did not occur to me then that Colin might have known something about my past, and might be deliberately pushing my buttons. Only after we were married did he let on that he knew Jamaica well, and that he had heard all about me and my family long before he met me. Jeanie had a house, Hopewell, outside Kingston in Irish Town. He had even stayed on the island for several months a few years before, on another property near Irish Town, Middleton. According to him, he planted a crop of ganja, for his own personal use of course, which the police got wind of. He recounted in true raconteur-fashion how he got home from a hard day's drinking to discover that the police had raided the property, forcing him to flee the island before he got into trouble. Whether he was merely entertaining me, or recounting something that really happened, I did not know then.

It was at this juncture that Colin gave the first indication that he was a tough operator. He said, 'Will you sign a document waiving all claims on my trust fund if things don't work out between us? I don't mean to be mercenary, but the income it generates is so small that it's not even enough for me to live off.'

'Sure,' I agreed, missing the warning light. Colin immediately went back into Jeanie's bedroom, got a sheet of paper from a writing pad and wrote out a comprehensive renunciation of my rights to alimony. This I gladly signed.

Disillusionment, however, was still in the future that first night. By the time we reached our beds, it was nearly daylight. I half expected the idea to have gone off the boil by the next day. Colin and Jeanie had other ideas, however. She made a few telephone calls and ascertained that we could not be married in New York for eleven days, but that we could marry forty-eight hours after establishing residency in Elkton, Maryland. 'I married Jackie, my second husband, in Elkton,' Jeanie said. 'It's the Gretna Green of the eastern seaboard. We can hire a car and drive there. What fun.'

'It might be more convenient for you if we did it here,' I said, still stalling.

'I couldn't wait eleven days,' Colin said almost recriminatingly. 'Don't you want us to be married as soon as possible?'

Melting in the heat of such ardour, I let brother and sister make their plans. Afterwards, Jeanie and Patricia Fleischmann, widow of the publisher of the *New Yorker*, took me for a girls' lunch, during which Jeanie once more swept aside my misgivings at the speed of it all. 'Colin really is a very sweet man,' she reassured me. 'And I'm so happy he's finally getting the happiness he deserves. His mother was absolutely beastly to him when he was a little boy. She had him to preserve her marriage to my father, and when that didn't work, and her lover, the Czar's nephew, Prince Dmitri of Russia, refused to marry her, she took out all her spite on Colin. He was such a sweet little boy, too.'

My sympathy duly engaged, I decided to stop trying to put on the brakes and start enjoying the romance of the whole episode. After all, how many times in a girl's life would she have the chance to elope with a handsome, dashing man? If I were going to throw caution to the winds and run off with a delectable stranger, I might as well enjoy it.

Romance aside, there were practicalities which had to be dealt with. My wedding dress was the first. Fortunately, I had a new evening dress all in white, which would save me traipsing around New York searching for a gown when I had no time to spare. And then there was the question of how to break the news to David that I was marrying someone else. I telephoned him and asked him if we could substitute our dinner date for that evening with a drink at seven, as I had something important to tell him. When he arrived, he found me accompanied by his good friend Roger Samet, whom I had asked to be there in case David needed comforting. I dropped my bombshell, they congratulated me and David and I remained friends.

Rather more onerous was the next task I had to face. If I were going to marry Colin, I had to tell him about my past difficulties. The next afternoon, while Colin was resting in his nieces' bedroom, I joined him. He stirred as soon as I entered the room.

'Hi,' he said easily, as if we had been together for years.

'Hi,' I mirrored. 'Listen, Colin, there's something we must talk about. It's rather awkward, I'm afraid.'

'You're not going to back out, are you?' he said with that terrified look on his face again.

'No, of course not,' I smiled.

'You told your parents and they're against it.'

I laughed. 'We agreed I wouldn't tell them until after-wards. Daddy can't prevent a fait accompli, but he can make a monumental fuss beforehand.'

'What's the problem, then?'

'I don't know if you're aware that I was brought up as a boy. Are you?'

'So?' he said, cool as a cucumber.

'Well, I mean to say it's well, sort of . . . well, you know, not exactly run-of-the-mill, is it?'

'Georgie, I don't care about bullshit like that. I told you, I can't stand bullshit. And I meant it.'

'I'm very relieved to hear that, but there's something else. I know you said you don't want children, but suppose you change your mind? I can't oblige, you know.'

'I'll never change my mind. I'm not keen on the little bug-gers,' he said with surprising vitriol.

With that hurdle out of the way, Colin, Jeanie and I went down to his trustees the following morning. They advanced him $2,000 from his trust fund of $225,000 so that he could buy me a wedding ring and pay for the elopement to Elkton.

Then we picked up a hire car, fetched Cusi, Jeanie's younger daughter, and set off for Maryland with me at the wheel (Colin couldn't drive).

The romance of it all could not have been more thrilling or in keeping with the spirit of the age. Instead of staying in a smart hotel, we stayed in a roadside motel. How real, I thought, excited at the novelty of fulfilling the forty-eight-hour residency requirement going from truckers' café to truckers' café, with only one detour for lunch in a more upmarket seafood restaurant. Colin was so easy-going, such fun, and so utterly endearing that I no longer minded the mad rush at all.

The afternoon before the wedding, we set off, ostensibly in search of a jeweller's shop to buy rings. Although men from our sort of background did not usually wear rings, Colin had hit upon the idea of a signet ring bearing his crest for his wedding-ring finger. I was only too happy to buy it for him, and did not think once about the fact that this ring cost much more than mine. Nor did it occur to me that this might be the first of many occasions on which he would exploit an opportunity to gain things he had always wanted but had never been able to afford.

Buying the rings, however, took second place to Colin's astonishingly thorough search for drugs to get him over his 'jet lag'. It was at this point that the warning bells should have rung, but I had no experience of anyone with a drug problem, so I put this extreme tenacity down to premarital nerves. We spent most of the day driving from drugstore to drugstore, hospital to hospital, town to town, looking for someone who would let him have 'just a few uppers and downers'. At one hospital, a policeman even asked to see his papers. When Colin produced his passport, he established his respectability by alluding to Princess Anne's kidnapping, which was big news at the time. Pointing to his title, he said, 'Her mother is my cousin. My father was the 11th Duke of Argyll, and the 9th Duke's wife was Her Royal Highness The Princess Louise, Queen Victoria's daughter.' Suitably bedazzled, the policeman asked him how the Queen was, and when he said he hadn't seen her for a while because he had been deep-sea diving in Fiji, he let him go.

This was the first I had heard of any connection between the royal and Argyll families. When we were safely out of earshot of the policeman, I asked, 'Are you really related to the Queen?'

'Yes,' Colin said. 'At Inveraray we even have a suite of rooms called Princess Louise's rooms. The one thing everyone loves more than a lord is royalty.'

Although the royal connection would later prove useful to my publishers in marketing my books on the royal family, at the time it was of no significance to me. I had met several members of the British royal family, starting at the age of about six or seven with Princess Alice of Athlone, as Queen Victoria's granddaughter and Queen Mary's sister-in-law was informally known. I found them all boring, and hated how most people stiffened into grotesque parodies of themselves as soon as a royal was present. My only concern was that I should not end up trapped in this surreal environment. 'I do hope that doesn't mean we'll have to be cheek and jowl with them when we're in England,' I said.

'Good God, no,' Colin laughed. 'I've never even met any of them. Pa was banned from court after his first divorce. He was the hereditary master of the Queen's household in Scotland, but he was never allowed into the royal presence. It upset him dreadfully, but there was nothing he could do about it. Princess Anne did come to Inveraray once. I wasn't there, but I heard the whole story. Ian went charging up to her and said, "I'm the Marquis of Lorne." She replied, "So?" turned on her heels and walked off. Cool eh?'

That evening, Patricia Fleischmann, who was my matron-of-honour, arrived by train with Kate, Jeanie's daughter from her marriage to Norman Mailer. We had a riotous dinner, all caught up in the unfolding drama. Afterwards, we turned in early so that we would be fresh for the big day. Colin and I had still not made love – we were never alone, not for one minute. I did not regard this as ominous: I had never had a lousy lover, so it did not occur to me that such a thing as sexual inadequacy could jump off the pages of women's magazines and land in my bed.

Saturday 23 March, 1974 was a chilly but sunny spring day. I awoke nervous as the dickens, but even surer than before that I was doing the right thing, for Colin had been so endearing and solicitous the night before. Patricia Fleischmann stayed with me as I dressed for the wedding, while Jeanie, Kate and Cusi kept Colin company in Patricia's room until it was time to go down to the courthouse for the marriage certificate. 'It's bad luck to see one another,' Jeanie had warned, and thereafter she resolutely kept us apart.

Only when we were about to be married did I see Colin. He was so handsome, so sweet and so funny that I floated through the ceremony on a cloud of romance. Only one thing spoiled it. Flashbulbs popped throughout, and even if Joe Dever, the society columnist, was Colin's best man, I still wondered how such a large contingent of the press had found out that we were getting married. The short answer to that was through the Campbells themselves. I was marrying into a family which measured its worth in terms of publicity instead of with the yardstick of sterling virtues.

Of the three siblings, Jeanie was the only one with a bona-fide relationship with the press. Through her mother, the Hon. Janet Aitken, she was the granddaughter of the first Lord Beaverbrook, the Canadian press baron who owned the *Express* newspapers and the *Evening Standard* in Britain. For many years Jeanie had written an American diary for the *Standard*, so she not only knew a plethora of journalists but also understood the way the press worked. Ian and Colin, who were not Aitken's children, had no link to the Beaverbrook dynasty. Such knowledge as they had had mostly been acquired through their disreputable father, who had 'worked' the print medium the way a cheap whore 'works' the street.

I did not know that the family had a history of whipping up perfectly ordinary situations into worldwide sensations. Twice in the last eighty years the Argyll family had gener-ated global scandals. The first had been the greatest scandal of the Victorian age – greater even than the Oscar Wilde debacle that followed shortly afterwards. This involved the previous Lord Colin Campbell, a syphilitic whose wife Gertrude refused to sleep with him for fear of reinfection after having been 'cured' of the disease, which nevertheless first crippled her and finally killed her at the age of fifty-three. His reaction was to enforce his conjugal rights, and when she retaliated by acquiring a legal separation, he tried to have her imprisoned in Paris on a trumped-up charge. When that failed, knowing that divorce was the greatest taboo of the age, he prepared an action against her on the grounds of adultery, citing three men as co-respondents (he added his doctor as a fourth for good measure when the man was ill advised enough to tender a bill for services rendered during the trial). Although he was not granted a divorce, the previous Lord Colin Campbell did succeed in making the previous Lady Colin Campbell the most notorious woman in the British Empire at a time when the sun never set on British territory.

The second global scandal involved Colin's father Ian and his third wife, the celebrated beauty Margaret Whigham Sweeny, whom he divorced, using his great-uncle Colin's divorce tactics (three co-respondents, with a fourth added when expedient), after Margaret refused to hand over £250,000 as the price for a 'clean' divorce in 1959. 'Big Ian', as the six foot Duke was known in the family (Colin's pint-sized elder brother was uncharitably called 'Little Ian'), exploited the mess he created for pecuniary advantage, selling stories about Margaret to tabloids such as the *Sunday People* in Britain. After the divorce, when Margaret silenced him through the courts, the despicable manner in which he had supplemented his paltry annual income of £1,000 became public. He then suffered the greatest ignominy a British gentleman can endure: he was booted out of his clubs on the grounds that he was not fit to associate with gentlemen.

Had I known the family's predilection for scandals, I would have grilled Colin very carefully before marrying him. And I certainly would not have married him once I found out that he admired his father. I deeply deplore destructive and ungentlemanly conduct. He, on the other hand, could see nothing wrong with it.

As it was, after our marriage I posed in blissful ignorance for the press with Colin standing proudly beside me. I had no inkling that I was being set up as a commodity for exploitation. I had become Lady Colin Campbell, an entity which had to be milked to keep Colin in a style to which he had never been accustomed. The first step along that road was to gain maximum publicity on both sides of the Atlantic to turn us into well-known personalities. If the marriage worked, Colin fully intended to use our public image as well as my private attributes and talents – and my father's money – to fill his empty coffers. And if it did not, he intended to follow the precedent of his father and great-great-uncle: he would create a scandal and sell stories about me to the newspapers on the back of it.

Of course, I had no idea what I had got myself into. I happily accompanied Colin, Jeanie, Patricia, Kate and Cusi to Joe Dever's club in Philadelphia, where the columnist graciously hosted our wedding breakfast. I was ecstatic. I had achieved everything I had ever wanted: I was married to a great guy, a great-looking guy, and a guy from a suitable background. True, he had no money, but we were both young and we could work, and you did not need much money living in Fiji, which is where we meant to reside. Money aside, he was perfect. I looked forward confidently to a happy marriage.

After the celebratory luncheon, Colin and I said goodbye to everyone and set off for the Endicott Hotel on Rittenhouse Square. As we checked in, my heart beat ever faster in anticipation of the pleasures that lay ahead. No sooner had the bellboy taken us upstairs, deposited our luggage and departed with his tip than Colin and I would fall into each other's arms and make mad and passionate love, sealing our marriage and marking the beginning of a good and constructive lifetime together.

Colin, however, had other ideas. Making no move to fill the empty space looming between us, he said, 'I'm exhausted. I still haven't recovered from my jet lag. You don't mind if I rest for a while, do you?'

Covering my disappointment, I said, 'Of course not. While you do that I'll phone Mummy and my brother and sisters and give them the news.' Somewhere in a corner of my mind into which I did not wish to delve, I did register how odd it was that he had not even kissed me since our marriage. The eternal optimist, I put it down to tiredness and looked forward to a show of ardour when he awoke.

When Colin finally surfaced, he did not leap upon me, as any of the other men I had been out with would have done. In fact, he suggested that we took a walk around the city, as this might be the only time we would ever be there. How perspicacious of him, I thought, misunderstanding his motives and setting a pattern which became the hallmark of the marriage as it lurched ever downwards to its ultimate destination.

Our great romance was certainly not following any script known to lovers. After we'd strolled around for a few minutes, Colin suggested we stopped in a 'pub' for a drink. We then went from 'pub' to 'pub', as he called the bars. Because I did not know him, I had no idea what to make of his behaviour; but I didn't like it one bit. However, I wasn't about to start out my marriage by being demanding, so I gave him his head and let him get on with it. When I got hungry, I said so, and we went somewhere nondescript where I ate and he drank. 'My stomach is bothering me,' he said. I seized upon that as the explanation for his strange conduct.

At about ten o'clock a buoyant Colin and a perplexed and increasingly annoyed Georgie were approaching Rittenhouse Square on the way back to the Endicott Hotel when a passerby stopped and asked Colin, who was smoking a cigarette, for a light. Within seconds he had asked this stranger back to our room. I was so taken aback I literally gasped. What's he trying to avoid? I wondered, developing a sinking feeling in the pit of my stomach.

I found out ten minutes later, after the hotel receptionist refused to let him take his 'friend' up to the room on the grounds that it was against hotel policy. He fulminated, I agreed it was a intrusion upon his liberty and we headed upstairs as the 'friend' was being led out by the hotel staff.

No sooner had we closed the door of our room than Colin began pacing the floor like a caged beast. Sucking on his cigarette, he stomped back and forth. 'I wouldn't take it so much to heart if I were you,' I said, thinking he was still annoyed at the hotel staff.

'It's nothing to do with that. I'm uptight because I might not be able to satisfy you. You see,' he said, dropping the first bombshell, 'I've never had a relationship with a girl in my life.'

Stunned, I said, 'I'm not sure I'm following you.'

'I'm not a virgin or anything like that. I've had sex with prostitutes. In fact, Pa sent me to a bordello when I was sixteen. He said that was the best way to break your duck.'

Suppressing the thought that this was surely a conversation which we should have had before the wedding, and wondering where Jeanie had got the idea that Colin was some sort of Lothario, I resolved to be gracious and constructive. In a funny sort of way, I was suddenly almost relieved that it was something which I believed to be trivial. 'There's no rush, Colin. We barely know each other. We have a lifetime to get to know one another. I'm happy to wait,' I said, the momentary relief evaporating fast.

There were two king-sized beds in the suite, and although Colin and I started out sharing one bed (exchanging a kiss so chaste he might have been my son), within minutes he had got up, muttered something about jet lag and gone to the other bed. I've never heard anyone make such a production about jet lag before, I thought, noting that he had been in America for nearly a week now. Given the previous day's palaver over the uppers and downers, I wondered if I had married the male version of a drama queen.

Hopeful that this was not the case, and eager to begin married life, I drove us back to New York the following afternoon. Roger Samet had lent us his apartment, which became the scene for the second bombshell.

That night, as we were about to go to bed, Colin said, 'I wasn't totally honest with you yesterday. I have a hung-up about physical contact. So-and-so' – he named a male relation some years older than himself – 'used to force himself upon me when I was a little boy.' He went into such graphic detail that good taste alone prevents me from recounting the instances of fellatio and intercourse which he described, but, suffice it to say, I was staggered. And, of course, sympathetic.

'How terrible for you,' I said, my heart going out to him as it would to anyone who had been so abused. 'Why didn't your parents stop it?'

'They didn't know. Pa was always off somewhere with Margaret or Mathilda [his two step-mothers] and Ma wouldn't've believed me. God, that woman was a bitch. I cannot tell you how much I hated her.'

'Oh, Colin,' I said, rising from where I was sitting and cradling his head in my lap. He winced as I uttered words of compassion.

When I had finished playing Mummy to the wounded little boy Colin was now presenting himself as, I said, 'What I don't understand is how you could have seemed so desperate to get me into bed when we first met.'

'That was just to let you know I liked you. I knew you wouldn't say yes.'

'But Jeanie said you used to be quite a ladies' man, losing respect for them once they obliged.'

'That may be what she thinks, but it ain't like that. Not one bit.'

Sorry as I was for my new husband, I knew that I could not tolerate a marriage without sex or affection. Gently but firmly, I made this clear, but assured him that I was prepared to be patient. In return, he would have to make an effort to overcome his antipathy to what was, after all, no source of pain, but one of life's fundamental joys.

I must confess that I did wonder whether I had made a

terrible mistake. It chilled my blood that Colin hated his mother. I was a firm believer in the psychological principle of transference, whereby the feelings an adult male has for his wife are coloured by those he has for his mother, both during and beyond childhood. But I realised it was too late to back out of the marriage now. Unless I wanted to look an utter fool, I would have to hang in there and try to turn the situation round.

Despite my positive attitude, I was annoyed that Colin hadn't told me about his 'hang-ups' before our wedding. I appreciated that he was probably aware that I wouldn't have gone through with it, but thought it best not to labour the point now. Any comment I made about my rights would seem like a recrimination, and that would have been unproductive in the long term. If I wanted this marriage to work, I had to accept the unpalatable facts, take them in my stride and overcome them. I had successfully dealt with one monumental problem before, and I was confident that I had the strength of character to face this one.

Whatever his shortcomings, Colin was a dedicated hedonist, and the four days we stayed in New York on our so-called honeymoon were great fun. He was highly sociable, and we had one long party with friends of Colin's such as the interior designer Harrison Cultra and his boyfriend, Richard Barker. They had been friends and tenants of Colin's mother at her house in Rhinebeck. They were also close to my good friend Mary Michele Rutherfurd, and I grew to like them both tremendously.

Colin, meanwhile, was smoking so much pot that even I, who smoked none, was getting high by simply being in the same apartment as him. But in 1974, so many people smoked pot recreationally that I thought nothing of his indulgence.

One evening, we were sitting in Roger's living room talking to a friend of Jeanie's named Joe. Without warning, Colin informed me: 'You're too sophisticated to live in Fiji. We'll stay in New York. I'll get a job in PR.' I was none too thrilled that he had made the decision without consulting me, but because New York was preferable to Fiji, I said nothing. Later, I tried to convince him that we should move to London, but having spent so much of his childhood in New York with his American mother, he wanted to stay there. 'The English are too uptight,' he reasoned, 'and anyway, a title goes further in New York.'

Of course, my family were eager to meet my new husband, so we made plans to fly out to Jamaica. My parents' reaction had been typical of their contrasting characters. Strongly sentimental, Mummy was caught up in the romance of it all and was perfectly prepared to give Colin a chance. My father, however, was another story. Upon hearing that I had married, his first question had been, 'What does he do?' When I told him deep-sea diving, Daddy asked what Colin's annual income was. The grunt in response to the $12,000 per annum I quoted put me on my guard. On the morning of our departure, I decided I had better warn Colin about my father. Daddy and I still had a highly volatile relationship. We might go for days or weeks in complete harmony; equally, there could be an unforeseen eruption within an hour of my arrival. I explained that Daddy was known to have a fiery temper, that he often regretted his explosions, and that Colin was not to take it to heart if there was one.

Colin seemed genuinely interested in what I had to say, so I also told him, in considerable detail, about the impact the medical mismanagement of my condition had had upon my relationship with my father. When I had finished, Colin, who was sitting on the floor in front of the matching sofas, said 'This is just uncanny. We have so much in common. Your father, my mother. Ain't this great?' This was hardly the response the situation warranted or I expected. I wondered whether he had actually absorbed much of what I had said. At least his reaction was positive, I told myself.

That first afternoon in Jamaica when Daddy met Colin, he ominously refused to tell me what he thought of my husband after interviewing (no other word is appropriate) him for twenty minutes. Only when our marriage had hit its first major rock did my brother Mickey reveal Daddy's prescient comment after that encounter: 'George's picked up a drunken bum. I only hope he doesn't think I'm going to support him.'

Regrettably, Colin expected precisely that. Indeed his principal reason for marrying me was that I was Michael Ziadie's daughter.

When a man marries a woman for her money, he then has to work out how best to get his hands on it. For Colin this tricky problem was compounded by the fact that the money wasn't mine anyway. In truth I had none. The only thing of value I had was my jewellery collection, which, while not excessive, was certainly considerable. Within forty-eight hours of returning to New York after our wedding Colin started trying to persuade me to take my jewellery, most of which had come from my parents and my Aunt Marjorie, to the jeweller's near Roger's apartment for an appraisal with a view to selling some of it. 'We'll need the money to furnish an apartment,' he said.

He had reckoned without my feminine wiles. I was certainly not about to part with any of my jewels. Although appearing to acquiesce, I got the jewellers to provide the lowest possible quotation, the breakdown value, for a Fabergé bracelet and tiara, both of which were made from gold-plated silver. I then informed Colin of the appraisal, which was hundreds of times less than the pieces were worth. 'It wouldn't suit us to sell at all,' I said.

Colin then began what turned out to be an intermittent but continuous campaign to gain access to Daddy's money. 'Get your father to settle an annual income on you.'

'Daddy's not like that,' I'd explained when he first brought up the subject in New York. Undeterred, he mentioned the matter again, the morning after our arrival in Jamaica as he, Mummy and I were having breakfast. Kicking him under the table, I quickly invented some excuse to get him alone in our bedroom. 'Please don't embarrass me in front of Mummy. Daddy will never agree to something like that,' I said. 'He thinks that men have a duty to support their wives. Approaching him won't only be fruitless, it will mean he'll never have any respect for you. I cannot tell you how humiliating that would be for me. I'd sooner starve than put myself in that position.'

But as I was to learn, Colin was nothing if not determined and resourceful. By midday my new husband was making the first of a series of unaccountably frequent telephone calls to his brother Ian in Scotland. I had no idea what they were talking about – I was too well brought up to eavesdrop – but even Mummy said, 'What on earth can be so important that he has to phone his brother every two minutes?' In those days, long-distance calls were expensive, especially in Jamaica, where not only were the charges substantially higher than in most places but also attracted a tax of nearly 100 per cent per call.

The same afternoon Daddy took a telephone call from the *Daily Telegraph* in London. 'We have been informed that your daughter changed sex. Is that true?'

'No, it is not,' my father said. 'Where did you get that from?'

'I'm not at liberty to tell you, but it was an impeccable source.'

A wave of panic swept over me when Daddy recounted the conversation to me. I could hardly believe that after four years my worst nightmare might be about to become a reality. 'Keep calm,' Mummy counselled. 'They can't print something that isn't true.'

'They wouldn't dare,' Daddy boomed. 'I'd sue them for every penny they have.'

Reassured, I calmed down. Within ten minutes, though, my father's niece, Doreen Forbes, rang from the *Gleaner*, where she worked. The British tabloid the *Sunday People*, Doreen said, had sent through a request for a stringer to check me out following a tip-off from a 'well-placed source'. The *Gleaner* had asked their social columnist, Violetta de Barovier-Riel, to deal with the matter, but Violetta, who was a family friend, had refused to do so. Doreen said they were looking for a replacement as she was speaking, and warned us to expect another call within a few minutes. 'Don't talk to them, Uncle Mike. I'm going to Theodore Seely right now to ask him to put a stop to this.'

This time I absolutely freaked out. I became completely hysterical. 'You must get a hold of yourself,' Mummy kept saying as I bayed like a caged animal about to be immersed in boiling water. Colin said something I took at the time to be an attempt to console me. 'The publicity doesn't matter to me. You can sell your story for a small fortune and the controversy will help you get your book published.' Thinking how sweet but misguided he was, I didn't bother to respond. Not that I could talk, for I was in such a state I could only howl and cry uncontrollably until Mummy forced two valium tablets down my throat.

Just as the tranquillisers were taking effect, Doreen phoned through to tell us that Theodore Seely had no intention of publishing, or helping anyone else to publish, a scandalous story about me. Once more he had mentioned Mummy's charity work, and asked if we would grant one of his journalists an interview on the specific and non-controversial subject of the marriage. Needless to say, we agreed with grateful hearts.

'Go and lie down until they get here,' Mummy advised.

'I'll come and keep you company,' Colin said. As soon as we were lying down, he reached over to my side of the twin beds which were pushed together as one. 'Come here,' he said, taking my hand in his. He pulled me on top of him, brought my head down to his, and initiated the first kiss of our marriage. 'I'll have to teach him how to kiss,' I thought, delighted that the second nightmare of the past few days was coming to an end with the first. Talk about wishful thinking.

Without further preamble, Colin inserted himself into me. Any man with any experience or sensitivity would have known that a woman isn't a light switch. Obviously I'll have to teach him how to make love was well, I thought as the encounter reached a quick conclusion. Even though he was no good in bed, at least the marriage had been consummated, which gave me hope for the future.

In that, as in so much else, my optimism was to prove misplaced. Thereafter, carnal relations (for that is all they can be called) took place on a sporadic basis. In total there were no more than five or six encounters, and each was as sensually sterile as the first. Kissing was out, and Colin didn't want his body touched, nor was he inclined to touch mine. He was always totally passive, lying back with eyes tightly shut and expecting me to do all the work until he had achieved his quick climax, at which point he pulled himself away unceremoniously. Talk about inadequate: he was every bit as unsensual and asexual as I had sensed when we were first introduced, and I ended up feeling like a necrophiliac.

In the first days of our marriage, though, I happily flung myself into the preparations for the first of our four wedding receptions, the Jamaican reception, which was to be followed by similar events in London, Scotland and New York. The last of these never took place. By that time the marriage had so degenerated that I told Patricia Fleischmann, our hostess, not to bother.

Despite the wrinkles in the background, Colin made a real attempt to fit into the family and get along with all my friends. If he was demanding and needy, he was nevertheless powerfully charming and good fun, and I really thought he was a great guy, if a little screwed up. Certainly, he smoked too much grass, drank too much booze and took too many uppers and downers, which he had purchased in quantity as soon as we arrived in Jamaica, where you could still buy just about any drug over the counter without a prescription. It was as a result of this preoccupation with drugs that I learned that Colin had lived in Jamaica, and about Middleton and his ganja crop.

Undoubtedly, the charmer I had married was full of surprises. Complexes, too, all of which I then thought he was admirably open about. What he was actually doing was parading them so that everyone would sympathise with his hard lot in life. It gave him the attention he craved and the excuse he needed to do nothing about helping himself. Day after day, Colin sat on the back veranda telling Mummy and me and whichever friends dropped in about how he had no faith in marriage, because his parents had seven marriages between them; how terribly he had been neglected by both of them (he saw his father only once between his parents' divorce when he was five and when he went to school in Scotland at twelve); how his mother never loved him because he was a mere second son and would never be the Duke; how he had hated her while growing up, and spurned her when he was an adult and she wanted to have a relationship with him; how his brother made him feel unwelcome at Inveraray Castle, despite the fact that he did not own it, but was a mere tenant there.

Sympathise I certainly did. This, after all, was 1974, and peace and love had given way to 'Don't be judgemental.' And, more to the point, having suffered in my own life, I identified strongly with underdogs. And if I had had any doubt that Colin was deserving of pity, I needed only to look at the state of his wardrobe for living proof of the deprivation to which he laid claim. His worldly goods were easily held by one medium-sized and battered suitcase. He had one pair of shoes; a navy blue velvet smoking jacket that had seen better days; one ruffled dress shirt with a frayed collar; one bow tie; three pairs of cheap socks; three or four old shirts for day wear; one turtle-necked sweater and casual suit, which we had bought the day before our wedding between purchasing the rings and looking for his drugs. The day after our arrival in Jamaica, I rang my Aunt Hilda, who worked with my father, and asked her to send up an extensive list of clothes and shoes from my father's shop. It would have been too mortifying to drag around a husband who looked like a tramp.

It was at this point that Colin started saying, 'I hope you don't think I married you for your father's money.'

'What money?' I asked, the thought having never occurred to me. 'How could you marry me for Daddy's money when he isn't a rich man? David Koch is rich, Ari Onassis is rich. Daddy is merely comfortable. I'd have to be paranoid to think anyone would want to marry me for

Daddy's crumbs when there are people with huge loaves out there.' Talk about naïve. While I regarded my father as having no real money, in the eyes of others, especially some-one with a paltry income of $12,000 per annum and no real prospects of earning much more than that, he was seriously rich.

Money seemed to be a subject dear to Colin's heart. His major preoccupation now, the jewellery escapade having failed, was how we could generate the capital to furnish our apartment in New York. 'The furniture has got to be antique. Nothing but,' he stipulated. Anything else would be infra dig for Lord and Lady Colin Campbell.

'Don't worry,' I would reassure him, thrilled that someone who had lived such a hippy lifestyle seemed to care so much about his surroundings. 'Daddy and Mummy are giving us money, Mummy is going to sneak me another whack on her own and Auntie and Grandma have also promised large cheques. And Aunt Hilda's phoning all the Ziadie and Azan relations to tell them not to weigh me down with the usual load of silver, china and crystal, but to bring cash. By the time they're through throwing money at us, I'd be very surprised if we can't furnish two apartments.'

I was right. With my wedding present money, we were able to buy superb antiques for the apartment I found on East Eighty-Third Street between Lexington and Third avenues. And that was after the apartment remained empty for four months while we headed for the United Kingdom, where Colin was able to enjoy the novel experience of being flush with cash for the first time in his life.

Those were heady days indeed. We stayed with my cousin Toni de Acevedo off the King's Road (Colin did not want to stay with his brother, towards whom he had strong feelings of antipathy, as well as the occasional fraternal tug, though Ian did tender an invitation) until Charles Delevigne found us a sweet cottage on Coulson Street in Chelsea, which interconnected with Mary Michele Rutherfurd's flat on Lincoln Street. I took Colin to Jermyn Street to augment his wardrobe. All my friends were so happy for me that just seeing their faces was pure pleasure. Even the press reports of our marriage were wholly flattering. Colin and I had become the Romeo and Juliet of 1974, my husband cast as the ruggedly individualistic aristocrat and me as the beauty with the brains and the bread. Colin's brother, the Duke of Argyll, organised two wedding receptions for us, one in London at his little house in Park Walk, the other in Scotland at the ancestral home, Inveraray Castle. Although we fared less well in the wedding-present department than we had in Jamaica, I did not mind, for many of the people I met were warm and charming, and all, without exception, were welcoming.

Ian and his wife Iona could not have been more welcoming, either. In fact Ian seemed most excited by our marriage and the attendant hoopla. On our first afternoon in London, he insisted that Colin and I came over for tea. When we arrived, he proudly presented his brother with a folder filled with press cuttings. 'You're a star now,' he said to Colin, before launching into a long explanation of how he had kept the kettle of press interest aboil with stories about Colin's adventurousness, my beauty and exotic ancestry, the 'hooley' he planned to have for us and so on. I was frankly surprised that he cared about what I regarded as trivia, and that he was so well informed about my antecedents. So that was how Colin had been spending Daddy's money when he'd been chattering away non-stop to his brother from Jamaica.

Colin was thrilled with the press coverage. Up to this point in his life, he had been ignored by the papers. He was the only member of his notorious family deemed too insignificant to be written about. Lords, after all, were sufficiently commonplace in Britain to be of no interest unless they did something noteworthy or notorious. Cutting a drugged and drunken swathe through the Americas and the Antipodes might have qualified, but since that was hush-hush, it took marriage to me to catapult him into the limelight.

'I don't see how you can say your brother is jealous of

you,' I said to Colin once we were safely back at Toni's flat. 'He struck me as genuinely pleased for you.'

'There'll be a catch,' Colin said. 'Depend on it.'

Ian's conduct the following evening belied any indication of sibling rivalry, and I wondered whether Colin was being paranoid. Ian and Iona took us to Mr Chow's, the fashionable Knightsbridge restaurant owned by Michael and Tina Chow, for dinner. Colin and I mentioned that the *Sunday Express*, a Beaverbrook newspaper, had given me a hard time about my past during an interview earlier that day. I was especially distraught about the source Colin said they had given him: an ex-boyfriend of mine who knew my family in Jamaica. Ian was sympathy itself. Iona, who seemed to have a limited attention span when the subject of conversation strayed too far from herself, either stared goodnaturedly around the celebrity-packed restaurant or repaired to the loo for extended periods.

Moreover, Ian came across as genuinely interested in the circumstances of my wrongly assigned gender. Accustomed to an environment in which no one ever spoke about such an awkward matter to one's face, I was delighted to have acquired a brother-in-law who was keen to know what life had been like for me. So I told him everything – not only about how the mistake had been made, and how it had been compounded, including my frustration at not being sent to Johns Hopkins in Baltimore, but even about how the solution had resulted in me having two birth certificates.

As much as the brothers loved publicity, I was reluctant to be written about more than was absolutely necessary. As I was the linchpin, and my co-operation was essential if the bandwagon were to continue to roll, they both employed their considerable skills of persuasion to conquer my fear of the press. They were terribly plausible. 'The papers can't print lies about you. If they do, you can sue.'

'Wives in this family are celebrated as great beauties. You have a duty to the family to co-operate in flattering publicity.'

'The publicity we're/you're getting will do your book good. It will help you to get it published.'

'Every report says how beautiful you are. A few more articles and you'll knock Margaret off her perch.'

My vanity did not require confirmation of my supposed beauty, nor was I competitive. The fabled Margaret, Duchess of Argyll could sit upon the throne of great beauty forever for all I cared. I thought that co-operating with puff pieces when two newspapers now had brought up the explosive issue of my background was begging for trouble, and I did not see why any publisher would be influenced by the superficial celebrity of an author of a work on philosophy – the book either stood on its own merits or collapsed accordingly. But I was grateful for the warm and kindly way in which Colin and Ian had taken my past in their stride. I was mindful, thanks to Daddy's warnings over the years, that there could have been a less enlightened response. For that reason, and that reason only, I stopped short of point-blank refusal to accommodate their quest for publicity.

While I was being querulous about the degree of media attention we had received to date, unbeknown to me, Ian was beavering away setting up an even greater barrage than had hit us so far. The result was that Colin, Ian, Iona and I flew into Glasgow to be greeted by a solid phalanx of photographers and reporters, who were not content with an interview at the airport, but had to follow us as far as the home of Iona's father, Sir Ivar Colquhoun of Luss, on Loch Lomond. It now emerged that the press were not interested in Colin. All the questions were aimed at me. Our marriage was nothing but a peg – had they been able to mention it without referring to Colin Campbell, they would undoubtedly have done so.

I didn't like this new development one bit. I dreaded the possibility of yet another journalist grilling me about my private life the way Lady Olga Maitland had done when she had interviewed us for the *Sunday Express*. I had found the experience deeply invasive, sullying in fact, as if someone were asking for an inspection of my body. I drew a metaphorical line underneath all this press nonsense and resolved to keep out of the media's way from then on.

When the newspapers containing the stories were delivered, Ian and Colin pored over the reports in the library, devouring each word and savouring each phrase as if they were consuming the most delicious meal. 'This is great,' Colin said.

'Marvellous, old boy,' agreed Ian, who had been born in Portugal and raised in France and America, and tended to overcompensate for his un-British background and mainly American heritage with an exaggerated English accent. 'We must get the chaps from *Tatler* and William Hickey to come up for the reception.'

'I hate to be a party-pooper,' I said. 'But I really couldn't function with the press at something as private as my wedding reception.'

'We wouldn't want the latest addition to the family being uncomfortable, now would we, brother?' Ian said in his stilted but charming way. 'It was just a thought, Georgie.' He looked up from the paper and smiled benignly at me.

But I was going to be fried alive in the fat of publicity. The question wasn't whether this would happen, but when.

7

Inveraray Castle is every child's idea of a fairytale castle. Its four towers were castellated into neo-Gothic cones during the reign of Queen Victoria, whose daughter Louise was then the Duchess of Argyll. It nestles beside Loch Fyne, with the Highlands behind it, in as picturesque a setting as can be imagined.

Compared to English stately homes such as Chatsworth or Longleat, Inveraray Castle is small. But that merely adds to its charm, making it cosy and homely rather than splendidly impressive. Despite the fine French furniture procured before the French Revolution by the then Duke and his wife, Elizabeth Gunning, it invites you to kick off your slippers and put up your feet.

When I first saw Inveraray Castle, this feeling of homeliness was enhanced by the modesty in which the current Duke and Duchess lived. They were tended only by a butler and his wife, helped, on a part-time basis, by a couple of cleaners, one of whom I was assured would loathe me because I was used to a full complement of servants and she was supposedly rabidly left wing. In the event, I found Mrs Lindsey a delight, and at first Inveraray even worked its magic upon my marriage.

For the first few days, the tensions in Colin's and Ian's relationship were relaxed, along with those in our marriage. Colin became warm and affectionate instead of distant and elusive. We even made love twice (lousy both times, but at least his heart seemed to be in it). I expected us to go onwards and upwards, building a nurturing relationship from this foundation.

It was in this frame of mind that I set out with Colin and Ian for a tour of the Argyll estate and its surroundings. We passed Innischonnel Castle. 'That's the original Campbell stronghold,' Ian said, pointing to the ruins. 'I'll let Colin have a life tenancy on it if you two agree to restore it.'

'I don't know where we'd get the money from,' I remarked.

'Maybe you should ask your father,' Colin suggested.

'It wouldn't cost much to do up,' said the impecunious Ian, expansively, as if large sums passed daily through his hands. 'No more than £250,000.'

'Daddy would never put his money into any enterprise he didn't own,' I said, 'even if he had money like that to spare, which I'm sure he doesn't.'

'Sure he does,' replied Ian, much to my surprise. 'Colin told me about your mother's jewels.' Colin had been present when Mummy brought home a selection from the bank to choose from for our Jamaican wedding reception. 'And Carolyn Nathan [a Jamaican socialite friend who had just been staying at Inveraray] said you Ziadies are rolling in it.'

'Daddy will never hand a large sum over to anyone until he's dead,' I insisted, hoping to close the subject.

'Why don't you ask?' Colin suggested.

'Yes, good idea,' Ian chipped in. 'Nothing ventured, nothing gained. He can only say no.'

'You know what Daddy's like,' I said to Colin.

By this time, Ian must have realised that this line of persuasion wasn't going to work with me. I could tell from the look Ian gave me that he was not exactly thrilled that I was being so obstructive of his plans to have his brother and sister-in-law living nearby in Scottish splendour, and I could see, for the first time, what Colin had meant when he said that Little Ian wasn't all sweetness and light. Ian then confirmed that observation with a catty comment directed at baby brother: 'I see you picked yourself a wet one.'

It was easy, when looking at Ian's precarious financial predicament, to see why aristocrats with large houses and heavy responsibilities now had to put practicality to the fore of their thinking. Inveraray had been built in the eighteenth century, when the Argyll family had been wealthier and more influential than they were now. It might have been smaller and more comfortable than other stately homes, but it was still a large house and very difficult to keep warm. It was not centrally heated, nor could Ian and Iona afford even to install, much less run, electric radiators and it was rather pathetic to see them rattling around in it trying to maintain what they called 'standards'. These included hot-water bottles, which Iona herself scurried around popping underneath the guests' pillows before they retired to their freezing beds at night. And this was at the height of a particularly warm spring.

Inveraray gave me another unwelcome insight into human nature. The British upper classes, I soon discovered, were nothing like the Americans, Continentals or Jamaicans. They would do anything – be nice to people they despised, tolerate scorn and abuse, most likely even silently bear witness to the stabbing of their own mother – just to receive an invitation to stay in a stately home. And if that invitation wasn't forthcoming, they would resort to staying at a nearby bed-and-breakfast, from where they would launch an embarrassing series of phone calls to ensure that they were received for a quick drink or tea at the very least. This enabled them to return to London and drop the odd comment such as, 'When I was at Inveraray, I said to Ian/Iona/Colin/Georgie . . .' as if they had been in residence as house guests. To people like these, friendship had less to do with liking someone than with forming associations based on the right social and material connections. This chilled me spiritually, but I did not pass judgement; I simply gave thanks for having British friends like Mary Anne Innes-Ker and Diana Ballard, who liked me for myself.

Along with the bona-fide house guests that old sinking feeling reappeared: something I couldn't put my finger on was wrong again with my marriage. I confided in both Mary Michele Rutherfurd and my cousin Toni, who agreed with my mundane analysis that Colin was probably possessive and didn't like sharing me with my friends. Confident that we would recapture our intimacy once they had departed from Inveraray, I was not worried. Nor was I tempted to push my friends and family aside to accommodate the jealousy of a man. So I threw myself into enjoying their company, and, to give Colin his due, he made every effort to be hospitable.

It wasn't until we all went to visit Glencoe that I discovered the family into which I had married was still regarded in many parts of Scotland as the world's original war criminals. Colin ill advisedly dropped his name in an attempt to expedite lunch at a restaurant near Glencoe. The waitress refused to serve any of us. 'I don't soil my hands feeding Campbells,' she said. The name Campbell was synonymous with treachery and evil to many Scots because of the Massacre of Glencoe, which took place in 1692, at a time when the Highland clans' tradition of hospitality compelled them to offer shelter even to their enemies. The Earl of Argyll ordered his men to seek refuge at Glencoe with his enemies, the MacDonalds, and then, when night had fallen and their hosts were asleep, to slay every last man, woman and child.

Glencoe, it emerged, was the most ignoble act in a thousand-year history of Campbell savagery and treachery, but there were many other lesser crimes, some of which the present Countess of Airlie entertainingly recounted to a party of us when I visited Cortachy Castle later. Others I learned about from just about every Scot I met. There were so many instances of betrayal, deceit, rape, pillage, disembowelment – even the setting alight of children – that they soon blended into one in my memory. But the common theme was clear: the Campbells of Argyll had a just reputation for cruelty and treachery.

I took the view time distanced the current Campbells from their forebears. Nearly 300 years had elapsed since the Massacre of Glencoe, and the other incidents were part of the past, too. I regarded myself as being far too fair-minded to believe in 'bad blood', or to stain someone's slate with the sins of his father, never mind a long line of vicious and treacherous ancestors. I was surprised by the fierce antipathy towards the family that persisted, but I did not feel any of it had anything to do with me.

We left Inveraray to stay with Jeanie's Aitken cousin, Alan Ramsay, at Galashiels in the Borders. On the way there, Colin told me that I could never be buried in the Campbell burial site at Iona because I was a Catholic and the Campbells had been anti-Catholic traditionally, even though Jeanie and Margaret Argyll were also of my religion. 'Pa would never have let me marry you if he'd been alive,' he sneered. 'A bloody Catholic and a bloody colonial.' I was too shocked by this sudden unaccountable malice to reply.

Colin quickly reverted to being pleasant after that first attack, but he remained as emotionally distant as he had been before our stay at Inveraray. I thought perhaps life would improve once we had left Scotland and moved into a place of our own in London, so I was grateful when we said goodbye to Galashiels and drove down to our little cottage in Coulson Street. It was to be our first marital home, since we had not yet lived in the New York apartment, and I was as excited as any new bride. I was looking forward to seeing my many London friends; Colin had a few, too, so we both got on the 'blower', as he called the telephone, and organised our diaries.

On the May bank holiday Monday, I set off with him for a drink in the neighbourhood pub, the Queen's Head on Tryon Street. Colin's stepmother, Mathilda, for whom he had professed undying love, was due to visit us from Paris. Ian was rather less fond of Mathilda: they were involved in a protracted legal suit over chattels which he wanted and she claimed were hers by right. After his second pint of beer, Colin became moody and started to talk disparagingly about Mathilda. Obviously, at Inveraray he had allowed his brother to influence him against her. 'But I thought you liked her,' I said.

'All women are bitches,' he sneered, in the same ugly tone he'd used at Galashiels.

This was so patently ridiculous that I could not treat it as anything other than a joke. 'Come on, Colin,' I laughed, jollying him along, 'you know that's not true. You've always said you liked Mathilda. How could she be a bitch? And I'm no bitch.'

For a long and lingering moment time stood still. Colin looked at me. I could tell from his expression that he understood what I was trying to do. For a while I thought he would scale the hurdle. For a split second it seemed he would break into a grin, but the hurdle was evidently too high. Instead his cheeks sank in and his mouth turned downwards. An expression of pure venom darkened his face. 'All women are bitches. My mother was a bitch, Mathilda is a bitch, and you're a bitch,' he said, grabbing my wrist and spilling my Coca-Cola.

With that, he stood up, still clutching my wrist, silently yanked me out of my seat and manhandled me into the car. He stood aside while I opened the door then pitched me in roughly. I stretched across to his side and opened the passenger door for him. He climbed in, sucking deeply and moodily on a Dunhill cigarette. As I drove the short distance to our cottage, I tried to pour oil on troubled water with expressions of wifely concern. 'Shut up, you stupid bitch,' he spat as we pulled up. No one had ever called me stupid before, and, whatever else I was, I was even less of a fool than a bitch. Partly through nerves, and partly because of the preposterousness of his insult, I started to laugh.

Colin leaped out of the car, stalked to my side before I had a chance to open the door and hauled me out. His fingers pressed into my right arm and he shoved me across the pavement, digging deeper into my flesh while I searched my handbag for the house keys. 'You're hurting me,' I said.

'Hurry up, you stupid cunt,' he said in a voice so laden with malevolence that it chilled my blood. Instead of relaxing his grip, he tightened it.

As soon as I managed to get the key in the lock and turn it, he kicked open the door and threw me through it, kicking it shut with his foot. He shoved me across the sitting room to the sofa, and pushed me down on it by the shoulders. By this time, I was laughing hysterically.

'Shut up, you bitch.' He stood menacingly over me, glowering with such irrational poisonousness that I hovered between hysteria and amusement at the sheer ludicrousness of all this.

I had no experience of violent men, and I could not quite grasp what was happening. 'Let me go upstairs and compose myself,' I said between giggles.

'You ain't going anywhere, you cunt. You're gonna stay right here and shut that stupid trap of yours.'

'I can't,' I said between giggles that were now most definitely hysterical.

'You stupid bitch,' he said again. It was as if his body and soul had fused into one awful mass of irrationality. He clenched and unclenched his fists, swinging them ominously on either side of my face.

'Let me go upstairs,' I repeated in a panic as I tried to make my escape. He pushed my shoulders down with his fists. 'Sit down and shut up.' With that, he clenched his fists again and smashed them into the right side of my face again and again.

As the bones collapsed, I felt an explosion of pain. With an atavistic surge of strength, I jumped up, knocking him over. I didn't need to look in the mirror to know I was injured, but when I did, I was horrified. I saw the face of a monster, one half sunken in and misshapen. 'Look at what you've done to my face!' I shrieked, lunging at the beast on the floor and pounding him with my own fists until he captured both wrists and restrained me. 'You monster, you beast!' I kept repeating. 'You've destroyed my face!'

As soon as I could get up, I headed for the telephone and called Dr Michael Yates, the house doctor for the Connaught Hotel, who my cousin Toni had used as a general practitioner since the days when she lived there. It was not the first time I had had to call him: before we went to Inveraray, Colin had overdone the amphetamines and needed an antidote to dewire him. I told Michael what had happened now, and he instructed me to meet him at the casualty department of St George's Hospital on Hyde Park Corner.

When I hung up, a contrite Colin was waiting for me, having marshalled the full battery of his considerable powers of persuasion. The insane scene of destruction was at an end as suddenly as it had begun. Swearing that he had not intended to maim me, he begged my forgiveness and pleaded with me not to tell anyone else what he had done. 'I never meant to hurt you,' he cried. 'I don't know how it happened. You must believe me, Georgie. I love you.' It was the first time he had used those three magical words. Now the manipulative Colin repeated them over and over again.

Paradoxically, the fact that I had done nothing to trigger this abuse made it easier for me to accept it. Had I shared some responsibility, I would have been angrier than I was, if only because I would have been angry with myself for contributing to something that had resulted in such damage to my face. As it was, I did not feel angry, although the enormity of what had happened descended upon me with immediate and crushing weight. Unless plastic surgeons could repair the damage, I would never be called beautiful again. Who knows, I thought, I might even have to live out the rest of my life looking grotesque. This prospect made me feel physically sick, but I realised that my psychological survival depended upon me preparing myself for that eventuality. Preparation would help to shore up whatever resources I needed to maintain a positive attitude, for the one thing I could not afford was to have my spirit destroyed too. No woman who has enjoyed a reputation for beauty confronts the loss of her looks with equanimity, and I was no exception. My future options with men had suddenly been restricted in a major way, and that consideration alone made me more amenable to Colin's blandishments than I might otherwise have been.

Colin was overcome with remorse. All the way to the hospital, he begged and pleaded for forgiveness. 'It will never happen again. I don't know what came over me,' he kept repeating.

'Your problem is you drink too much and take too many drugs,' I said.

'I swear I'll cut down,' he vowed, desperation oozing from every pore. 'Please, please say you'll stay with me. You're the best thing that ever happened to me.'

'As long as you give me your word of honour,' I said, 'that you'll stop drinking so much. And you must stop drugs altogether.' To me, someone's word of honour was carved in stone.

'On my father's grave,' said Colin, who hero-worshipped his father. Then he launched into a long spiel about how he could end up in prison for assault if the police ever found out, and how they'd be sure to if the press got wind of it, which they would if I told anyone. All the papers had spies everywhere, he said, and someone in the hospital would be sure to betray us. This being a world I knew nothing about, and recognising the logic of his argument, I agreed to cover up for him. In truth, it was almost a relief to do so, for there can be few fates more demeaning for a woman than to have her own husband ruin her looks for no reason at all.

If I expected Colin to behave with consideration thereafter, I was in for a surprise. As soon as we reached the hospital and it became apparent that the process of examination, X-rays and treatment would be time-consuming, he made some excuse about the stress and strain of the hospital being too much for him to cope with and fled, doubtless to hit the bottle.

I didn't care. I was relieved to be rid of my persecutor-cum-husband. Dr Murdoch, the first doctor to examine me, asked how the injuries had happened. 'I fell down the stairs,' I lied.

'That's what they all say,' he said kindly, his eyes full of compassion. 'For what it's worth, injuries like yours can't be sustained in a fall.'

'Then you know.'

'Yes. I know.'

As luck would have it, Colin had done his worst on a bank holiday and most of the consultants were away. Mr Warner, the chief plastic surgeon, was on the golf course; the dental surgeon, who needed to be in attendance to realign my jaw, was not around either. By now the shock had worn off and I was in agony. Thank God Michael Yates showed up quickly, and buzzed back and forth between various members of the hospital staff, encouraging them to interrupt everyone's holiday and perform the reconstructive surgery sooner rather than later.

Once I was checked in, I telephoned my little sister Margaret at school. She immediately came to the hospital and, though she was as much of a support and comfort as she had always been, I refrained from telling her the truth. I didn't want the rest of the family to find out.

One person who did know all about the cause of my injuries was Mary Michele Rutherfurd. She lived in the building adjoining ours, and the two flats had an interconnecting door which we often used. You couldn't drop a pin in our cottage without Mary Michele hearing it in her flat.

At nine o'clock that evening, Mr Warner and his team reconstructed my face into what would become, once it had healed, as close an approximation of the original as any artist could have achieved.

The episode was undoubtedly a turning point in the marriage, but it was one which I hoped at the time would set us on a more positive path. I was tempted to leave Colin, but I did not want to discard a husband who had promised to alter his behaviour to search for another when my looks might never be restored. Moreover, I genuinely believed that it had been an isolated aberration that would never be repeated. But such joy as there had been had gone out of our marriage, and Colin's problems would have to be solved

before we stood a chance. It was a time of reflection as much
as of recovery, and I used the peace and quiet of enforced
bed rest to face the issues squarely.

I could no longer say in all truth that I either loved or was
in love with my husband. I had been halfway there when
we'd married, but he had failed to fulfil his spoken and
unspoken promise. Worse than that, he was so woefully
inadequate in enjoying any of the pleasures, much less living
up to the duties, of matrimony that I was frankly perplexed
as to why he had married me at all. It certainly wasn't for
sex, affection, or companionship, or any of the normal things
men wanted. I still could not believe it had been for money,
since I personally didn't have any.

I no longer wanted to stay with Colin, but at the same
time, I was aware that I had made a vow to God when I had
made my marriage vows. The Catholicism of my youth and
of my family had taken deeper root than I could have imagined, and the fact that our marriage had not been solemnised
by a priest did not affect, in my opinion, the validity of that
vow. The contract was between God and me, and I would
have to stay until a way out which did not involve me in
breaking my word presented itself.

Meanwhile, my husband was doing nothing positive
towards improving our relationship. His idea of cutting
down on his drinking was not to start until 11.30 a.m. Then
he would lurch home from the pub and pull out all the stops
to gain my sympathy. Day in, day out, he went on and on
and on about how unhappy his life had been; his lack of
faith in marriage; how his suffering at the incestuous hands
of his male relation had blighted his life and caused him to
turn to drink and drugs in an attempt to blot out the pain.
How there were times when he was so consumed with
hatred for his mother that he hated all women, and that I
mustn't take any manifestation of that sentiment personally.

It was clear that Colin was a total mess, and that something must have been responsible, but it never occurred to
me that the true reason might have been something as
simple as the fact that he was a spoiled and arrogant brat

who had been overindulged and underdisciplined by both his parents, and that his taste for intoxication had blown whatever brains he had once had. After all, no one could have had the hundreds of LSD trips he claimed, or taken the mescalin which induced flashbacks and had prompted one of his incarcerations in the Priory, the fashionable drink-and-drugs 'bin' in Roehampton, not to mention the cocaine he snorted and the heroin he smoked, and expected to remain either happy or sensible.

In the weeks after my release from hospital, our relationship was undergoing a fundamental shift. Because I now accepted that he was incapable of fulfilling the role of husband, and because his attempts to gain my sympathy cast me in the role of nurturer, I was being manoeuvred into playing mother and nanny rather than wife and sexual partner. Indeed, sex was now as dead as the dodo he had within his trousers. I saw the danger of a partnership based on these new dynamics, but I did not see what choice I had. It takes two to tango, and there was hardly any point in dancing sexily around the room on my own when my husband had passed out after a hard morning's or afternoon's, or evening's drinking.

By asking Colin to reduce his drinking and give up his drug-taking, I was threatening the very things he held dearest. Within days of my injury, he came up with a scheme that would allow him to continue as before, keep me docile and satisfy his desire for more money in the bank. Moreover, he introduced it, as he would thereafter introduce every other such strategy, with a breathtaking brazenness that blinded me from cottoning on to what he was up to until it was too late.

'I didn't tell you before, because I didn't want to hurt you, but I've had something on my mind. The *Sunday Express* mentioned to me the other day that your ex-boyfriend Ian Hamilton has been phoning them up and telling them that you're a man.'

This, of course, was a complete lie, but I swallowed it whole. I simply could not envisage my own husband

making up such a contemptible story. What possible motive
Ian could have for doing such a thing perplexed me until
Colin reasoned, 'He's obviously still keen on you. It's nothing but sour grapes. Since he can't have you, he wants to
destroy you.' Colin now set about convincing me that I
should ignore his little foibles, like drinking and drug-
taking, because I had cause to be grateful to him. He was
my protector, and I had a duty to teach Ian a lesson. 'You
must sue him for slander,' he advised. When I baulked at
such a noxious step, he demanded I do it for him if not for
myself. 'Put yourself in my shoes,' he said. 'Do you have
any idea how embarrassing it is to have everyone saying
my wife's a man? It's enough to drive even a teetotaller to
drink.'

Of course Colin has a right to be upset, I thought, bitterly
hurt that someone with whom I thought I was on good
terms could have been so malicious, but I didn't want to
sue. 'I'd much rather sort this out behind the scenes,' I said.

'Sue him and he'll have to settle,' Colin insisted.

'I can't sue him. We have friends in common, I know his
family and his knows mine. It would make things very awkward for everyone. What would they say to each other when
they ran into each other at the racetrack or at parties?'

'You put your friends and family before me, then wonder
why this marriage isn't working,' Colin grumbled.

He demanded that we consulted Peter St John-Howe, a
friend who was a solicitor. When Peter and his wife came
round for dinner to discuss the matter, I took him to one
side and told him that I really did not want an open breach.
Peter gamely came back with advice that pleased Colin but
at the same time took my reluctance into account. We were
to threaten to sue without actually doing so. Perhaps we
could get a friend to arrange a meeting between Ian and
ourselves, make the threat, and get Ian to agree to a settlement whereby he undertook not to repeat his allegation.

Kari Lai, through whom I had met Ian, set up the meeting
at her Eaton Square flat. 'Georgie, I did not phone up the
Sunday Express or any other newspaper and tell them

anything about you. I have never phoned up a newspaper in my life to give them a story about anyone,' Ian stated firmly. 'Why would I tell them that you're a man when you were my girlfriend?'

'That's exactly what I want to know,' I retorted bitterly.

'I didn't do it, Georgie. You must believe me. I would never do anything like that. Why on earth should I?'

'Sour grapes,' Colin volunteered. 'You couldn't keep her and I have her.'

'This is unbelievable,' Ian said plaintively. 'Georgie, you know me and I know you. Can you say that you truly believe I'm capable of something like that?'

'No, Ian, I really didn't believe that you were. That's what made it so shocking. And hurtful.'

'It's not true,' he repeated. 'I didn't do it, Georgie, I didn't.' He certainly seemed to be telling the truth. I wondered whether British newspapers would tell a bare-faced lie just to ferret out a story.

'This is pointless,' Colin said. 'The *Sunday Express* told me you did it. They have no reason to lie. You're either going to pay us £15,000 in damages or we're going to sue you for slander.'

I could not believe what I was hearing. St John-Howe had specifically told us not to discuss money, explaining, 'In Britain, you can't quantify damages for defamation. It's not like America.' When Colin pressed him, he said he thought we might get about £3,000 if the case went to Court.

'You see, Colin,' I'd said, 'it's hardly worth the bother financially, so we may as well settle it privately.' Now here he was demanding five times that amount.

'That's blackmail,' Ian said. 'Withdraw your threat or I'll go to the police.'

Although I was furious with Colin, I was not about to let Ian walk away believing that he was the injured party, just in case he really had made that call. 'It's not blackmail, Ian. If it were anything, it would have to be extortion. But Colin is not trying to extort money out of you. He feels you've damaged his reputation and he simply wants compensation for the damage you've caused. If you go to the police and report him for blackmail, you'll look a real idiot.'

Thereafter the discussion degenerated into accusations and counter-accusations, and I kept out of it as much as possible. Only after they had nearly come to blows did Ian depart. On the way home I was so angry I could barely contain myself. 'How could you have done that?' I demanded. 'You put yourself in the wrong. Peter told you not to ask for money, just an apology and an undertaking not to repeat the slander. Was this whole thing about silencing someone who has been spreading lies about your wife, or was it nothing but a covert attempt to extort money out of someone who you know has some?'

No sooner were the words out of my mouth that I knew I had hit upon the truth, or at least a part of it.

'He should pay for the lies he's told about you,' said Colin. 'Don't you care that he's humiliated us before the whole world?'

'How do I know the *Sunday Express* is telling the truth? Ian was awfully credible.'

'OK, OK,' replied Colin irritably. 'So I might have made a mistake. Maybe they did set us up. Maybe your stupid boyfriend wasn't lying. Is it my fault the newspapers are hassling me because of *your background*? Why are you so angry with *me*? I was only trying to protect you and make the bastard pay for hurting you.'

It did not yet strike me that the whole story could have been Colin's own creation, but that is what I now believe. However, I did feel in my heart of hearts that he had shown scant concern for my wishes and feelings and that he was trying to exploit the situation financially and me emotionally. This proved to be another huge nail in the coffin of our marriage.

At the time I was searching for an agent in London to represent my book on philosophy, so on several occasions I used that as an excuse to bring up the subject of how inextricably linked happiness is with sound values, attitudes and behaviour. Colin seemed incapable of making the connection between actions and consequences. Unable to grasp the notion that no one is above life's rules, he always seemed to think that he was a special case, that he was the one person who was entitled to enjoy the benefits of happiness while being poisonous, of sobriety while drunk, of thoughtfulness while being thoughtless, of being treated lovingly while behaving hatefully, of being loved while caring about no one but himself. Frustrating as it was to have acquired the role of Sunday-school teacher on top of all the others, I persevered, not because I seemed to be getting through, but because I did not know what else to do.

Help came from an unexpected quarter. Alan Ramsay's ex-wife, Frances Beveridge, who had known Colin all his life, and was only too aware of his problems with drink and drugs, saw me floundering and she came to my aid. 'The first thing he needs to do is give up drinking. I'll arrange an appointment with a doctor who can convince him to do so,' she said, 'then both of you can come and stay with us for the last few weeks of your time in England. That will relieve you of the burden that I know Colin can be.'

That Sunday, Colin and a relieved and hopeful Georgie drove down to Surrey to see this doctor. He clearly spelled out the options: drink and you destroy your life and marriage; give up booze and you give your life and your marriage a chance. Colin then tried a new tack: he tried to lay the blame at my door. He was just warming to his theme, that Frances and I were exaggerating his drinking, when I stopped him with a raised finger and one word. 'Cheekbone,' I said. He took the hint. Not wishing the Beveridges, the doctor, or anyone else to know about that incident, he hastily agreed to go 'on the wagon'.

But if I thought that this leopard was going to change his spots simply because he had changed his watering hole, I was in for a big disappointment. It was now July, and we had had no marital relations since Inveraray. Nor was sex the only dead issue, either. He still had his 'hang-up about physical contact', which ruled out affection as well. Moreover, he had no interest in me personally. He couldn't

My mother, seen here leading in *Patriotic Lady* (her favourite racehorse) was an ideal role model for any girl who wanted to be stylish and glamorous

My father, photographed here in Mexico in the mid-1960s

'Auntie', as we children called our mother's only sister Marjorie, was a figure of adoration

My maternal grandmother, May Smedmore, was a woman fifty years ahead of her time – she lived in complete harmony with her husband and her lover until her daughters were safely married before achieving the divorce she had long wanted

Me, aged about five, with my younger
sister Sharman

Me, aged between sixteen and seventeen
beside the swimming pool at home with my
best friend, Suzy Surridge

By eighteen I had escaped from the prison of a false identity and was living as myself in
New York. Here I am with Fred Dryer, the famous Giant football star, who went on to
become a television actor with his own series

Modelling, aged eighteen. One of the most agreeable surprises of my life
was to discover that many people regarded me as beautiful

At the Army Training Camp at Newcastle with my brother Mickey and sisters Sharman *(left)* and Margaret *(right)*

Jamaica in the early 1970s with sexy Mark Shand *(in the hat)*, brother of Camilla Parker-Bowles

Whenever I wasn't jetting up and down between London, New York and Jamaica, I dabbled as a model and dress designer. Here I am modelling a particularly daring outfit for the time

Tucker Fredrickson, the Giant's quarterback, was a famous sportsman and instrumental in introducing me to my first love

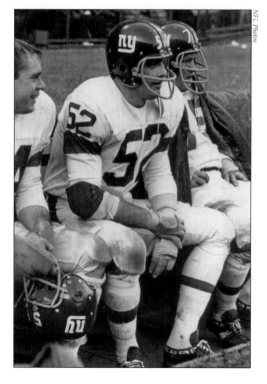

Bill Swain – my first great love and linebacker for the New York Giants and Detroit Lions – was a hunk on and off the football field

Like my contemporaries, my main aim in life was to be a wife. I really thought I was in heaven when I married an archetypal romantic hero named Lord Colin Campbell. This is a week after our American marriage at my parents' Jamaican house, photographed by Cookie Kinkead

After my divorce, I tried to pick up the pieces and return to my old life. Here as a model, this time photographed by Peta Gay MacMillan

Of all the people who knew the inside story of my marriage and divorce, none defended me more stalwartly than Colin's step-mother Margaret, Duchess of Argyll, seen here with me and businessman Daniel Hodson at the England Ball in 1976

Jardine-Matheson heir James Buchanan-Jardine, the next man to play a large part in my life, was everything my husband had seemed to be but was not

As I approached my thirties, I had a romance with the acclaimed English actor Larry Lamb. We have remained close friends

Friends are of crucial importance to single women, and I was lucky in having excellent ones throughout the solo years. None was more supportive or generous than the writer Cathrine Olsen, pictured here with her husband Sir James Mancham when I was staying at their Majorca villa

Margaret Thatcher

One of the most fascinating experiences of my life was working as Social Secretary to the Libyan Ambassador

The press went wild over the sumptuousness of the Ambassador's dinner dance, especially over the eminence of the guests, who included the Earl of Longford and Prince Paul of Romania

Once I started writing professionally, most of my social engagements were purely private, such as the one where I am speaking to Prince Michael of Kent at a luncheon he hosted

During my charity work my path inevitably crossed with that of the royals. Here I am with Prince Edward at a ball which I helped to organise for St John's Ambulance

My cousin Peter Jonas, Managing Director of the English National Opera, 1986

Simpson's Piccadilly widow Heddy Simpson, seen here in the background *(back to camera)* talking to me *(right)* with her heiress daughter Georgina and her actor husband Anthony Andrews *(standing left)*

In Vienna with a representative group of friends: J.Javier Mora; Ondine Smulders; Porfirio Munoz Ledo; and Hugo Villalobos Velasco at the Technike Ball

The Guards Polo Cup match at Windsor Great Park, where my camera and I were on the guest side of the fence as the other journalists stayed behind security ropes. The result was that I captured the Queen dropping something, bending over in her typical unpretentious way to pick it up, and being pre-empted by Brigadier Thwaites

The Maypole Ball in 1991, with the Duchess of York as guest of honour

Ivana Trump's engagement party to Riccardo Mazzuchelli speaking to my friend Harry, Duke of Northumberland, Syon House

One of the high points of my life was being received by His Holiness the Pope in a private audience at the Vatican

The high point of my life was becoming a mother when I adopted my two sons, Dima *(right)* and Misha *(left)* (seen here in the baggage trolley as we leave Moscow for London in July 1993)

Feeding Misha and cuddling Dima two weeks after getting them back to London

My country house with the boys and *(left to right)* Princess Georg zu Bentheim, Prince Maximilien zu Bentheim, Renate Manecke, and my two eldest dogs, Tum Tum and Popsie Miranda

A godmother and loyal friend has been Anna Lady Brocklebank

At one of Andy and Patti Wong's extravaganzas with Greek shipping heir Manoli Mavroleon

My brother Mickey photographed in front of his desk shortly before he fell ill

My adored boys Misha and Dima. Never was a mother more richly blessed

Rafting down the Milk River in Ocho Rios, Jamaica, in a £40,000 Norman Hartnell dress which the fashion house lent me

have cared less how I felt about anything, unless he stood to gain something from it. This became painfully evident when, a few weeks after the Ian Hamilton episode, he came up with another get-rich-quick-and-keep-the-wife-grateful-that-I'm-standing-by-her scheme. I went into Frances' drawing room to find Colin in full flow. 'The *Sunday Express* are a danger which must be eliminated,' he was saying to Frances.

'Why are you stirring up a hornet's nest?' I asked. 'Can't you let things be?'

'What happens if the *Sunday Express* print that story? It isn't only you and your family at stake. My family's reputation is on the line, too.'

Using the nag's version of Chinese water torture to break down my resistance, Colin went on and on about it for weeks. 'You have no objection to people knowing you've always been female even though you were brought up as a boy. Nor do I. But we both object to people thinking you are a man. The press will jump at the chance to report your story. If you don't give it to a sympathetic paper like the *Express*, sooner or later a hostile one will print it. I know how the press works, you don't. You've got to do it, and do it now. And if you're going to give it to them, you may as well sell it.'

Finally, worn down by all this, I took the first tentative step towards agreeing.

'Everyone does it,' said Colin. 'Pa did it all the time. How do you think he bankrolled his divorce?'

'Colin, I'm sure any journalist would respect one more if one didn't sell a story of that nature. If you truly believe there is a threat, surely the sensible thing is for us to choose the newspaper ourselves? They'd be doing us the favour of printing what we want.'

That amused Colin no end. 'Newspapers don't do people favours, Georgie,' he sneered. 'It's use and be used.'

'But we don't need the money.'

'We will. Sooner or later, we will.'

Although I dreaded the possibility of any personal

publicity, Colin had now got me to the stage where I saw the wisdom of making a pre-emptive strike to preclude any misrepresentation of the facts. 'Phone Olga Maitland. Go to lunch with her. Fly the idea past her,' Colin said. 'She's one of us. She'll keep her trap shut if it doesn't suit us to go through with it.'

Reluctantly, I got in touch with Olga, the Scottish aristocrat who had interviewed us for the *Sunday Express*. We met for lunch at Walton's. She told me the story wasn't worth anything like the tens of thousands Colin hoped for – at any rate, not in the decorous form I was insisting upon. I heaved a sigh of relief, especially when she advised me that any worries we had about it appearing in an inaccurate form were groundless. 'No newspaper would dare print something like that without proof,' she said.

Returning to the Beveridges' flat, I walked in on a discussion of the subject between Frances, her first husband Alan Ramsay, Colin and my brother. Mickey had returned that very day from Jamaica. He was saying to Colin, 'One doesn't deny rumours, Colin. Have you lost possession of your senses? No, no, a thousand nos. I will not allow you to bring my sister and our family into disrepute. Georgie will not be making any statement on her personal life, and that's all there is to that.' I have never been more grateful for Mickey's domineering character than I was at that moment.

In August we returned to New York, to real life. Since our apartment was still empty, immediately after dropping off our luggage we had to go shopping for beds. Colin opted for twin beds pushed together: a statement of separation, and a harbinger of ills to come if ever there was one. My spirits spiralled ever more downwards.

Two and a half weeks after our arrival, real trouble loomed. Colin received a letter from the attorney who handled his late mother's estate. The bottom line was that the kitty was empty. This was the only extra source of income for Colin or Ian, beyond the $12,000 per annum each brother received from their $225,000 stake in their maternal great-grandfather's trust. Colin, of course, freaked out.

The estate already owed Colin about $20,000. His mother had guaranteed a bank loan so that Ian could purchase his Park Walk house in London, but Ian had never made any repayments on the loan. It was hardly surprising, when he had no job of work and such a paltry income. The bank were demanding repayment of the outstanding amount, $21,011.23, and the executors of the guarantor's estate were obliged to satisfy the debt. It had cleaned out the account, and there was no money to settle the estate's debt to Colin. Worse, the Priory, where Colin had been treated for his drink and drug problems before he met me, was threatening to sue him for over £2,000 in unpaid fees. Unless the estate could come up with the money, Colin would suffer while Ian benefited from funds he owed his brother.

Colin was beside himself with worry that people would discover not only that he had drink and drug problems, but financial ones, too, if the Priory sued him. He placed the blame for the fix he was in squarely on his brother. They fired telephone calls and letters back and forth across the Atlantic, Colin demanding that Ian make good his debt; Ian refusing to acknowledge responsibility for his failure to do so. The only way Ian could settle the matter was to sell his Park Walk house, and this he was adamant he would not do.

Colin then turned his attention to me. Couldn't I get Daddy to help? I most certainly could not. My father would have said to Colin, 'Get your brother to fulfil his responsibilities and discharge his debt to you.' Colin then suggested using a portion of the money I had received from my family to furnish our marital home. We had already spent a lot of it on antiques since returning to New York. I reminded him of that, and of the fact that he had also dipped into it at a rate of knots in England, frittering it away on daily visits to the trichologist Philip Kingsley, even though he had a full head of healthy hair; standing round after round for a multitude of strangers in bars indulging in extravagances such as chauffeur-driven limousines to take him two or three blocks, when a taxi, or his feet, would have done the job just as well. We needed what was left to finish the apartment. The problem wasn't mine, and I wasn't about to become involved with it. He and Ian must sort it out among themselves. Moreover, the money Daddy, Mummy, Auntie, and Grandma had given us was specifically intended for our marital home. What would I say when they came to visit us and discovered that I had never completed the job?

By now I knew Colin well enough to anticipate that he would wait until I least expected it and then clear out the account. Not for nothing did he admire his father, who had been resourceful enough to steal his first wife Janet Aitken's diamond tiara on their honeymoon to settle his gambling debts. To prevent this I spent my own money before he had a chance to get his hands on it, ploughing every last cent into items we needed for the apartment. It left us very little to live on, but that, I reasoned, was no bad thing. It would force Colin to curtail his spending, and focus both our minds on generating income through something he seemed to find very distasteful: work.

As I saw it, my greatest opportunity to make some money was the book I had written, which I hadn't yet placed. I set about finding a literary agent with renewed vigour. At the time, Barbara Taylor Bradford lived on the same block as us. She very kindly put me in touch with her literary agent, Stephanie Bennett, who agreed to represent me. It would take Stephanie nearly four months to find the right publisher, but when she did so, it was one of the literary world's brightest stars: Howard Kaminsky, then head of Warner's book division.

In the meantime, I started looking for a job in the only sensible way I could think of: I wrote to people I knew, such as Bill Paley, who was the head of CBS. While I awaited their replies, I worked on the apartment while Colin pursued his primary activity: drinking. 'I thought you were giving up drinking and finding a job in public relations?' I finally said.

'PR isn't my thing,' he replied, quick as a flash. 'I'll try my hand at writing instead.'

'And what will you write?' I inquired with curiosity.

'A travelogue.'

'A *travelogue*?'

'Yeah,' he said edgily. 'You have said yourself how interesting my travels have been. Just you wait and see. It will
sell like hot cakes. The public will be intrigued to see how
the other half lives. It might even outsell your philosophy
book.'

I could hardly believe what I was hearing. 'Colin, a book
is a major project. It takes time and dedication to write. We
agreed that we'd both earn a living.'

'I'm not having you strong-arm me into taking a job I
don't want,' he said. 'You get a job. I've got my income. That
will be my contribution.'

'It's not enough.'

'Then get your cheapskate father to support us.' He
stormed off to the bar, slamming the door.

Obviously Colin's tactic was an attempt to force me to
appeal to Daddy for help, but I would sooner have chopped
off my right arm than have humiliated myself like that. So I
battened down the hatches and waited for my husband to
come to his senses.

Colin's response was to taunt me about why he'd married
me. 'Are you stupid enough to think it's because I loved
you? I don't love you. I only married you because of your
reputation as a great beauty and your father's money.
Doesn't he know that's how things are done when money
marries a name? My father didn't work a day in his life. His
wives supported him. That's what wives are for. That's what
you are for, you stupid bitch.'

Like any other woman, I wanted to be desired for myself,
not for my merits as a trophy or for my father's worldly
goods. His words had an unsettling ring of truth, but I was
not going to play the victim. When he persisted in rubbing
salt in that particular wound, I finally hit back. 'If that's the
case, you really must be dumb. Whoever heard of a man
marrying a girl without money on the off-chance that her
father will part with some of his?'

Predictably, now that Colin was back on the booze, things
went from bad to worse. Every morning he'd leave the

apartment, hit the bar and lurch back in mid-afternoon, ostensibly for lunch, which I had eaten an hour or two before and which he was usually too drunk to consume in any case. Then he'd collapse in a sodden, stinking heap on the sofa or bed. He'd crank himself up at about six, demand food, which he'd guzzle down like a hog, grunting and burping and grimacing. 'My stomach,' became his constant refrain, but I no longer had any sympathy for him. I pointed out that he was bound to develop alcoholic gastritis if he continued to abuse himself. His response was to guzzle more alcohol to dull the pain it had caused in the first place.

I don't know how much more of this I can stand, I often thought. By this time, I dearly wanted to leave him, but two things held me back. The first was my marriage vows, which I did not in all conscience feel I could break before enduring as much as was humanly possible, and I had not yet reached the end of my tether. There is no doubt that my medical history had a bearing upon my attitude as well. In those days, all divorce was construed as a failure on the part of one or both parties to the marriage. I was desperate not to fail, for I did not want anything to reflect adversely on my performance as an individual, or worse, a woman.

I tried to lead as normal a life as possible. Above all this meant seeing friends, irrespective of Colin's state, or whether he tagged along or not – and he not only broke arrangements but was an unpredictable companion when he did turn up. Mark Friend was then living in New York, and I often saw him. We would go together to see Huntington Hartford in his beautiful apartment at Beekman Place, or the Cuevas (Rockefeller) family at their house in the East Sixties. Barbara Taylor Bradford was also a good friend, as was Sarah Spencer-Churchill, and I saw a lot of them, too, though I always met Sarah on my own. Charles Dismukes the attorney and Charles Patterson of Hammacher–Schlemmer were also firm friends, as were Harrison Cultra and his partner, Dick Barker, whom I'd met shortly after my wedding. I also kept in close touch with Frances Bacal, my guardian when I was at FIT, who was as horrified as all my other friends by Colin's antics. But everyone except Sarah put up a brave front whenever he was present, drunkenly holding the floor or lurching around like a robot with fused joints. No matter how kind they were, however, the sad fact remained that my husband was an excruciating embarrassment.

It was with considerable relief that I received a letter from Bill Paley late in August. He wanted to offer me a job at CBS. A meeting was arranged for mid-September.

In the meantime, I awoke each morning to a sodden addict delivering recommendations as to how I should 'play' my meeting with someone he had never even met. I was careful not to rock the boat. After five weeks on the booze and drugs (Colin had three doctors supplying him with valium, and dealers with God knows what else), he was a complete stranger to reason or civility. It was pointless discussing anything with him, so whenever I couldn't escape or ensure the presence of a third party, I just let his ravings wash over me.

Two days before my meeting with Bill Paley, Colin stumbled over to me in an approximation of good-natured drunkenness and held my chin upwards to give me a kiss on the cheek (this was very unusual, but he was well pleased with what he construed as my submissive acceptance of his hectoring). 'Everyshing'sh gonna be awright when you get the job, jusht you wait and shee,' he said, and collapsed on top of me, breaking three of my ribs.

After the doctor left, Colin was more solicitous than he'd been since the early days of our marriage, but by the following day, he had returned to his customary frame of mind. 'You'd better get that job from that rich Yid. I don't care if you have to screw him as long as you get it. We need the bread.'

'You disgust me,' I said, the words popping out before I had a chance to swallow them.

'I disgust you? *I* disgust *you*? You, a little colonial are disgusted by the son of the Duke of Argyll, chief of the Clan Campbell and Lord of the Isles? Thanks to me, you're related to the fucking Queen of England, you stupid cunt. I'll show you what disgust is all about.'

With that, he launched himself in, fists flying. After the initial flurry of blows, I thought he had stopped. After all, when he smashed up my face, it had all been over in moments. But this time it was different. As I was getting up off the floor he turned around, his face frighteningly distorted, aimed very deliberately at my trunk, and kicked me as hard as he could in the same ribs he had broken the day before.

Winded, I wondered if I was going to die. Initially, I could do nothing. Only when the shock of the impact wore off did I gulp as hard as possible, hoping to get some air into my lungs, which felt as if they had collapsed. Colin stood over me, glowering, an expression of satisfaction besmirching what I had once seen as a handsome face. That expression intrigued me. I had seen it in enough films, and once before on a living face (his, when he had first hit me). It was pure, unadulterated viciousness. 'Get up,' he ordered. Unable to breathe, much less speak, I was certainly not in a fit state to get up. He launched into a frenzy of kicking, all the while screaming, 'If you won't get up, take these like a woman.'

I cannot describe how terrifying it is to be kicked by a man doing a convincing impersonation of a crazed fiend, especially one who is nearly seven inches taller and several stone heavier than you. The need to escape was atavistic. I could still barely breathe, but my instinct for survival propelled me to try scurrying for the bedroom. Colin thwarted my every attempt to flee, dragging me back with brutal relish. Sometimes it was by my hair; others by my neck or arms; once by an ankle. 'You'll never escape from me,' yelled a crazed voice like something from a bad 1940s Hollywood movie.

For nearly an hour Colin continued to abuse. Finally, even he grew tired, and he collapsed, wet with the effort, on to the sofa. It's over, I thought automatically, so punch-drunk I could no longer feel relief or any other emotion. But my brain was still functioning. I dragged myself to the bedroom and on to the bed, planning to telephone the doctor as soon as I could summon up the strength. I was in acute pain. I had had a bad cold as well as the broken ribs from the day before, and these new injuries – whatever they were – left me in agony every time I tried to breathe or, worse still, had to cough. When I felt stable enough to call the doctor, I picked up the telephone by the bed.

I don't know whether the click of the telephone in the drawing room alerted Colin, or whether he was lying in wait for me to 'make a mistake', as he put it, or indeed whether he just happened to be coming into the room, but I never did get to speak to the doctor. He strode in, arms folded, legs apart. 'Put it down,' he ordered. He crossed over to the phone, grabbed it out of my hand and erupted into a frenzy of furious blows. 'You bitch, who are you phoning? What are you going to do? Tell people I beat you up? What sort of wife tells on her husband? You're worse than my fucking mother.'

As the blows rained down upon me, I lowered my head and covered it with my arms, trying to protect my skull, which was taking the greater part of the punishment. At the first opportune moment, I made a dash for the front door, hoping to get outside to safety. But Colin blocked my exit and dragged me back, beating and kicking me. Thereafter, every time I tried to escape, the same thing happened. Throughout, he kept saying, as if it were something to be proud of, 'Don't worry. I'm not touching your face,' and 'You'll never get away from me. Never.'

The attacks went on for over six hours. When the abuse had still not stopped after midnight, I realised I would have to be resourceful if I were going to get out of the apartment alive. I went into the bathroom while Colin lay prone on the sofa, gathering his strength for a further bout. Opening the medicine chest, I took out all of his valium tablets. There must have been about a hundred. Good, I thought, flushing all but six down the lavatory, let the bastard think I've taken them all. I swallowed the six tablets in the certain knowledge that they would do me no lasting harm, remembering what constituted a safe dose from the time I had tried to force my father's hand in Jamaica.

I have no recollection of what happened after the tablets took effect. Patricia Fleischmann later told me that Colin rang her and said I'd tried to kill myself. She telephoned for an ambulance, which took me to the Lennox Hill Hospital. The first thing I remember was the medical team asking me my name. They also asked me what I'd taken and how many, and I told them. They nevertheless took the precaution of pumping my stomach, and I will never forget the terrible sensation as they inserted the tube, or my struggle to stop them.

The next day I was interviewed by a psychiatrist. All suicide attempts were treated as criminal matters in New York in those days, for suicide was against the law. You could not be released until you were perceived as being no threat to yourself. 'I did not try to kill myself,' I insisted, repeating what I had told the medical staff the night before. I explained how it seemed the only way to escape from a battering that had gone on for over six hours. And the evidence was there for all to see. My ribs had been rebroken; my body was a mass of bruises and contusions. My neck was completely discoloured from the innumerable times Colin had choked me. My arms were covered in finger marks and bruises from kicks; my legs looked like a Rorschach test. My bosom was a splodge of purple. My back, which I had not yet seen, was so black and blue that not one square inch of white flesh remained, and my little sister would tell me that it remained marked for over a year thereafter.

'You need Al-Anon,' the psychiatrist said. I must have looked perplexed, for she then explained, 'You've never heard of it? It's like Alcoholics Anonymous, only it's for the victims of alcoholics.' She wrote the name and a telephone number on a notepad, tore off the piece of paper and handed it to me with an expression of profound kindness. 'We can release you, if you want,' she said. 'But is it safe for you to return home?'

'I'm sure it is,' I replied, keen to get out of the hospital.

Because Colin Campbell was my next of kin, the hospital contacted him to pick me up. One would imagine that anyone who had so brutalised his wife would have turned up full of remorse, but once we were in the taxi on the way home, it became apparent that Colin felt anything but guilty. 'Don't you try to stick me with the blame for your suicide attempt,' he said, colder than an icy river. 'It's your own trip.'

Shocked, I asked, 'What are you talking about? I didn't try to kill myself. Taking those tablets was the only way to escape from you. I don't want to die, I want to live. And I'll tell you, that's one thing I haven't been able to do since you entered my life.'

No sooner had we stepped through the door to the apartment than Colin started haranguing me. This time I rose to the occasion. 'Wasn't it enough that last night you proved what a big man you are by beating up a defenceless woman? You want another shot? Is that it? You haven't had enough of a fix at beating up someone who is half your size? Well, go find someone your own size to beat up, you perverted bully,' I screamed. 'This isn't last night and I'm not going to be silent. I'll scream down the building if that's what it takes to keep you away from me.'

His response was to move towards me menacingly, his lip curled in his now characteristic expression of malevolence. Without saying a world, I stepped towards the coffee table, picked up my silver cigarette box and hurled it at him. He side-stepped the missile and it crashed through the huge picture window and down into East Eighty-Third Street below. Without missing a beat, I grabbed the purple Scottish cut-glass fruit bowl Maggie Weir had given us as a wedding present, and flung it across at him. Regrettably, that, too, missed.

'You cunt,' he snapped, storming off. It proved to me that the way to deal with a bully is not to be nice, or kind or gracious, but to pick up a bigger club than the one he is using and hit him with it, with more force and, it is to be hoped, more painful consequences.

Exhausted, I went to bed. At six o'clock, Sal, the doorman, awoke me by ringing the buzzer. 'Mrs Campbell, Mr Barker is on the way up to see you,' he said. My God, I remembered, I'd arranged to have Dick Barker over for a drink.

Before I had a chance to change out of the shorts and T-shirt I'd been sleeping in, Dick was ringing the doorbell. Dick, of course, was gay, so I didn't think twice about my appearance on opening the door to him. He gasped. 'My God, Georgie, what's happened to you?'

'Colin,' I said simply.

'I knew he was violent, but I never expected him to be violent with you. You can't stay here,' he said dramatically.

He crossed over to the desk, picked up the telephone and called Margaret Hawkins, a good friend of his and recent friend of ours, whose father was the president of Ireland at the time.

'Get your passport. Don't bother with anything else – not even your toothbrush,' Dick said to me once he had rung off.

I spent the night at Margaret's and the following morning, Dick put me on a plane to my sister Sharman in Canada. When my brother-in-law saw me, he insisted upon examining me. Afterwards, he declared, 'This is the worst case of wife-beating I've seen in all my years as a doctor. I've got to phone Uncle Mike. He'll kill that lunatic when he hears what he's done to you.'

Oh my God, I thought. That's all I need, Daddy being brought into this. Dreading the inevitable recriminations and criticism, I stood by as Ken made the call and described my condition. To my surprise, Daddy, for once, did not put me in the wrong. 'I knew he was no good from the moment I clapped eyes on him,' he said. 'Come back home and I'll arrange a divorce for you.' Coming from a devout Catholic like my father, it was support indeed. But I knew it wasn't right to return to Jamaica, to being the daughter, when I had the potential to be my own person in New York. So I decided to return to the apartment I had found and paid for and the life I hoped to make for myself. Colin was the problem, so he could leave.

It was a penitent husband to whom I returned. My department had really scared him. Doubtless the prospect of living solely off his own paltry income, or worse, actually having to work for a living, had brought him to his senses. I was still young, and a lot less worldly-wise than I am now, so I listened while Colin once more swore undying remorse, as he had done the previous May. I agreed to give him one last chance. Once more he made empty promises to give up drinking (he had a drink in his hand at the time) and the drugs which, it now emerged, he had been taking all along. I shuddered to think what he had been up to, or where he had got them. 'I don't want to know,' I said. 'If the police pick you up, I want to be able to say in all truth that I didn't know what you were up to, or when. Just make sure you don't bring *anything* into this flat. When I say *anything*, I mean *anything*. From grass to LSD to cocaine, whatever. If you think I'm going to end up serving fifteen years in an American prison because you're too self-indulgent to say no to the things that are ruining your life and your health, you can think again. And Colin, if you think you can lie to my face and sneak behind my back the way you did after your last set of undying promises, let me spell out the consequences to you. They're spelled D-I-V-O-R-C-E.'

This time Colin did make an effort. He cut back on his drinking for all of a week or so, and stopped all but the prescription drugs. He tried to be an agreeable companion while I regained my strength. He even managed to convince me that he wanted to have sex with me. Ironically enough, this encounter proved to be the straw that broke the camel's back.

I was ill with pleurisy and in pain from my bruises and broken ribs. Colin had been unusually nice to me since I had awoken that morning. He always seemed to be nicer after he had spoken to his brother, and he had done so late the night before. Quite what the connection was eluded me at the time, though I now see that it was his way of allaying any suspicions I might have had about the contingency plans they were laying in case the marriage failed.

Colin came into the bedroom and offered himself with the romantic enticement, 'I'm horny. How about it?' He hurled himself down on his side of the twin beds and lay back like a quadriplegic, leaving me to get on with the job of giving him pleasure. As I looked at this long, passive log of a man, with his slender, lipstick-sized penis waving uncertainly between his skinny, unmuscular legs, I realised I felt absolutely nothing for him. He might have been a block of cement for all I cared. I tried to go through the motions, but, as I moved towards him, the sight that greeted me made me retch. The bounds of taste prevent me from describing in detail the condition of his body: suffice it to say that cleanliness was not his strong point. I fled to the bathroom and was promptly sick. That was it: Colin Campbell would never again get within spitting distance of me, not unless he changed so radically that he was unrecognisable from the dirty slob from whom I had just had to escape.

The following afternoon, Colin came into the bedroom, where I was reading, and said, 'Since you like sex so much, and I don't, I won't mind if you have lovers, as long as you're discreet.'

'I beg your pardon?' I was nonplussed.

'No, really. I've not been a very good husband in that department' – I wondered in which department he thought he had been a good husband – 'and if that's what it takes to keep you happy, it's fine by me.'

'That's very thoughtful of you, but you've misread the situation entirely. I don't want to hive off various aspects of matrimony for different men. The point of having a husband is to have as many of those aspects as possible in one package.'

At the time, I thought Colin was trying to hang on to me regardless of the cost. Now, however, I see it differently. I am convinced he realised that I meant business when I threatened to divorce him, and this, I believe, was his first attempt at setting me up for the sting. He wanted to divorce me the way his father had divorced his stepmother, or his great-uncle Colin had divorced his great-aunt Gertrude. Sensationally, for adultery, and with multiple co-respondents.

Meanwhile, Bill Paley rescheduled our appointment and did offer me a job. I opted to work as an editor at the CBS-owned publishing company, Holt Rhinehart Winston. But I had been more severely affected by the battering than I had realised, and when I had my first meeting at Holt Rhinehart, I was uncharacteristically unable to express myself. Halfway through each thought, I lost the thread. It was apparent to both the editor to whom I was speaking, and to me, that something was wrong. We agreed to end the meeting and resume it when I felt better.

That evening, I telephoned my brother-in-law Ken and told him what had happened. I mentioned that there had been other, less dramatic episodes, but that I had always managed to retrieve my powers of concentration before the problem became obvious. 'You should go to your own doctor,' he suggested. 'But it seems to me you're suffering from a delayed reaction to what Colin put you through. I wouldn't worry about it if I were you; in the circumstances, it's an appropriate response, and you'll get over it soon enough.'

Sadly, I did not recover soon enough to work for Holt Rhinehart. I simply did not see how I could cope with a demanding job as a book editor when my concentration was so impaired that I could not string ten words together without unexpected delays. I telephoned Bill Paley, thanked him for his help and interest, explained that I hadn't been feeling well recently, and promised to be in touch when he was gracious enough to say, 'I'm always here when you need me.'

Colin, of course, didn't care what happened with Holt Rhinehart. All he cared about was the fat salary he had been counting on. He was once again drinking like a fish, and the marriage, I finally accepted, was on its last legs. Soon he would do something to make it keel over and then I would leave with a clear conscience.

We still needed money, so I got a less taxing job as a receptionist with a company on East Fifty-Eighth Street to

keep us going in the short term. While I was at work, Colin
was supposed to be writing his fascinating travelogue. By
the end of the first week, he had written two paragraphs. By
the end of four weeks, he had managed only four long-
hand pages.

To escape the misery at home as much as to try to find a
cure for Colin's ills, I went to Al-Anon. Of course, they had
no magical cure; they merely confirmed my fear that there
was nothing more I could do to help Colin. He was suffering from a degenerative condition which affected him
mentally, emotionally, spiritually, physically and intellectually. Only he could help himself, and if he did not want
to, no one else could. I carried on attending Al-Anon meetings, mainly in the hope that Colin would follow my
example by going to Alcoholics Anonymous and see the
light. Although I held the programme in high esteem, for
someone like me, who had already had to develop strong
spiritual and emotional resources, the twelve steps were
like teaching Grandmother to suck eggs. Colin disparaged
all my attempts to get him to go to Alcoholics Anonymous.
'I don't need AA. I can give up drinking any time I want.
Why do you want to deprive me of my one little pleasure
in life?' A friend who was a member did convince him to
go once. 'They're nothing but a bunch of losers sitting
around a dingy church hall talking about how drink ruined
their lives,' he said when he got back. 'Drink hasn't ruined
mine.'

My last attempt to galvanise Colin into action was to warn
him that he had pushed me to the point where I wanted a
separation. I didn't want to walk away feeling I had left any
stone unturned. 'If you leave me, I'll destroy you,' he said.
'I'll destroy you the way my father destroyed Margaret and
my great-uncle destroyed my great-aunt. No woman walks
out on an Argyll unless we want her to.'

'There's no need to be nasty. I'm only trying to alert you to
the choice you're forcing upon us both. And please don't
threaten me. There's nothing you can do to harm me.'

'I'll destroy you. Destroy. Like this,' he said, snuffing out his lighted cigarette between two fingers and crushing it until the tobacco scattered over the Persian carpet.

What I did not appreciate was that Colin Campbell not only meant every word, but that incapable as he was in a positive sense, he also had the ability to carry out his threat.

8

'I want a divorce,' I said at last. It was November 1974. The marriage was eight months and an eternity too old.

Colin did not ask why. He knew. The previous evening he had started to shove me around, a precursor to the battering that would ensue if I did not break the cycle. I had bolted for the telephone and called the police, despite his objections, informing him that he'd have to kill me to prevent me. The people at Al-Anon had advised this course of action, and they'd been right. He had backed off. But for how long? I had gone to bed to the accompaniment of a diatribe of abuse and threats about what awaited me in the not-too-distant future.

'In September I told you if you ever touched me again, except lovingly, the marriage was over,' I told him now over the telephone, checking the offices adjoining the reception area to make sure that no one could overhear. I had chosen to bring down the axe from the office because that was the only way of keeping the conversation neat and clean. 'I'm here looking at my bruised arms. My neck looks as if a strangler has been practising on it. You and I both know that it's only a matter of time before you savage me again the way you did in September.'

'Georgie, please,' he blubbered, genuine panic in his voice. 'Please don't leave me. You're the best thing that ever happened to me.'

I'd heard that before. 'Colin, don't make this more difficult than it has to be,' I said as agreeably and politely as I could. 'My mind is made up. It's not as if you haven't had plenty of warning. I want you to pack up all your stuff and have it out of the apartment before I return home this afternoon. Perhaps you could ask Jeanie to put you up until you get somewhere else to live.'

Colin started to cry. 'Colin,' I said when he was still sobbing after what seemed an age, 'I really can't stay on the line any longer. I have work to do. Just please make this easy for both of us by doing as I ask. I really don't want to see you when I get home later. I've had more than enough of scenes.'

Within the hour, Colin phoned back. (When our telephone bill came in, I was intrigued to note that he had used the intervening time to call his brother in Scotland.) 'Georgie, I have a proposition. Please listen to the whole of it before you say no. You're right. I do have a problem with violence, and drink and drugs. I know you want out. I can't blame you. I've treated you appallingly, and you deserve better. But you *are* the best thing that ever happened to me. Even though you don't realise the good effect you've been having on me, I have been listening to the things you've said. I don't want to move out to Jeanie's; her apartment's so chaotic. If I give up drinking and go to AA, can I stay here with you until I'm fit enough to find somewhere else to live?'

'How long are we talking about?' I asked, expecting him to come back with something exploitative like six months.

'A month, maybe six weeks,' he said, taking the wind out of my sails and leading me to believe that he was sincere. It was not so much to ask. We were man and wife, after all, and I hoped that we would maintain cordial relations after the divorce, once the strains and stresses of living together were at an end.

'Only as long as you don't touch a drop of alcohol or any drugs.'

'If I'm not drinking I'll need my valium.'

'In AA they say a cross-addict shouldn't take any mood-altering substance, especially if they're already addicted to it.'

'I'll need something to calm me down. And in any event, why should you care what I take now that we're not together? Your concern should be that I don't endanger you.'

'OK. No drinking, AA, and you move out in the new year.'

'It's a deal.'

Sad though I was to see my marriage fail, it was a monumental relief to have acknowledged that the corpse was indeed lifeless. Throughout the previous month, I had felt as if I were carrying the whole world on my shoulders. I hadn't felt so oppressed since I was a teenager. Now, as I made plans to return to London once my book deal had been finalised, I felt that this huge load had been lifted off me.

Two weeks later, Ian Argyll came to New York. He stayed with his sister Jeanie. The problem of where the brothers were going to get the money to pay off their debts and prevent Colin from being sued by the Priory had not yet been solved, but they both seemed to think that it could be sorted out without sacrifice by either of them. I was perplexed by this new optimism, for I could not see where they would get the money from. As I overheard them talking amiably, and saw that the cloud which had cast such a pall over their relationship had lifted, I was pleased for them. It was genuinely good to see harmony restored. They even travelled by subway together to the offices of Cusack & Stiles, the executors of their mother's estate, in the Wall Street district, to sort out the problem.

I never did learn what the solution was. When I asked Ian, at a luncheon party Jeanie had for him immediately after their meeting, he replied with the venom that was obviously a family characteristic, 'You've made a big mistake taking me on, Georgie. You'll pay for it.'

'I have no idea what you're talking about,' I said, puzzled.

'Oh, you do, you do,' he said. 'Colin told me all.'

When I got home from work that evening, I asked Colin what he had told Ian. He denied saying anything, but I had a shrewd idea that since he was so desperate for Cusack & Stiles to get the money from Ian to settle his debt, he had blamed me for all the pressure he had been applying for the previous three months. I asked him about the outcome of the meeting with the executors. 'It's been sorted,' was all he would say.

'How?'

'It's too complicated to go into,' he replied shiftily, making it clear that the subject was closed.

The next few weeks were odd, especially after I resigned from my job when they did not want to give me time off to attend an important meeting about the publication of my book. Colin spent a great deal of time brooding on the sofa, smoking cigarette after cigarette. Now that he wasn't drinking, he was even more uncommunicative, albeit much more civil. When he wasn't lost in his own world, he was on the phone to his brother, who had returned to the United Kingdom. They seemed to have formed a new closeness, for which I was glad. Maybe Colin could go and stay at Inveraray when we separated.

At times, Colin was actually pleasant. Now that the marriage was over, he even wanted to know about my youth. This surprised me, for he had shown no interest when I had wanted to tell him all about it. Not realising that he was gathering information for a big betrayal, I was perplexed by his behaviour, but not suspicious. All the same, I did not discuss the subject – the last thing I was going to do was share raw and distressing emotions with someone who had proved himself to be callous and unreliable.

By this time, I knew from Stephanie Bennett that Warner wanted to publish my book. According to her, Howard Kaminsky had read it and loved not only the ideas, but also the way I wrote. He wanted to meet me for lunch before making a final offer, so we fixed a date for early December. I took to Howard Kaminsky straight away. He was everything I liked in a person: straightforward, dynamic, intelligent, open-minded, adventurous. Then we hit a hitch. 'You're not a doctor or someone with a degree in philosophy. We'll have a problem promoting the book unless you incorporate the reasons why you've reached your conclusions. In other words, you have to put in your past.'

'That's the one thing I'll never do,' I said. 'Much as I'd love you to publish the book, it's not a price I'm prepared to pay.'

'Any other publisher you go to will tell you the same thing. Tell her, Stephanie,' he said.

'It's true, Georgie. And Howard will be behind you in a way few other publishers will. This is your best bet.'

'Then I regret to say it has to be no,' I said.

When I got home, I was greeted by a most interested ex-husband-to-be. I told him what had happened, and he tried to talk me into changing my mind and accepting the offer immediately. But there was no possibility of that. I would sooner have had my legs amputated than violate my own privacy and subject myself to the humiliation of everyone knowing the pain and distress I had been through.

On the morning of Friday 13 December 1974, the telephone rang. I answered it. 'My name's Jolyon Wilde. I'm an English journalist working for the *Evening Standard* in London. We understand that you and your husband are planning to return to London. I'd like to interview you about that.'

'I'm afraid I don't give personal interviews,' I said, as Colin gesticulated furiously for me to hand the telephone over to him. He invited the man to come around at four that afternoon.

'God, those newspapers discover everything,' Colin said to me as soon as he rang off. 'How did they know we're thinking of going back to London?'

'You're the one who knows how they function, not me,' I said idly.

'Don't let on that we're separating,' Colin pleaded.

'I'm not planning to be here.'

'But you must. If you're not here, they'll smell a rat. You

want us to remain friends, don't you? That won't be easy if the press say there's a wedge between us.'

'OK,' I agreed, happy to spare him any embarrassment if it kept things on an even keel between us. We had not done too badly on that score so far; indeed, Colin was even coming as my family's guest to Jamaica for Christmas. They still did not know about the impending divorce, and I wanted to tell them face to face.

Jolyon Wilde turned out to be a pugilistic Brit with so much attitude you could have canned it. For about an hour he reeled off the most asinine questions; then he asked if he could take pictures. Colin consented with relish. I went along with it to keep him sweet. It was only after the pictures were safely in the can, and my co-operation could thereby be presented to an unsuspecting public as having been freely given, that Wilde pulled off his gloves. 'Before I leave, I have a question I'd like you to clear up for me.' His tone was completely different, and he was looking at me as if he had the right to inspect me naked. 'We've received reliable information that you changed your sex. Is that true?'

I was so enraged by his duplicity and impertinence that I was shaking as I replied. 'How dare you! Is that what you came about?'

'Did you or didn't you?' he demanded.

'How dare you! Where did you get that from?' I reiterated, softly but so angrily that Colin shot me a look of concern.

I thought he was charging to my rescue when he said, 'Mr Wilde, my wife has never changed her sex. She can prove it, too. Georgie, get your birth certificate and show it to him.'

'Absolutely not,' I said. 'He is not entitled to any explanation or proof, and none will be forthcoming.'

'Lady Colin, if you won't answer the question, I'll have no option but to think you have something to hide.'

'I have nothing to hide. You simply have no right to information of a personal nature. Moreover, you tricked your way into this apartment.'

'You've upset my wife,' said Colin protectively. 'You will appreciate that no woman likes having her femininity questioned. But Georgie,' he continued in so reasonable a tone I could scarcely believe it was the Colin I knew, 'I'm sure he isn't trying to be offensive. He's only trying to earn a crust of bread. Give the guy a break. Go on, show him your birth certificate. It's the safest way of getting Fleet Street off our backs.'

Against my better instincts, I went to find the document and handed it to Colin, who passed it to Wilde. 'You didn't change your sex!' he blurted out, nonplussed. He seemed so surprised that the person who gave him the information must have sounded very authoritative indeed.

When Wilde left, I telephoned Barbara Taylor Bradford, who had been a working journalist from the age of about seventeen. 'I know Jeffrey Bright,' she said, 'who represents most of the British papers here. I'll ask him to sniff around and find out what's happening.'

Within the hour, Barbara had crushing news. 'Jolyon Wilde does not represent the London *Evening Standard*. He is acting on behalf of the *Sunday People*.' I had never even heard of that tabloid, but it was familiar enough to Colin and his brother: it was the same newspaper their father had used to make himself some money and to smash the remnants of their stepmother Margaret's reputation. 'Jeffrey represents the *Sunday People* here, but they brought in Wilde because he has a reputation as a killer,' Barbara went on. 'They were going to do a real hatchet job on you. Jeffrey said he wouldn't touch it. But you don't have anything to worry about. Showing Wilde that birth certificate was the best thing you could have done. He now accepts there's no truth in the information they received.'

That would have been the end of the matter had Colin and others not wanted the story published. But they had been beavering away behind the scenes with the aim of dishing up a perverted account of my private life for public consumption. The introduction of the birth certificate had been unplanned, I later learned from Colin. For some reason he became worried that I might suspect he was behind this latest bit of press interest. Knowing that there were two birth certificates, and that the amended version was accessible to anyone who wished to obtain it from the registrar of births, deaths and marriages in Jamaica, he could point the *Sunday People* towards the proof that I had once been registered in the male gender at the same time as he appeared to be protecting me. It was a diabolic act of deception, but brilliant. And, more importantly, ultimately it worked, for I did not suspect his part in the enterprise for a moment.

But for the moment, of course, by raising the other birth certificate, Colin had thrown a spanner into the machinery of his own plot. Wilde was now so convinced that the rumours were unfounded that he told London they were barking up the wrong tree, and nobody checked the Jamaican certificate. Unbeknown to me, Colin was expecting the story to be published on the very day we were flying to Jamaica for Christmas.

When it did not appear, Colin embarked upon a flurry of telephone calls between Scotland and Jamaica, all at my parents' expense, of course. Colin would later tell me, in February 1975, that he had a partner in Britain who rescued the mess he had made of their carefully made plans. How true this was, I did not know then and I do not know now. Obviously it was in his interest to minimise the part he had played, and it is quite possible that he was the sole as well as prime mover in this sordid scheme. All I know with any certainty is that someone tipped off the *Sunday People* that I had two birth certificates, something that only Colin, Ian, my parents, the registrar of births, deaths and marriages and I then knew. The *Sunday People*, I was told, sent two journalists out to Jamaica to dig up the dirt on me. Although they were able to get hold of the amended birth certificate, they encountered a solid wall of resistance from friends, relations, staff and servants alike, despite offering bribes to both the rich (who were insulted) and the poor (who were too honourable and decent to succumb). The *Sunday People* now had no option but to bounce the story back into the lap of its paid hitman, Jolyon Wilde.

Meanwhile, in Jamaica, Colin was back on the bottle in a big way, using the 'pressure' of the interview with Wilde as an excuse. Now I can see why he needed to drink, but at the time I was incredulous. 'What pressure? You gave the interview of your own accord. Why make a mountain out of a molehill?'

That Christmas vacation was anything but a holiday. Colin was totally out of control. But this time my anxiety about the comfort of others was tempered with self-interest, and his behaviour was so irrational that it made the task of announcing the impending divorce much easier. On several occasions my cousin, Abe Azan, who was a doctor, even had to administer sedatives intravenously to calm down Colin, who would work himself up into such valium-, amphetamine- and alcohol-induced states that he seemed in danger of exploding.

By Christmas Day, his behaviour was so bizarre that I could scarcely believe it myself. My father's nephew, Winston Ziadie, his charming wife Carole and their children came to visit after mass. Their three-year-old son Troy was the most beautiful child you could imagine, and Colin took an unexpected shine to him. So Colin doesn't dislike all children, I thought, happy to see some good in him. In the hurly-burly of a family gathering of twenty or more people, I did not notice Colin leave the back verandah, but some time later Sharman said to me, 'You'd better go up to the pool. Colin's up there with Troy.' He was in no condition to be in charge of a toddler beside a swimming pool, so I went up to fetch them. Colin was sitting on the verandah with Troy on his lap. 'Come on, give Uncle Colin another hug,' he was saying drunkenly, his mouth open like a guppy in search of food. Troy seemed uneasy, as if he didn't know what was going on, and wasn't too sure whether he liked it, either.

'So how are things going?' I greeted them. 'I'm going to take Troy down to Carole and Winston.'

When I returned, I let my instincts do all the work. 'I am not going back to New York with you and I want you to file for divorce as soon as you get back. This separation/non-separation has gone on long enough. The failure of this marriage has been entirely due to you, and you're going to accept the responsibility and pay the price, both financially and morally. After the divorce, I'll return to New York, ship my stuff to London and close down the apartment.'

'It's not what you think,' he reiterated.

'I haven't said anything about what I think.'

'You don't need to. It's written all over your face.'

'Colin, you've known since last month that I want a divorce, so don't act as if this is the be-all and end-all.'

I snapped. So he wanted to put ideas in my head, did he? Fine. 'Then you tell me this, Colin. If it's what you are insisting I thought, even though it hadn't occurred to me, why the sudden interest in Troy when you've always gone on and on about how you can't stand children.'

'He's cute.'

'So is Andrew.' Andrew was my sister's little boy of the same age.

'But Andrew isn't beautiful.'

'Shades of Oscar Wilde in the witness box. You obviously don't realise the significance of what you're saying,' I said.

'I swear it's not what you think,' he said again.

'Whether it is or isn't makes not a scrap of difference. No one knows about this, and no one will. I'd be too ashamed to repeat it to anyone, if only because it reflects so appallingly upon my choice of husband. But if this conversation is anything to go by, no wonder,' I said bitterly, 'you never wanted children.'

Thereafter, until after the divorce, I spent as little time with Colin as I could. Although I remained civil, I spoke to him only when I had to. No words will ever convey how utterly bereft I was. I felt an utter fool for having stayed and stayed and stayed with someone who patently had not been worth the trouble. My one consolation was that enough time had elapsed since the wedding for me to leave without the brevity of the marriage being ridiculous, or its failure reflecting upon my femininity. Had I been able to walk away with at least a vestige of respect for Colin, I might have had less of a sensation of having been sullied, but now there was nothing I could do but swallow hard, throw back my shoulders and hope that I could live down a marriage made in hell.

Colin, meanwhile, was playing an altogether more mercenary game. On 28 December, Jolyon Wilde telephoned Colin at Duncan's on the north coast of Jamaica, where we were staying as the guests of Judy Ann MacMillan, the Jamaican artist who is my oldest friend (our mothers were best friends when we were children). This time he was moving in for the kill.

In the Jamaican countryside in the days before mobile phones made everyone accessible, no private country houses or beach cottages had telephones. We were contactable only through the hotel adjoining the MacMillan beach cottage. As a result, I had to suffer the indignity of talking to Wilde about the most private matter of my life on a public telephone in a public place.

'We know you changed your sex,' he insisted when Colin handed me over. 'I've got your original birth certificate in front of me. It says you were born George William Ziadie, male, and that your name was changed to Georgia Arianna Ziadie, female, in 1971.'

'If you had read it carefully, you would have noted that it states that the birth certificate was amended, which means that my sex was not changed. Birth certificates in British territories can only ever be amended if a genuine mistake was made at the time of registration. They cannot be altered if the person in question changed sex.'

'Your sex was changed at Johns Hopkins Hospital in Baltimore. There's no point in denying it. We have the proof.'

'How odd it is that you have proof of something that never happened, at a place I've never been to in my life,' I said icily.

In an effort to gain my co-operation, Wilde then began mentioning what he must have thought were large sums of money. 'You can make ten, maybe twenty thousand pounds out of this if you give us the exclusive.'

'Just who is "us"?' I asked, laying a trap for him.

'The *Sunday People*.'

'Ah. The same publication you were representing when you spoke to me on Friday 13 December.'

'That's right,' he said, almost proudly.

'Now, Mr Wilde,' I said with exaggerated politeness. 'You tell me, what sort of person puts her trust in someone who has already shown himself to be untrustworthy?'

'You're making a big mistake,' he said nastily. 'If you don't co-operate, we can still write the story and it will be harder on you.'

'In other words, if I don't sell you my foot, you'll chop off my hand?'

'That's about it.'

I pointed out that I did not need the money he was offering. Remembering what Olga Maitland had said in London when we had gone to lunch at Walton's, I said, 'I'll sue you if you print anything about me that isn't true. I did not change my sex and you cannot say I did.'

Eventually Wilde asked to speak to Colin. 'And why on earth would you want to speak to him?' I asked.

'He has a right to comment on his wife, doesn't he?'

I leaned on the railing while Colin stood listening to whatever it was Wilde was saying. I was delighted when he responded with, 'My wife is as much a woman as any, and more than most.' He then motioned to me to get him a drink, which entailed going to the house for my purse before fetching one from the hotel bar. I was itching to stay and listen, but I did not want to antagonise Colin. I couldn't take the chance of him turning against me at such a crucial moment. Obviously, he was getting rid of me so that he could say things to Wilde behind my back that he would never have dared say in front of me.

It was only after the article was published that I learned what Colin had said. The opening sentence of the article was: Lord Colin Campbell last night revealed that his wife of nine months was once a man. I was incandescent with rage when I finally saw this treacherous epistle, which was not until several days after it was published. In the interim I had only my brother's word from London that the story had been 'terrible' and was a 'pack of lies'. He could not read the article out to me because he had not kept it ('Too disgusting,' he said), which was touching, but frustrating too. In the days before fax machines and overnight courier services, both Jolyon Wilde and Colin Campbell had relied upon my isolation to achieve their objective.

'Wilde says he gave you a break and made the story tame. The only reason he did that is because I promised him an exclusive on your life story if he went easy on you,' said Colin.

'You *what*? You *promised* him *my life story*? Let me get this straight. You, my ex-husband-to-be, promised him *my* life story? By what right did you promise someone something to which you have no right?' I shrieked.

'I was only trying to help,' Colin said lamely. 'I thought it would make things better for you.'

'When I left you talking to Wilde, I was under the impression that he didn't have enough information to run *any* story *at all*,' I countered, little realising how close I was to the truth. 'Just who were you helping, Colin? Me, or my deadliest enemy?'

'I know the press better than you.' That old line. 'If I hadn't done what I did, he'd have hacked you to death. You should be thanking me. You can learn from my experience. Since you don't want the focus to be on you, let's sell our joint story. Wilde has promised me he'll let you deny the allegations of a sex change.'

'How very magnanimous of him. The cheek of it,' I exploded. My sisters and parents were listening on the back verandah, disgust at Colin written all over their faces. 'He's going to allow me to deny the very slur he created, as if it were some favour. A slur, incidentally, Colin, which he put into your mouth. How come you're not furious with him for taking such a liberty when you've smashed me and others around merely for being nice to you?'

'Don't take this so personally. It won't do you any good.

The only way to achieve your ends is to give him what he wants. We can make a packet for ourselves in the process and the publicity will do your book good. Stop being so negative. Now that you've had this publicity, your reason for refusing to publish the book with Warner's disappears. Don't you see the advantage?'

'All I see is that you've been fine-tuning the details of a deal which you have every reason to know I would never have allowed you to strike. What I want to know is, when did these discussions with Wilde take place?'

'I've phoned him and he's phoned me.'

'You've phoned him?' I screamed. 'When and where?'

'Here. I even spoke to him this morning.'

'You have one hell of a nerve, using my parents' money to set up a story which I don't want to sell. Listen to me, and listen very carefully.' I enunciated every word exaggeratedly. '*I will never – repeat, never – sell the story of my life to a newspaper*. Apples will have to grow on lilac trees before I would ever even spit in the direction of Jolyon Wilde, or that rag he represents. What I find astonishing in all of this isn't that Wilde will write this sort of disgusting material, but that any husband of mine, even one as debauched and deranged as you, would try to edge me in the direction of someone who has done his level best to destroy my reputation.'

My parents warned me not to give Colin any more information about myself or any of the family. 'Keep your mouth shut and he won't have any information to purvey,' Mummy advised. 'Mark my words, if you don't keep a lid on that Judas, he's going to sell you down the river.' Controversy then raged within the family for the next week on the question of whether I should return to New York with Colin. I wanted to stay in Jamaica, a decision my father supported. But my mother and Sharman argued that I must return, otherwise I would be leaving myself open to the possibility of him selling a story claiming he had dumped me. Against my better instincts, but appreciating the logic of their argument, I boarded a flight for New York on Sunday 5 January 1975. Colin Campbell was with me, full of assurances that we

would find a way to defeat the slurs which had now cir-
cumnavigated the globe on the front pages of just about
every tabloid from Fleet Street to Freetown.

Within half an hour of our arrival at the apartment in
New York, I answered the door to be confronted by the
pinched features of Jolyon Wilde. Without a word, I went to
close the door, but he pitched his weight against it, elbowed
me in the side and forced his way in.

'What gives you the right to force your way into my
home?' I demanded.

'You husband invited me.'

'My husband *invited* you?' I echoed in disbelief.

'How else would I know when you were arriving?'

'And what, pray, did you do that for?' I hissed at Colin.

Both men answered at the same time, Colin once more
mouthing his nonsense about 'our' story; Wilde cutting
straight to the bottom line. 'He's said I can have the rights to
your life story. I'm here to collect.'

'How can he give you the rights to something that is
mine? Colin,' I commanded, 'tell him that the rights to my
life story are mine. Only I can give them to anyone, and if I
were going to give them to someone, it wouldn't be him.'

Colin stood there silently, red and sweaty from alcohol.

'Tell her,' Wilde said. 'Tell her, goddamnit.'

'I don't see how he could have done something like that
when he knows how much I loathe you. You falsely said
that I changed my sex and even had the audacity to quote
me saying that.'

'Your husband said you wouldn't mind. Without it there
wouldn't have been a story. No serialisation of your life
story, no story.'

'You have the gall to stand here, in front of me and my
husband, and say that he authorised you to lie about me?'

'He didn't say it was a lie. He said it was the truth.'

'He couldn't have done that, Mr Wilde, because it is most
certainly *not* the truth. And he knows it.'

I looked from Wilde to Colin and back. I couldn't tell
which of the three of us was more furious. 'Are you going to

stand there like a spineless jerk and let him say this about
you to my face and yours, or are you going to behave like a
man?' I demanded of Colin.

'He misquoted me in the article and he's misquoting me
now,' Colin said, knowing very well that to have said anything else would have meant instant ejection from the
apartment and my life.

'I did not misquote you,' Wilde insisted, and they started
squabbling over who had said what to whom. Oaths flew for
a good few minutes and then Colin began pummelling
Wilde with his fists. Soon they were on the floor, and Wilde
was coming off the better.

Displayed on the wall beside the sofa was a Fijian war
club which Colin claimed had been given to him by a
descendant of the last warrior king. I grabbed it and swung
it behind Wilde, screaming to him to get up, otherwise I'd
club him. He spun around, saw the club, sprang off Colin
and jumped towards me, seizing the weapon. He hit Colin
with it once on the forehead, threw it down, screamed
obscenities at us and ran out of the door, adding for good
measure a few blows to my body as I clung on to his sleeve.
'Stop that man,' I screamed all the way down the stairs,
through the lobby, past the doorman and into the street. This
being New York, of course no one did a thing.

Rushing back upstairs, I saw that Colin's wound was only
superficial. I challenged him about what Wilde had said. He
categorically denied every word. 'In that case, you won't
mind pressing charges against him for assault. I certainly
will, if the few punches he gave me qualify. This might be a
blessing in disguise. He'll have to be tried. We can tell the
court, and all the newspapers *you* will get to attend, how
he's conned us into this sorry pass.'

The police arrived within fifteen minutes. 'If we take a
statement tonight, we have to report your husband's condition,' they said. Colin was so drunk he could barely stand.
'My advice is, let him sleep it off. Tomorrow he can go
downtown and make a report.' So we rose bright and early
the following day and Colin filed a complaint against Wilde

for assault. We then went with the police to serve the papers. I was jubilant. The truth would be established and my reputation restored.

But things are not always cut and dried especially if you cannot be sure where the allegiances of others lie. Two days later, I returned home in the afternoon and overheard Colin on the telephone. I did something which would have been unthinkable even a few weeks before: I eavesdropped. He was speaking to his brother, who seemed to be insisting that I had definitely changed my sex, and that it had definitely been at Johns Hopkins. Colin was saying that he had no doubt I was speaking the truth, but I was stonewalling him about the details. Implying that there were plans for other stories in the pipeline, he said I had no idea what was happening. I felt faint.

I opened the door noisily. 'I have to go now,' Colin said. 'I'll call you later.'

'Hi,' I said. 'Who was that?'

'Get out, you fucking bitch. Get out. I want you out of here right now.'

'What's got into you?' I inquired pleasantly.

'You tricked me into marriage. I want you out of here. Get out, get out, get out!' he screamed.

'Are you insane? How could I have tricked you into marriage when you're the one who made all the running?'

'I never knew anything about your past until after I married you.'

'That's a lie, and you know it.'

'Get out. If you don't get out right now, I'll throw you out bodily. This time I might kill you, so you'd better do as I say.'

'Don't you try to frighten me with threats, you big bully,' I said. 'Lay a finger on me and I'll have the police here quicker than you can say boo.' I made towards the telephone. He blocked my way, glowering.

I serenely opened my handbag to take out a cigarette. 'If that's what it takes, I have all day,' I said calmly, reaching into the bag, lighting the cigarette and inhaling deeply. He stormed off to the desk, grabbed the telephone, and dialled.

'Barbara, it's Colin. You'd better come over here and talk some sense into your friend. If you don't, I can't be held responsible for what I might do.'

Within minutes, Barbara Taylor Bradford had arrived to find Colin shrieking that he would kill me if I didn't do as he wanted. I was adamant that I would not leave. 'This apartment was furnished with my family's money. I've paid the rent. If you want to leave, you leave,' I said.

'Barbara, if she doesn't get out, I'll kill her,' Colin threatened.

'Georgie, he sounds like he means it. Please come with me.'

'Absolutely not,' I said.

'Please. I'd never forgive myself if I left you here and he harmed you.'

'OK, Barbara,' I said. 'I'll leave. Not because this lout is threatening me, but because I don't want you involved in yet another of the sorry sagas he creates.'

I went inside to pack an overnight bag. Afterwards, I walked over with Barbara to her apartment. From there, I called Mary Michele Rutherfurd and went to stay with her.

I did not expect Colin to succeed in selling me out to the gutter press – after all, he had none of the information Wilde wanted. But I was beside myself; I felt so betrayed, so defiled, after all the kindness and decency my family and I had shown him. And he knew only too well that he would not only be hurting me, but also my family. They, too, found the publicity distressing; they, too, loathed having their names trawled through the mud.

I was still in a state of distress when my literary agent, telephoned me the next day. 'Georgie, I have some bad news for you. Colin has dropped his complaint against Wilde and has sold a story about you to the *Sunday People*. He's claiming he knew nothing about your medical history until a week after your marriage. He says that's the reason why your marriage has broken up.'

The shock was so severe that my system seemed to fuse for a split second. It was as if my internal motor had switched off momentarily, and when it restarted, it did so at half the power and half the speed. For the next seven years, nothing I did could rid me of this sensation. But medical science had yet to recognise post-traumatic stress syndrome, so one simply had to dust oneself down and try to rev one-self up. At times the inability to see what the future holds is merciful. I am glad now that I had no idea how long and dreadfully slow my climb out of the pit which Colin Campbell dug for me would be. Each day I thought, If I do this, or that, things will fall into place and I'll begin the ascent back to the spiritual plane I inhabited before. I never doubted I would regain the lost territory, but to have known in advance how long it would take would have daunted me.

The first and most immediate effect of Stephanie's news was shock. This has its benefits, for you can actually function automatically when you are dazed, and this is that I did. 'Georgie, Wilde wants an interview with you to rebut Colin's claims,' Stephanie said.

'That will only give him an even bigger story,' I replied. I felt as if I were talking to her from somewhere far away.

'Not necessarily. How you handle it will determine what he can use. I'll come with you if you want. But you must speak to your lawyer about this, for Colin is now threatening to sue you for divorce on the grounds that you are a man. You have to give this interview, Georgie. It will be so damn-ing if you don't.'

I telephoned Charles Dismukes, a respected lawyer. He confirmed Stephanie's advice. 'Give the journalist one quote and only one. "My husband knew all about my medical his-tory right from the outset." Answer questions so that he can't quote you as having said anything else. You want to make it clear that you've been dragged into this article against your will. You mustn't co-operate with any other aspect of it. You want it to remain Colin's article. Later, we might use it as grounds for divorce. It should qualify as cru-elty.'

Appalling as I found the idea of granting Wilde an inter-view, I consented. 'He mustn't set foot in this building,'

Mary Michele's father, Boss, cautioned. I asked Stephanie to arrange for us to go to Wilde's office. The date was set for two days hence, the day after Colin's final interview.

Mary Michele and her mother Jacqueline were standing nearby when I put down the phone. I promptly collapsed into their arms, the floodgates opening. 'There, there,' Jacqueline said, patting my shoulder gently. 'Let it out. It will do you good.' Poor Jacqueline could have had no idea how literally I would take her recommendation. For the remainder of that day, and the whole of the following one, I was either crying or bent over the lavatory bowl being sick. Unable to keep down the soup she kept spoon-feeding me, by the weekend I had lost twenty pounds in weight.

Colin Campbell burst into this torture chamber of his own creation with all the sensitivity of a psychopath. At about seven o'clock on Friday morning, Mary Michele came into my bedroom and shook me awake. 'Colin's on the phone.'

'Hi,' he said jauntily, as if I were a fellow conspirator. 'I phoned to say it's OK for you to come back now.'

'Ah,' was all I could manage.

'The interview with Jolyon went great guns. Come back tomorrow after he drops my cheque over. But don't come before in case they're watching the apartment. We can't be seen together until after the story appears on Sunday.'

'Is this some sort of joke?' I asked.

'Why the fuck do you always have to spoil everything by being so uptight? I've made us enough to keep the Priory quiet for a while. Ian won't have to sell the Park Walk house if we milk our reconciliation for a few more thou'. I'll let everyone know Wilde misquoted us. We'll all be happy.'

'Well,' I said bitterly, 'I've lived to see the day when green is grey and bad good.'

'Christ, you're a fucking pain. Are you or aren't you coming back?'

'Absolutely not. Just give me one reason why.'

'Because you love me,' he said.

'You really are sicker than I thought.'

Early that afternoon, Stephanie picked me up and took

me downtown to Wilde's office. At least, I thought, I will be able to pick his brain. By now it was clear that there had been a conspiracy to sacrifice me on the altar of greed and penury, but I still had nothing but unproven suspicions and dropped hints to go on.

Wilde, it transpired, also wanted something from me. He hoped to draw me into a public slanging match with the jerk I was married to. 'We know Colin is an alcoholic and has mistreated you,' he said. 'Just tell your side of the story.'

'Mr Wilde, one does not slag off one's husband in the gutter press. Not even if one's husband deserves it. It is just not done,' I said. On and on and on we danced for about four hours, until Wilde realised that there was no way I was going to relent.

'I have to tell you,' he said, 'I admire you. You've got guts and you've got class.' I wondered if he had any regrets about the things he'd written, but not for long.

I succeeded in gaining some valuable insights into how the whole business had been set up. 'We could never have written the story if we hadn't got that tip about your two birth certificates,' he said. 'I really swallowed your line when you showed me the one in your apartment.'

'What tip?' I asked.

'The one from the informant who said that you had two birth certificates: one amended, the other abridged.'

'Was he the same person who told you I'd been treated at Johns Hopkins?'

'Yes.'

'When you said "we" got the tip, did you mean yourself here in New York, or the *Sunday People* in London?' I inquired chattily.

'London. The informant was never in touch with me. He was in direct touch with London. He's the one who revived the story after you killed it dead by showing me the birth certificate.'

My head spun as I tried to work out who the hell would do something so awful. It must have been Colin, and Wilde must be covering for him, I decided. It was not until later that I learned from Colin that Ian was the person who passed that crucial bit of information to the *Sunday People*. Obviously he believed that I had been a patient at Johns Hopkins, a fact he confirmed to me in writing shortly afterwards.

Colin, meanwhile, was on the attack again. When I went to the apartment with Mary Michele to get some clothes, he confirmed what I'd heard from Stephanie. 'Ian's advised me to divorce you on the grounds of being a man. The *Sunday People* have provided him with the proof we need. We have chapter and verse on you. You can't escape us now. Ian says the case will cause an even greater sensation than Pa's divorce. The $2,500 the *Sunday People* paid for the story of our separation is chickenfeed compared to what we'll make.'

'I only hope he's going to be handling your financial arrangements,' I said. 'Stephanie tells me you could've got ten times what you did. Not only did you sell me down the drain, you sold yourself as well, you inadequate jerk.'

'He is. He helped Pa with his divorce. He flew over from Canada – he was at McGill University,' Colin explained to Mary Michele, 'to be with him throughout the trial.' He turned to me. 'You didn't know that, did you?' he said proudly.

'If that's your game plan, you'd better think about the consequences very carefully. I'm your wife, and will remain so until we are divorced.'

'I'll get the marriage annulled.'

'No, you won't. Nor will you get a divorce on those grounds. If you try, I will contest the divorce and defeat you. Then, when I've won and we're still married, I won't divorce you. I'll have you committed to an asylum and *throw away the key*. Think about it. I'm your next of kin until we're divorced.'

The following Tuesday I departed for Jamaica without telling Colin that I was going. My beloved Aunt Marjorie was there staying with my parents, who were overwrought about Colin's betrayal. Daddy, especially, felt acutely the tarnishing of his good name. I was still as devastated as I had been at the Rutherfurds'. I spent a week lying on the chaise-longue on the back verandah or in the drawing room crying and being consoled by Mummy and Auntie.

Once I resurfaced, my sense of humour returned. Colin had figured out where I was and was inundating the house with telephone calls. I took the first one about ten days after arriving in Jamaica.

'I love you. I know you love me. I made a mistake. I'm sorry. It will never happen again. Please come back,' he pleaded.

'Ah, now that you realise you can't make the money you hoped by betraying me, you want your old punch bag back, do you?' I was enjoying putting the boot in.

'It's not that. I do love you. Wilde and Ian convinced me you'd made a fool of me.'

'And just how did they accomplish that, dear Colin?'

'When he came to New York, Ian said everyone in Scotland was laughing behind my back because I had married a man. He told me to get shot of you. He said if I did it right we'd solve our financial problems and be rid of you in one stroke. That's how this all came about. I swear it wasn't my idea.'

'That I can believe.' I didn't think he had the brains for a venture of this scale.

'And Wilde did misquote me,' Colin said, lapsing into his lost and injured little-boy tone. 'I didn't say those terrible things about you.'

I still hadn't seen the second story he'd sold, so I asked, 'Why don't you tell me precisely what you did and didn't say?'

'I said you were a passionate wife on our wedding night.'

'If you must stoop to discussing your wife's sexual performance in the gutter press, you could at least refrain from lying. We didn't have sex on our wedding night.'

'I didn't want anyone to think there was anything wrong with you.'

'No, Colin. You didn't want anyone thinking there was anything wrong with *you*.'

'Right, right,' he said awkwardly, aware that he'd needed to throw me a concession if he wanted to get the conversation back on track. 'I'm going to the travel agent. I'll send you your ticket. Come back.'

'You do that and we'll see.' I had to get back to New York somehow, and frankly, if Colin was going to pay, so much the better. I was unhappy about being such a drain on my parents' resources.

For the next two and a half weeks, I played cat and mouse with the rat, and Mummy and I had quite a lot of fun at Colin's expense. Sometimes he'd telephone six times in an hour. 'Say I'm out, Rupert,' I'd instruct the butler, who was also in on the joke and would give the game away just enough to drive Colin crazy. On other occasions, I'd take a call and say, 'I'm coming back on Wednesday,' and then not show up. It was childish and silly, but it was a laugh in the graveyard at the expense of the killer of my reputation and peace of mind, and we needed some light relief. I don't regret doing it at all.

At last I received the article Colin had sold from my brother in London, and I knew I had to return to New York to defeat his lies with proof. That meant moving back in with Colin for long enough to invalidate his claims that my medical history was the true reason for the collapse of our marriage. I would also have to gather evidence against him to use in case he changed tack yet again and tried to orchestrate a sensational divorce. That called for getting hold of documents which would completely disprove his version of events, as well as the letters from his files which had been written to his father by his hosts in Australia and New Zealand and concerned his brushes with the law while stoned and violent or drunk and disorderly. These went back to the mid-1960s, and clearly showed that he had always been disturbed.

The next item on the agenda was to smoke Ian Argyll out of his lair. That was easy enough to accomplish. As a precondition of returning to New York, I had stipulated once again that Colin had to give up drinking and drug-taking.

'I'll need your help,' he had replied, hoping to manipulate me as he had done before, but I am not the sort of person who makes the same mistake twice. I used his appeal to protect myself and ensnare his brother. I telephoned him in Scotland. 'Ian, I need your help. Colin wants me to go back to him, but I told him I wouldn't until he's dried out. He can't afford hospital prices in America and there's no question of my family paying, especially after what Colin just did with the press.'

'Why don't you arrange for him to be hospitalised in Jamaica?' Ian suggested shrewdly.

'I couldn't possible do that. My father says he'll kill Colin if he ever sets eyes on him again.'

'But it would be so much cheaper in Jamaica,' Ian persisted.

'But not as cheap as Scotland, where it will be *free*,' I said, my voice positively trilling with barely concealed relish. 'What I need is your support. If I suggest to Colin that he returns to Scotland for treatment, will you back me up?'

'Of course, Georgie, of course. I'm happy to do anything I can to help.'

'I so hoped I could rely upon you.'

Later that afternoon, Colin was on the telephone, in an hysterical state. 'Ian says you want to commit me. He said you were on the blower to him asking for his co-operation.'

'Now why would I need his co-operation when I'm your next of kin?' I recounted my conversation with Ian verbatim. 'But you can thank him for showing me his true colours.'

I returned to New York to 'sign divorce papers and steer the action safely through to a civilised conclusion', as I put it to Colin. He was now off the sauce. He still took his valium, but that was now a matter of complete indifference to me as I couldn't have cared less whether he lived or died. Frankly, there were times when I hated him so much that I wished he'd just take the whole lot and put us both out of our misery. Colin, however, was not one to punish himself – all anger and blame had to be directed outwards. I was determined that this time I would not be the butt of his sadistic inclinations.

It was apparent to me from the moment of my arrival at 170 East Eighty-Third Street that Colin Campbell was hoping the marriage would pick up where it had left off. Whistle in the dark, I thought, making it clear that he had to provide me with a divorce. He instructed Cusack & Stiles to make the arrangements for the quickest and cheapest (he was paying) no-fault divorce available. This turned out to be divorcing in Santo Domingo. Meanwhile, I was determined to get Colin to recant the lies he had sold. By this time the peculiar idea that we would remain together after the divorce had taken hold in his head. I said nothing to disabuse him of that notion, recognising as I did that I would be lucky indeed if I could achieve a scandal-free divorce and a scandal-ridding proclamation as well.

While Colin was trying to keep me sweet, Ian was trying to break up what Colin must have told him was a reconciliation. He became increasingly strident in his accusations about my medical history, telling Colin he knew for a fact that I was a man who had been 'hacked up' by the 'butchers' at Johns Hopkins. I told him the next time he phoned the apartment never to ring my home again, then wrote him a letter which left him in no doubt that I knew what he had been up to.

I could not now wait to see the backs of both brothers. I had ceased using the name Campbell. Apart from putting distance between myself and a creep like Colin, it was a slap in the face to him, for he truly believed that his was one of the greatest aristocratic names in the British peerage. By dropping it, I was showing the contempt I felt for him and all he represented, and the contrasting pride I had in my own antecedents. It was like a red rag to a bull. Colin nagged me mercilessly to resume using my married name, but for once, I wasn't tempted to give in. Now his persistence served only to stiffen my resolve: I loved seeing him frustrated and impotent. Now it wasn't he who was tormenting me; by withholding what he wanted, I was tormenting him.

In March Colin started to drink again. I serenely continued with my own life. I was in New York for a purpose, and

I was going to see the project through to a successful conclusion. I saw my friends and even went on one or two dates
with men like Nick Simunek and to the odd amusing party.
One was the vernissage of the artist Sarah Churchill (Sir
Winston's daughter, otherwise Lady Audley). Upon meeting
me, David Frost archly said, 'I've been reading all about you.
Anyone married to your husband deserves all our sympa-
thies.' Appreciative though I was of the kindness behind the
sentiment, I found it mortifying that Colin Campbell had
managed to turn me into a figure of curiosity and pity.

Sometimes I went along to Al-Anon meetings. These I
found no more satisfying than before, but at least the people
there reduced the sense of isolation that Colin's bizarre
behaviour created. It was simply impossible to speak about
it to normal people without feeling a deep sense of embarrassment that anyone associated with me could reduce
himself – and, by association, me – to such a condition.

In Colin's view, of course, he had good reason to resume
drinking. Despite having been perspicacious enough to
have had me sign a prenuptial agreement, he had discovered from his lawyers that it did not fulfil its intention of
protecting his trust fund. He had overstepped the mark,
and had got me to sign away all my rights to alimony,
instead of just some of them. 'I'll be only too happy to sign
a separation agreement,' I said. 'I don't want maintenance.'

'That ain't possible,' he said. 'You have to have some
maintenance. If you don't, the agreement ain't valid.'

I knew from Charles Dismukes that I was entitled to 50
per cent of everything Colin possessed in New York, which,
incidentally, was where his trust fund originated. Colin told
me that Richard Steel, the senior partner at Cusack & Stiles,
was suggesting 15 per cent – $26,000 – though I later over-
heard him telling someone else that the figure Steel had
recommended was 25 per cent. Either way, it was hardly
compensation for someone scarred by his violence and
whose reputation he had destroyed, but I just wanted to be
rid of Colin, so I agreed. Colin used the opportunity the
drafting of the separation agreement afforded him to exploit

me financially. 'If you're getting a slice of my trust fund, I should have the furniture,' he pointed out.

'You must be joking. I'm saving you 35 per cent of what you owe me under New York State law. Why should I give you the furniture? Your money didn't buy it. It's not yours. Regard my share of your trust fund as compensation for all the abuse you subjected me to. And remember, this marriage has failed because of you. You should feel enough guilt to carry the can without complaint.'

Money, however, brought out the beast in Colin that my refusal to use his name did not. Within days, he was employing his old standby: brute force. On each occasion I called the police. In those days, however, domestic violence was not treated with the seriousness it is now, so they always talked to Colin and calmed him down while I stood by imploring them to throw him into the slammer. Colin did once prevent me from calling the police by repeatedly chopping me on the back of the head with his hand, judo-style. Deciding that it was easier to pretend I had passed out cold than to struggle for the telephone, I lay down on the floor, eyes shut. 'Fuck,' he said, bending over to examine me. 'I hope the bitch isn't dead. Fuck. Stupid cunt.' While I tried hard not to burst out laughing, despite the pain, he did something interesting and unexpected. He telephoned his brother and gave him an elaborate explanation.

This gave him a new idea. Within a couple of weeks, Ian was in New York, and while he was there, my death became Colin's latest obsession, a topic he persisted in returning to even after his brother had left the city. 'It's easy to get a contract out on you. I've been told how. I know who can arrange the hit. You'd better watch your step, or you might never make it crossing the road.' I no longer dismissed the Campbell ravings out of hand – too much that I had never believed possible had already come true. So I telephoned my parents and told them about the threats to my life. If I did die, they would know what to do and who to go after.

'Just sign the furniture over to him,' my mother counselled.

'It's only money,' Daddy said. 'That's what this is all about, money. Just sign the damned furniture away and let's get rid of the drunken bum.'

'If I do that, we won't be rid of him. We'll only encourage him.'

At first my parents allowed me to do as I saw fit, but when Colin bombarded them with five days of round-the-clock telephone calls – all collect, naturally – Daddy snapped. 'Sign the goddamned furniture over to him if you know what's good for you!' he screamed at me. 'I'm fed up with the mess and the problems. It's our money and I'm your father. I'm ordering you. Sign the furniture over to the leech.'

Against my better judgements, I agreed that Colin could have the furniture. No sooner had I done so than up he bobbed with a new demand. 'It's humiliating that you're insisting the lawyers refer to you as Georgia Ziadie in the separation and divorce papers. Just for those, let them call you Campbell,' he suggested.

'Absolutely not. My name is Georgia Ziadie, and that's the name they're going to use.'

Colin nagged on and on until watching his discomfort was no longer satisfying. I was secretly relieved when he came up with a compromise that saved both our faces: using the name Georgia Ziadie Campbell.

'I'll do it only if you give the *Sunday People* an interview after the divorce saying that everything you said before is a lie,' I said, deciding that I might as well use the situation to strike a bargain.

'Done,' he said.

So the end was in sight at long last. In May Colin flew down to Santo Domingo for two days to get a no-fault, mutual-consent divorce. On the day the decree was granted, I celebrated the occasion with dinner and a romantic interlude with Bill Madden. It was the only time my marital bed was ever the scene of good sex.

My second objective had still not been achieved to my satisfaction. Although Colin went along with a story in the

Sunday People which asserted that we were reconciled when we were in fact divorced, he would not recant his lies about me being a man, or about knowing nothing about my medical history until after our wedding.

I announced that I was returning to London, which thereafter became the focal point of my existence, even though I did not officially establish residency there until 1981.

'But I thought we were staying together,' was Colin's response.

'I never said that. You said it,' I reminded him. 'You surely don't think I'd stay with a man I'm not married to, when he can't even clear up misconceptions of his own creation?'

'I'll come with you.'

'This is a free country. If you want to come with me, you can come as far as Heathrow Airport. Thereafter, you're on your own.'

For a marriage that had begun with such romance, and had been conducted in an atmosphere of abuse and exploitation, at least it had ended civilly.

As I closed down the apartment and packed up my possessions for shipment to London, I made a vow to myself. Never again would I give anyone the opportunity to do to me what Colin Campbell had done, nor would I ever allow anyone, myself included, to use a medical problem for which I had had no responsibility as a club with which to batter me.

9

The end of any marriage is a time for grieving, and grieve I did. I wept for the loss of my dreams, for all the good times I had not had, for all the efforts I had made which had come to nought, for all the pain and suffering and degradation I had endured, for the loss of my innocence, for my introduction to disenchantment, evil and destructiveness. My one consolation was that the trauma was now at an end. I had spent all but the first six weeks of my marriage recovering from broken bones and beatings, and it was a tremendous relief to know that I would now be conducting my life without further physical violence or pain.

Free at last of Colin, I also noticed how deeply I was able to sleep. Ever since his first death threat in March, I had been sleeping with one eye open, so to speak, in case he tried to 'top me', as he had put it.

Hungry once more for life and its pleasures, as soon as I was settled at Richard Adeney's house in Notting Hill, where my brother was living, I picked up the telephone and called my friends, and even an attractive man from my single days. Count Giorgio Emo di Capodilista was a scion of a grand Italian family I had met through my ex-boyfriend David Koch. He seemed genuinely pleased to hear from me, and took me to dinner at the Chelsea Rendezvous, then back to his Belgravia mews house, where we did what all adult heterosexuals did in the 1970s.

Attractive and thoughtful though Giorgio was, I decided that I could not circumvent the grieving process by distracting myself with men. I would have to go through it before I could enjoy being with another man. As well as the emotional distress, there were physical effects of what I had suffered to be dealt with. I weighed less than a hundred pounds and could barely eat. And night after night, I had terrible nightmares in which Colin Campbell was beating me or trying to kill me. Sometimes these could be quite embarrassing, for I would scream out in my sleep. 'Wake up,' Mickey would say, coming into my bedroom. 'You're having another nightmare.'

To spread the burden until I found a place of my own, after a time I went to stay with Mary Anne Innes-Ker. 'You married into the most notorious family in the British aristocracy,' she said. 'There is bad blood there. You should never have married Colin. It was doomed to failure before you took the vows.' Each day I made a concerted effort to find myself somewhere to live. I yearned for stability. Finally, I stumbled upon just what I wanted: a sweet little house on Denbigh Street in Notting Hill. 'Don't take it,' my brother counselled. 'It's too expensive [it was the princely sum of £50 per week]. Why saddle yourself with responsibilities after what you've been through? Give yourself a rest. Share a flat.'

Dulany Howland, the American friend who subsequently married into the famous Hunt family from Texas, came up with what seemed the ideal solution, and I moved into a flat in Green Street, Mayfair with a female friend of his and an English chap called Richie Self. A few days later Richie had a dinner party. I was returning from the theatre as the guests were leaving, and ran into Joanna Pinches (now better known as Joanna Wood), the English interior designer, who introduced me to the others. The following day Richie came into my bedroom after work. 'James Adeane, who was here last night, is smitten by you. He thinks you're devastatingly beautiful. He wants to meet you.' I remembered James as being tall, dark and handsome.

'Richie, I'm not up to meeting anyone yet. I've only just been divorced, and frankly, the last thing I want right now is another man.'

'Don't say no so readily. He's one of the most eligible bachelors in England. He has two estates; he is the grandson of the Canadian multimillionaire Sir James Dunn, and his Uncle Michael is the Queen's private secretary.'

'Richie, there are times when I feel so drained I can barely put one foot in front of the other. This is not a good time for me.'

'He'll be sympathetic. He knows what suffering is all about. His mother committed suicide.'

'Richie, it's sweet of you, but the answer has to be no.'

It was the beginning of months of persuasion. I even received an invitation to go cruising in the Mediterranean on a yacht James was taking there, even though my sole encounter with him remained that chance meeting in the hallway at Green Street.

When I did finally meet James properly, I liked him immediately. He was every bit as good-looking as I remembered, and had a voice that rumbled and a warmth that was detectable beneath a taciturn, almost brusque exterior. Like Bill Swain, he was sufficiently like Daddy to trigger whatever elements of a father complex I had. But life had taught me to remain true to my instincts, and I stuck to my decision.

Any temptation I had to do otherwise – and I did have them – was quashed when the dark and simmering presence of Colin Campbell in the background thrust itself to the fore once more. He had been in touch, promising one thing one day and delivering the opposite the next, and I had tolerated this because he had said he would give a true version of events to a popular tabloid, the *News of the World* – on the condition, of course, that I sold them an interview. I went along with all this, and even allowed myself to be interviewed, only to have Colin pull the plug and refuse to talk on the grounds that he saw no reason to give them two stories for the price of one.

Now he had seen my article, and freaked out. 'You blame me for the break-up of our marriage. You say I took out my moodiness on you.'

'It is a highly sanitised version of the truth. How can you object to it?'

'And you want me to take back what I said?' he observed angrily.

'Yes, Colin. Because what you said wasn't even an exaggeration. It was an outright lie. Surely you see the difference.'

If he did, he gave no indication of it. We were now back to where we had been before the signing of the separation agreement, and true to form, he was blowing hot and cold. One morning he telephoned me and begged me, for the umpteenth time, to resume using the name Campbell. The same afternoon he rang again, this time to accuse me of hanging on to his family silver, which he had asked me to look after until he found somewhere permanent to live. I drove it round to where he was staying and dumped it on the pavement. Then he was hospitalised for surgery to his stomach, shot by years of abuse, and asked me to visit. But when I arrived, he told me to keep it short, as he didn't want his friends knowing he was still seeing me. I promptly left and refused to return despite his relentless entreaties.

The last straw was when I picked up the *Daily Express*, owned by Colin's half-sister Jeanie's uncle, Sir Max Aitken, and saw an interview he had given in the William Hickey gossip column. He had repeated his lies about his ignorance of my medical history, and had stated that this, and my inability to have children, were the reasons for the break-up of our marriage. He needed to marry a woman who could give him children, he said, to secure the Argyll dukedom's line of succession (something he has singularly failed to do in the two decades that have since elapsed). He had divorced me out of a magnanimity, since an annulment would have destroyed me. Worse, his so-called revelations had been picked up by the *Evening News*, which took the opportunity, in the guise of reporting that I had been seen on the town with Princess Elizabeth of Yugoslavia, to repeat the canard.

Colin's perverse comments wiped out all the headway I had made towards recovery. Finally, I understood what he had meant when he had said he could destroy me. He would hound and abuse me, using the press instead of his fists to batter me. Moreover, he expected to get away with it, because he knew that the Jamaican political situation had now degenerated to the extent that my father was seriously worried that his assets would be nationalised, and that I would therefore not have the means to sue the newspapers.

He was right in his assumption that my father would not back me in expensive litigation, but he reckoned without my resourcefulness and determination. I tried to get the Hon. Vere Harmsworth, now Lord Rothermere, who owned the *Evening News* and whom I knew from Jamaica, and Max Aitken to publish corrections. When they waffled and flannelled and failed to deliver the goods, I sued them myself – and, for good measure, the *Sunday People* too. I was quite prepared to go without food to nail the lies. If something is important, one must make sacrifices.

The next year was a dark period indeed. Lawsuits in Britain were fraught with problems. First, there was no possibility of a contingency arrangement, which meant that you had to keep your lawyers 'in funds'. Then there was the bizarre system of solicitors doing some of the work, and barristers the rest, and you had to pay both for what was often the same thing. And barristers and solicitors charged twice the fees of their peers elsewhere, even in the United States.

Yet I had little choice but to pursue this course of action. Unless I could put a stop to these stories, each repetition would add credibility to them. This would doubtless have a cumulative effect, shrinking the number of men who would be interested in me, and quite possibly affecting my friendships as well. As it turned out, only a handful of people were ever put off, notably Davina Wodehouse, then Richie

Self's girlfriend, now Countess Alexander of Tunis. I am grateful to the rumours for weeding her and her ilk out of my circle of friends.

My counsel was the eminent QC David Eady. At first he was confident that the newspapers would settle quickly. I sincerely hoped so, for I was so afraid of spending any money at all on anything except the case, lest I be forced to throw in the towel, that I was living in a financial straight-jacket. I seldom entertained, which is fatal for a recent divorcee: not only do you invite more loneliness into your life than is healthy, but you also relegate control of a signifi-cant part of your social life to others.

The time had come to cut my ties with the past. It was never going to be possible to have a civil, civilised or posi-tive relationship with anyone as malevolent, changeable and cruel as Colin Campbell. I wrote him a letter telling him why I never wanted to see him again. And fed up with the British newspapers referring to me as Lady Colin Campbell, I instructed *The Times* to issue the following announcement in the court circular: Lady Colin Campbell wishes in future to be known by her maiden name, Miss Georgia Ziadie. Not one British newspaper ever respected my stated wish.

Although Colin Campbell did not reply to my letter, he reacted immediately to the announcement in *The Times*. Two or three times a day, every day, he plagued me about it. 'Stop phoning me,' I demanded.

'But it's so humiliating! The whole world knows that you don't consider one of the greatest titles in the land a fit name to bear.'

In October, I allowed Colin to come to Green Street to col-lect the paintings I was still holding for him because he refused to pick them up from Mickey. These did not include the pictures he had taken, unbeknown to her, from his own sister Jeanie's house in Jamaica. In New York, he had refused to have her come to our apartment in case she saw them. I had arranged for them to be returned to their rightful owner without telling Colin. He settled himself on the sofa and proceeded to prattle on and on about his wretched name.

'You're doing yourself no favours,' he said. 'You've played right into Ian's hands. He's banging around Scotland telling everyone you were forced to give up the name.'

I had no means of knowing whether Colin was telling the truth, but I was quite prepared to be manipulated into changing my mind if there were the slightest chance that he was. It certainly seemed in character for Ian. 'Is that a fact?' I said, my blood pressure rising. 'Well, it looks as if your brother's resourcefulness has won the day where your persistence failed.' I consoled myself with the likelihood that I would remarry within a year or two. Then I could safely kiss that hated name Campbell goodbye.

Colin departed with his pictures tucked under his arms. That's the last I'll ever see of you, I thought as he retreated down the stairs. But my luck was out. That evening, as I was dressing for a dinner party, Colin returned, and kept his finger on the buzzer until I let him in. 'Please come back to me,' he implored, slobbering over me while I tried to put on my make-up.

'Colin, you don't seem to understand English. I don't want to see you, I don't want to speak to you. I don't want to have anything to do with you. If you won't have the good grace to leave, at least sit on the bed and stop being a nuisance.'

James Adeane was calling to collect me, and when he rang the doorbell, Colin jumped up. 'Why don't you go down first?' I said, hoping to avoid an awkward confrontation.

'Nah. I want to see the man my wife's going out with.'

'Your ex-wife, you mean,' I said, walking out of the flat with him in front of me, bobbing and weaving down the stairs like a coconut tree buffeted by a storm.

At the front door, I introduced them. Colin's greeting was, 'What do you want with a bitch like her?'

'Goodbye, Colin,' I said, hoping it really was.

'I want a quiet word with my wife,' he demanded of James whose eyebrows shot me a look of sympathy.

'I don't have any money to get home. Can I borrow a quid?'

'You'll have to walk home, I'm afraid. I do not have the pound to lend you. Goodbye, Colin, and good luck,' I said with finality, taking James' arm. This small but pointed gesture of contempt must have done the trick, for I have never seen him since.

Returning to a normal existence was not an entirely smooth process. I had had so much publicity that it was impossible to walk into a roomful of strangers without half of them knowing 'all about me', or so they believed, and promptly 'enlightening' the other half as soon as my back was turned. This was truly galling. Not only did one have to labour under a host of misconceptions, but one had to do so without stripping oneself of one's dignity. This I accomplished by studiously avoiding direct mention of my personal life. Those who tried to bring it up were invariably met with a blast of icy reserve which chilled them into silence. Although I understood that people were bound to be curious, I had a right to my privacy and my dignity.

As I began to appreciate the enormity of what Colin Campbell had done, I decided that I would not waste my energy on hating him. I cut him out of my thoughts. There was no point in speculating about why any human being would be so evil. I was dismayed when a year elapsed and I still felt fragile and wounded. Admittedly the libel litigation did not help in this respect, since it was a constant reminder of traumas that would have been best consigned to the past, and the financial uncertainty did not enhance my feeling of security. I was only too aware that Colin Campbell and Ian Argyll had left me with an abiding distrust and fear of people, and I recognised that I could never have a fulfilling life unless I overcame those feelings. The solution seemed to be to get a job that made few demands of me but involved contact with people. My brother suggested I did as he had once done, and got a 'holiday' job at Harrods. So it was that I came to work in the cosmetics department from May to the end of September 1976.

Meanwhile, my social life was as busy as ever. Practically every evening I would be out for dinner with friends, or went to the opera or concerts with my brother Mickey, or beat a path to nightclubs like Annabel's or Tramp with beaux who did not mind chaste relationships. I was going everywhere, but my life was heading nowhere.

Providence stepped in in November. I was in Annabel's, on my way back to the table from the powder room, when Anka Dineley, whose London home, Aubrey House, was the venue for Prince Andrew's stag party, called out to me. I briefly stopped to say hello to her and her husband Peter. They introduced me to someone whose name I did not catch. I did not even notice if he was good-looking – I was still on my sabbatical, and the last thing on my mind was romance.

Two days later Anka telephoned me. 'Come for tea,' she suggested, making it clear she had an ulterior motive. When I got to Aubrey House, she told me that I had captured the heart of James Buchanan-Jardine. Christ, I thought, here we go again.

'He's a great guy,' Anka enthused. 'One of the best-looking men in London. He's a member of the family which owns Jardine-Matheson, the great Hong Kong trading company. He's got a great personality, he's about to be divorced, from the Earl of Carlisle's daughter Susan, and he lives in great style in the country, with butlers and the whole shooting match. Can I give him your number?'

'No,' I said.

'It doesn't have to be dinner. He'd take you for lunch or tea if you prefer.'

'Thanks, but no thanks. I can think of a few things I'd like less than to go out with someone I don't know at all.'

'Georgie,' Anka said. 'He's a great catch and a truly nice chap. As a friend, I'm telling you, don't squander this opportunity. He's crazy about you. You'll never meet anyone better.'

What the hell, I thought. 'OK, Anka. If he wants to see me so much, he can join my table for the Rainbow Ball next month. I'm on the committee and I have to get a table together in any case.'

On the evening of the ball, as I pulled on my strapless

peach silk chiffon ballgown and a matching jacket heavily embroidered with pearls and beads, I wondered if I would even like James. The moment our eyes connected I knew the answer. Here was my dream come true.

In December 1976, James Buchanan-Jardine was thirty years old. Although not tall (he was only five foot ten), he was my physical type – burly, masculine and muscular. He was one of the most classically handsome men I had ever seen: good, strong jaw, sensuous lips, straight nose, big hazel eyes with long lashes, noble forehead, brown hair. Before he even greeted me I felt my knees weaken and my pulse quicken. Without doubt there was a tremendous chemistry between us.

During dinner, James sat beside me and flirted with me shamelessly. He's my sort of man, I thought: frank, straightforward, open. I could never stand men who pussyfooted around, playing it cool and expecting a woman to extract their interest as if it were an infected tooth. So far so good. As the evening progressed, I discovered that James had a Jamaican connection. When he was a child, his father had bought Sir Frank Pringle's magnificent eighteenth-century house, where the Buchanan-Jardines lived in tropical splendour until things went sour as independence approached. That was all very well, but I hadn't forgotten that Colin's Jamaican links had not exactly turned out to be the bond he had presented them as.

As the ball wound down, James suggested that we went on to Annabel's. I made sure that my cousin Enrique Ziadie, who was my official partner for the evening, came along too. I was already thinking of ways of slowing down the desire which was emanating unmistakably from the Jardine quarter. I was not now prepared to become involved with any man until he showed me that he was worthy of my trust. If he couldn't wait, that was just too bad. I would sooner be manless than savaged again.

I must have rattled James with the chill of my reserve, which was already well enough developed for friends to describe it as astonishing hauteur, for he made sure that he came armed with moral support for our first date. We met at the typically Sloane restaurant, Pooh Corner, with Patrea and Alan More-Nisbet, friends of James' who own a stately home just outside Edinburgh. I enjoyed the evening: James had a good sense of humour, he was kind, and he seemed to like nothing better than a good laugh. Afterwards, we again went to Annabel's where we danced, safely familiarising ourselves with each other as the lust built and built to scarcely bearable levels. But not even a declaration of love and further dinner dates budged my tightly closed legs. I planned to keep them just as they were until I was sure that James was someone worth having.

I went to Jamaica for Christmas, while James went to Hong Kong to see whether he should move into tax exile for a few years. When I returned to England, I moved straight into a new flat, which I was sharing with a friend, Nikita Chahursky. James drove from Cambridgeshire, where he was living, to see me that first afternoon. Nature, I fear, finally got the better of my good intentions, but I never had any regrets, for James was an accomplished lover with a divine body.

As our relationship developed, I saw that James possessed the qualities I sought in a man. He was warm, loving and affectionate, and was capable of making a commitment – in my view, one of the most important factors in a successful relationship. He was loyal, with just the right mixture of conventional concern and aristocratic indifference to the opinions of others. Like me, he was gregarious and sociable, and he had an excellent sense of humour. More to the point, he loved me unconditionally. Once, when we were talking, he said, 'I love you just as you are. I don't care what people think you were. In fact, I wouldn't care if you'd been a goat.'

All in all, James, it must be said, was quite something. 'I can see James was here last night,' my cousin Enrique, who lived nearby, often said when he dropped in for coffee. 'Your eyes are sparkling like diamonds.'

'It's tiredness,' I used to reply in what became a stock

response. 'I never get any sleep. Four, five times a night, every night. I wish I could say no. I don't see how I can marry him – I'd have to spend all day sleeping.'

And by this time, James and I were discussing marriage. Although he was not yet divorced there was no doubt that they would be divorced. I admired the finesse with which he was handling the dissolution of his marriage. His kind-heartedness, decency and absence of malice, even with people he disliked, also impressed me, and went some way towards reducing my understandable terror of remarriage.

In the meantime, my libel actions were brought to a conclusion. The Jamaican government had recently tightened up exchange controls to such an extent that it was now impossible for my father to get money out of the country legally. He was not prepared to resort to smuggling out funds as many other people did, with the result that the greater part of his worth remained in Jamaica, waiting for the Manley regime to swoop in and swallow it. This it was in the process of doing, to the alarm of both my parents, my mother especially – she could hardly believe that my father would stand by and fail to take protective measures on the grounds of principle. Only when 90 per cent of his assets had been nationalised did he finally accept that the way to fight the Castro-admiring brigands who were engaged in legalised theft was not to allow himself to be crippled by his principles, but to secrete whatever was left.

So I could now no longer look to my parents for help, for the money they gave me to live on had dried up. Faced with the prospect of funding three separate libel actions with no resources, I had no choice but to settle, especially after listening to the advice of my QC, David Eady. 'The fact that the newspapers haven't settled has been a source of some perplexity, as you know,' he had said at our last conference. 'Sadly, I now believe they never will. Not that they expect to win – they never will, and they know that. But the sad fact is that they stand to make more money by taking this to a trial, even though they will lose. They might have to pay out, say, £20,000 in damages, plus another £50,000 or so in costs, but they'll make hundreds of thousands in increased sales resulting from coverage of the trial. I fear, Lady Colin, that the gruesome truth is, this will be the most sensational libel case of the century if it reaches court. They know it. That's why they're not settling.'

Disenchanted with a legal system that can allow the persecutor to profit at the expense of the victim, not to mention being sick to death with the perpetual hassle, I instructed my lawyers to settle. The *Daily Express* paid some of my costs, and all three newspapers agreed not to repeat the libels. Although the outcome fell some way short of victory, at least I had the satisfaction of depriving the press of the money-making circus they had hoped for.

By this time, James' plans for moving to Hong Kong were well advanced. 'Hong Kong is very much like Jamaica,' he said. 'You'll love it. Everyone knows everyone else. It's cosmopolitan and great fun.' Moreover, the name Jardine carried a tremendous amount of clout in Hong Kong because James' ancestors had been responsible for wresting the territory from Chinese control to British sovereignty. If not exactly the world, Hong Kong at least was my oyster, if I wanted it.

I might well have taken the plunge but for one small incident. One day James said, 'I have to go and see my cousin, Sybilla Edmonstone, this evening. She wants my help with something. I'll see you after dinner, if that's OK.'

He came back to my place at a respectable hour, about eleven. He was as loving and attentive as ever, but I noticed that he smelled of soap and that his hair was freshly combed. It was a dead giveaway. No man takes a shower and combs his hair after an innocent dinner. He'd just crawled out of bed, I concluded, waiting to see if he made romantic overtures. He did not, though he settled down to sleep with me in his arms.

As soon as he had drifted off to sleep, I clenched my fist, thumped him in the stomach – not hard enough to hurt; just enough to startle – and said, 'That's to let you know you didn't dupe me.'

James jumped up with a start. 'What's wrong, darling? Are you having a bad dream?'

It was just the response a philandering man would make. If a certain liberality of outlook had been inculculated into me with mother's milk, it did not mean that I was happy to catch my man pulling up his trousers after a bit of light relief. 'I don't want to make more of this than it deserves,' I said without the slightest degree of rancour. 'I just want you to know that I know that the help you gave Sybilla was rather too in-depth for my taste. Good night, James, sleep tight.'

'Night, darling,' replied a relieved James, sealing the air of harmony with a kiss.

Although neither James nor I alluded to that night again until Sybilla died some ten years later, it did consolidate my doubts. Even though I was of the firm opinion that most men cheat given half a chance (and that it's no big deal unless they bring home unwelcome presents or flaunt their acquisitions in one's face), in my fragile state I immediately began to ask myself questions that I might otherwise never have put into words.

What would happen if I went to Hong Kong and the relationship did not work? Now that I couldn't simply pick up the telephone and get Daddy to cough up enough dough to resettle me in the place of my choice, would I not be taking too great a chance in flying halfway round the world to be with a man I had known only for some seven months, and who, despite being abundantly loving, clearly had problems keeping his flies zipped up? Sure, James seemed to be a wonderful guy, but that might change when the familiarity of domesticity took hold. No, I decided, I would stay in London. I would not put my life in anyone's hands again, at least, not until I was sure that the lily would remain desirable even after it had lost its gilt. If that meant I lost James, then so be it. Much as I loved James, I simply could not face another trauma.

So I stayed in London, and James and I drifted apart. Eventually he met and married someone else, had two children, and I thought that that was the end of the story. When Vanessa Hoare had a party to introduce James' new wife to his friends, I was happy to attend and wish them well. I thought that was it as far as James and I were concerned but as it turned out, the best was yet to come.

10

If I wasn't going to be a married woman, I had to become a working one. It was not exactly a popular choice to have to make. In 1977, girls from backgrounds like mine seldom let a good man get away unsanctified by matrimony unless they believed someone of equal stature would come along. I confidently expected life to throw up one fabulous guy after another for my delectation; moreover, I was now absolutely sure that I would prefer to remain single unless I could find exactly the right man for me.

This attitude called into question the very structure upon which the establishment conducted itself. Why should I opt for a single life, with all its harsh realities, when I could just as easily choose marriage? Why should I choose to confront the issues that most women like me did their best to avoid? Did I really want a small flat instead of a large house? A tiny income instead of marital wealth? The struggle of facing the world on my own, instead of the safety net of matrimony? Not only my father, but many of my friends thought I was making life unnecessarily difficult for myself.

I no longer cared what Daddy or anyone else thought of me. Notoriety had given me a new indifference to the

opinion of others, because I had to live with people thinking
I was the opposite of what I was. Just to maintain a mod-
icum of equanimity, I had had to adopt a new set of values.
These new values gave me great freedom, and I was becoming aware that I could rid myself of many of society's
shackles. In other words, I could become an independent
woman.

First, however, I needed a job. At twenty-seven, I was too
old to model, and I did not want to return to dress-design-
ing. I toyed with the idea of writing, but decided against
doing anything that would not bring in a steady income. In
a quandary, I turned to Joe Fish, a wise and wonderful
American diplomat posted to the Court of St James's. 'What
you have to sell is class,' he said. 'Not many people have it,
and not many people can afford to buy it. Target the Arab
ambassadors. They've got the money; they'll like your class.
I'll send you a copy of the Diplomatic List.' (This was a
booklet put out by the Foreign and Commonwealth Office
which listed all the embassies, high commissions and diplomats accredited to London.) 'Write to each of the Arab
ambassadors. Keep the letter short – one, maybe two sen-
tences saying you're available for a suitable post. Brevity is a
sign of confidence. Then sit back, wait for the replies, and
we'll take things from there.'

The first to reply was the Libyan ambassador. He needed
a social secretary. Could I arrange an appointment with his
secretary? I was offered the job, and Joe said, 'Take it. It's a
good offer.' Although I had reservations because of Libya's
reputation for having links with the IRA, Joe talked me out
of them, pointing out that the Libyan embassy was a bona-
fide diplomatic mission with properly accredited diplomats.

Next, I needed a place of my own. Through Maxine
Franklin, the acclaimed Jamaican pianist, I found a flat at 10
West Eaton Place. Belgravia was not to my taste. Although
the smartest area in London, it was so sedate, so mono-
chrome (all the houses are painted in the same magnolia
gloss, by dictate of the Grosvenor Estate) and so quiet that I
felt I was becoming middle-aged overnight. But I counted

my blessings and moved in opposite Andrew Lloyd Webber and his first wife, Sarah.

Doing up the flat, searching for antiques and pictures, was fun. So, too, was my new job. Once the ambassador discovered that I was capable and reliable, he had me doing the work of a private secretary as well as a social one. This was fascinating, not only because one dealt with people at the very highest levels in government, business and the professions, but also because I was afforded a glimpse into the hypocrisy that underlay governmental posturing. If you picked up a newspaper any day of the week, you could read story after story about the dastardly Libyan regime. Yet, again on a daily basis, people from all the major British companies competed for contracts awarded by the Libyan government, while government ministers, diplomats from the Foreign and Commonwealth Office and members of the royal household were regular and frequent visitors. Libya, you see, had a great deal of money, and no matter how the West decried Colonel Gaddafi's politics, the lure of his lucre was infinitely more seductive. Hence the constant cap-in-hand appearances of the great and mighty, some of whom trooped all the way over from the United States. The Washington embassy did not have an ambassador, for political reasons, which made 'my ambassador' (as everyone in embassies referred to their head of mission) the West's primary route to the Libyan government.

I could not have been at the embassy for more than about two months when I was offered my first 'commission'. 'If you give us access to the ambassador whenever we want it, we'll give you a handsome commission paid anywhere in the world,' an eminent businessman said, handing me a box of chocolates. Had I heard right? Was I being offered a bribe for merely doing my job? Yes, I was, and it happened time and again. Nor was access the only thing I was being asked to provide. Denying access to competitors also had a price tag, and I gathered that it was even higher.

I wish I could say that the offers of commission presented me with a dilemma. Regrettably, they did not. I was too naïve to consider accepting money thinking it dishonourable to take outside remuneration for a service that the Libyan embassy was already paying me to provide. Nowadays, I would most likely take the money and laugh all the way to the bank, *baksheesh* being an accepted part of the Arab culture, though no amount of money could induce me even now to deny access to those who are entitled to it.

To my surprise, the least hypocritical segment of the supplicating population turned out to be the journalists. Those who covered diplomatic and governmental matters were not like the tabloid reporters. Where there was muck, they sought an explanation, not a wallow. Where there was good, they questioned its existence and its effects. In other words, they sought truth in a responsible and intelligent manner. Doubtless the fact that Britain had a Labour government, that Gaddafi was a believer in state largesse for his people, and that the journalists on assignment were frequently left wing had something to do with it, though not always. The right-wing *Daily Telegraph*'s diplomatic coverage, for instance, was invariably admirably even-handed, and I can think of no occasion on which any diplomatic correspondent deviated from the high standards everyone had a right to expect of him at all times.

When I had taken the job, I had not reckoned upon coming into contact with journalists. Indeed, had I known that it would become an everyday part of my routine, and that I would even be called upon to court the press in an attempt to improve Libya's image in the Western media, I would not have taken the post. The diplomatic editors, however, all respected my privacy and kept my personal life out of their writings and questionings. I cannot tell you how relieved and surprised I was to discover that there was a part of the British press that was actually ethical.

The Libyans themselves were also a revelation. 'My' ambassador could not have been a more decent, correct or honourable man. Mohammed Younis al Mismari had been Colonel Gaddafi's commanding officer before the revolution. He was a dead ringer for the young Omar Sharif, and even more charming. Happily married with several children, he treated me with the respect that an Arab gentleman accords a lady. When I left, the newspapers claimed that we had had an affair, which was entirely untrue. We did get on well, though, and with time he came to use me as a sounding board for what people in the West thought.

Once I was settled in my job, I realised that the wealth and caring attitude of the Libyans presented me with an ideal opportunity to benefit others. Each Libyan citizen who needed medical care not available at home was flown to London, put into one of the top hospitals, such as the London Clinic or the Princess Grace, and given the finest medical treatment free, while their families were housed in hotels and given spending money. I conceived the idea of channelling some of the altruism towards people I knew. 'Charities are constantly approaching me for help,' I said to the ambassador and Said Gaddafedam, Colonel Gaddafi's nephew, who headed the military section of the embassy, one day. 'Perhaps you would consider supporting some of the worthier causes? It would do Libya's reputation no end of good, especially if you sustain the support over a prolonged period. Drip, drip. Gradually people will begin to notice, and they'll associate Libya with worthwhile patronage.'

'That's good thinking,' Said said. 'We should do it.'

'Yes,' the ambassador agreed. 'You tell us what to support, and we'll support it, Georgia.' So began my charity work in Britain.

Charitable causes, however, were not the reason why I had been hired by the ambassador; social clout was. 'We want you to organise something to celebrate the eighth anniversary of the revolution. Something that lots of well-known people will come to. Can you do it?'

'I should think so,' I replied. This, I could see, would not be an easy task. It was one thing for Field-Marshal Lord This or the Most Honourable the Marquis of That to drink coffee with the ambassador during the day while on a contract crawl, for the British establishment thought nothing of befriending people with whom they would never socialise as long as there was a financial reward in sight. But the tricky part would be to get those same men out after dark, and, even more difficult, to have them accompanied by their wives. I set to work.

The British social set, I had discovered, were suckers for parties. Never before had I seen people, even those of sup- posedly great principle, who would forgive any atrocity, tolerate any failing, overlook any inadequacy, to be enter- tained elegantly by others. As long as the host or hostess lived in the right area, greeted them in a civil manner, got the butler to serve them champagne, had a footman or two pass- ing around a few canapés, they would arrive in droves. Whether or not they knew the host or hostess was irrele- vant. I decided that to persuade potential guests that the reception was going to be well worth attending, I would need to attract them with a healthy proportion of socialites, business tycoons and diplomats.

Before the invitation cards were even printed, I began the serious business of courting people via the media. The Libyan Ambassador's Dinner, as I named the event (thereby removing all associations of revolution, which would assuredly put off just about everyone my employers wanted to attract), was going to be the epitome of civilisation and sumptuousness in the contemporary recession-ridden British economy. In other words, it was going to be quintes- sentially aristocratic, with the best of champagnes, wines, food, brandy, liqueurs, bands, cabarets.

As word began filtering out through the gossip columns that I was organising the grandest, most lavish diplomatic reception ever held, I was inundated with calls. The press wanted more information (yes, the champagne would be Louis Roederer Cristal, not Dom Perignon; the Confrey Phillips Band was playing because it was generally acknowl- edged to be the finest dance band in the United Kingdom). All sorts of people wanted invitations. Some were already on the guest list, but others were truly surprising. One woman even took to writing me threatening letters when I refused to include her, and more than once I had to rescue Lizzy Thompson, my assistant, from tenacious supplicants with the curt comment, 'The list is closed. It's only a party, for God's sake. Develop some dignity and stop begging. Goodbye.' The guest list remained exactly as I had planned it, with one exception. Vanessa Redgrave, whose outstanding work for the Palestinian cause had earned much condemnation in the Western media, expressed an interest in attending through a mutual acquaintance. I decided that if anyone deserved to attend it was her, so I had the ambassador's chauffeur deliver her an invitation.

The dinner dominated my life for three months. Because this was an ambassadorial reception representing a sovereign state, each guest's invitation had to be addressed in the full, formal style laid down by Buckingham Palace. The embassy, of course, had no precedents, so I had to check each guest's correct title and decorations in *Who's Who* or *Debrett*'s, or with one of the official bodies such as Buckingham Palace or the Foreign Office. Talk about time-consuming – boring, too. My only consolation was the knowledge that the embassy would make no gaffes while I was in charge of social affairs.

Six weeks before the date, 29 September 1977, I handed all 2,000 invitations over to the postal section of the embassy and held my breath. Only when the replies came in would I know whether my campaign had worked. I was worried, not least because August is a notorious time of year for the conduct of any business. Everyone is on holiday in Scotland or the Mediterranean, so some of the replies would not be received until as late as mid-September. By then, however, I knew I was on to a winner. Not only had most of my young socialite friends accepted, but so too had eminent politicians like Reginald Maudling and Roy Mason (both cabinet ministers) and heavy-duty businessmen such as James Goldsmith and his then mistress Lady Annabel Birley (after whom Annabel's, the nightclub in Berkeley Square, is named).

The evening proved a huge success. Within the two tiers

of the great ballroom of the Grosvenor House Hotel, all 1,231 guests were treated to a spread most people hadn't even dreamed was possible. 'There are chauffeur-driven cars backed up on Park Lane beyond Marble Arch,' Peter Snow, the television journalist commented with admiration. 'I didn't know there were so many limousines in the whole of London. This is the diplomatic ball of the decade. How does it feel to have so much clout?'

And in a way, he was right – working at the Embassy had revealed that I did have a measure of clout. Most people I met now seemed impressed by me. Only the die-hard socialites still made the connection with Colin Campbell's lascivious tales, which, thankfully, seemed to have petered out. I could pick up the telephone and call just about anyone in the country and be put through to that person. Colin Campbell, I was beginning to discover, had been right about his title, even if he had got the wrong end of the stick as to why it impressed people. Only the aristocracy and royalty recognised the link with the dukedom of Argyll: most other people believed the family was related to the famous racing drivers, Sir Malcolm Campbell and his son, Donald. And when they learned the truth, they usually accepted it as a reasonable substitute. Thus ignorance and confusion, exacerbated by the commonness of the name Campbell, were responsible for the bedazzlement. I had no objections, as long as it worked in my favour. Life was certainly looking up after the years of doom and gloom; if not the purpose of my life, this was at least a pleasant enough diversion.

In December 1977, President Sadat's peace initiative with Israel resulted in the Camp David Accord, which now pitted Gaddafi against the very Western governments with whom he had so recently been cultivating good relations and a good image. 'Georgia,' the Ambassador said to me on 28 December, 'I didn't want to ruin your Christmas with this, but Tripoli now has different political needs from when we employed you, and the Foreign Ministry are asking if you would be gracious enough to resign. Every one appreciates all you've done, and of course we'll still continue to support the many worthy charities you foster.'

'I fully understand the predicament,' I said. 'You will have my resignation as soon as I can type it up.'

'You don't have to be so quick, Georgia,' he laughed. 'No one is throwing you out. Take your time, as much time as you want.' When they gave me my pay cheque, I was delighted that they had been kind enough to pay me till the spring.

After a month's rest I began searching for a new job. Four Lloyd's underwriters were advertising for someone to run their office, in those days adjoining the Wigmore Hall, one of London's premier concert venues. The job started at 10 a.m. (crucial for someone who was seldom in bed before two) and finished at 4 p.m. (most convenient for drinks parties and charity committee meetings). I turned up for my interview on a blisteringly cold February morning in a black diamond mink coat with matching muff. 'It's the muff that got you the job,' says David Hornsby, nephew of the Marquis of Reading, who has remained a close friend.

Although I earned less than I had at the embassy, I was far happier. I had far more in common with three of the four men for whom I worked. David, John Avedon, John Cregan and I shared a wicked sense of humour and had similar views on life and I felt a part of a whole instead of like a prized object on a pedestal. Nor was the work too arduous. There were whole days when there was nothing to do except read newspapers and organise my social life. When there was work to be done, I did it, of course, but even then, the three men, being gentlemen, understood that few things in Britain took second place to one's social life. If I were on the committee for an impending ball or concert, they happily let me jam the switchboard and shunt their work to one side until the big day had passed.

It was not all one-way traffic: I got them on to the List for Royal Ascot, and always made myself available to help impress clients at lunch in the Captain's Room at Lloyd's or for dinner in town with prospective American 'names'. Peter

Green, the chairman, was a good friend of John Cregan; John Avedon had a secret route through to Ian Posgate, the miracle-worker whose syndicates always made fortunes for those lucky enough to gain admission. Peter Cameron-Webb was another bigwig with whom we had a connection – his wife Ann was a close friend of mine through KIDS, the Marquis of Northampton's charity for handicapped children, whose fund-raising committee she chaired and I sat upon.

Looking back on the shambles that Lloyd's has become, it is hard to reconcile those heady days of ultra-respectability with the outright incompetence and thievery which recent developments revealed to be rife. They were nevertheless halcyon days for me. For three and a half years I enjoyed a security and companionship above and unusual in any job, which was largely based on the friendships I built up with my three bosses. Did I want to go to the south of France during summer? Borrow John Cregan's house at Gassin? Join David and John Avedon for smoked salmon and strawberries and cream in some little garden tucked away in the middle of nowhere? The pace was so leisurely that there was always time for laughter.

Like my Libyan employers, my Lloyd's bosses were protective when publicity reared its head, which it often did, now that my libel actions were settled. Nigel Dempster, the *Daily Mail*'s gossip columnist, had a particular obsession with me which exceeded even the snideness for which Richard Compton Miller, the slick curly-haired number from the *Daily Express*, was justly renowned. Handbags at dawn might have been their aim, but in my book men don't beat women up – not with words; not with innuendo; not even with column inches or handbags. Their poison prompted David Hornsby to volunteer to accompany me to one of my court appearances. The police were prosecuting Grania, Lady Duff Gordon for making menacing telephone calls to me in a case that was typical of the trigger a life such as mine can have upon the fantasies of others.

Grania Duff Gordon had once been a great beauty. A model for Balmain and the first wife of Sir Andrew Duff

Gordon, she drove herself out of a good marriage. Our paths only crossed once or twice and she seemed perfectly civilised. Then she conceived the bizarre idea that a small group of aristocrats, including one of the Fitzalan-Howards and me, was intent on selling Britain down the drain to the communists. Thereafter, she hounded us with telephone calls at all hours of the day and night.

At first I tried to be nice, and when that failed, under-standing. In the end I contacted the police, who charged her. She pleaded guilty, was fined and banned from communi-cating with me, a ban with which she complied until a year or so later. Then her obsessions took a sexual turn, focusing on some inelegant fantasies concerning me and her former boyfriend, Count Artur Tarnowski. This time I insisted that the police put a stop to her ravings without recourse to a trial. The last time, the press had been out in force for each of the three hearings, turning the whole thing into a circus. The mischief they would create with sexual stories could easily be imagined. Whether the police succeeded, or whether it was my friend Patricia Baldwin, who knew Grania's brother, I shall never know, but someone got Grania to get her claws out of me.

Not all of the fantasies for which I was the catalyst were so disturbed. Out of the blue, an eminent financier I knew approached me on behalf of a friend of his. 'He's the monarch of a Middle Eastern state. He wants a Western-style Queen. She has to be from a good family. She has to be good-looking. She must be good with people, for he wants her primarily for the public role she'll play. She's got to be intelligent, and she also has to have a good character, because she can't mess around on him once they're married. Do you know anyone who'd fit the bill?'

I compiled a list of possibilities with notes beside each name. The problem was, hardly any of the candidates had the looks, the charm and the character, and of the few who did have all three, not one was the type to go for such an arrangement. Feeling an utter failure, I met with my friend to convey the bad news. With only the most perfunctory of looks at the list over which I had slaved, he said, 'Do you want the role?'

'Don't be ridiculous. Where have you been living? Don't you read newspapers?' I asked irritably.

'So does what the papers say rule you out of the running?'

I gave no more than a slight nod of the head.

'In fact, Georgie, it's you he wants. He's seen you on television; he knows Lebanon well, and the Ziadie family. He's heard good reports about you.'

'I can't believe he wouldn't mind about my medical history.'

'Middle Easterners take a more compassionate view of birth defects than Westerners. He's also a pragmatist. No one will ever write a word against you in any Middle Eastern publication, at least not while you're Queen. Those rulers stick together and look out for each other's interests. Even the English papers will lay off once the British government has a quiet word with the newspaper-owners. Which they will – you can depend upon it.'

I was so taken aback I didn't know what to say. 'Why are you negotiating on his behalf?' I finally managed.

'I'm not negotiating. That will come later, when his representatives hammer out a marriage contract with your father's representatives. This is his way of showing you that he's not old fashioned and that he's thoughtful.' Otherwise, I suppose he'd simply have approached Daddy, cutting me and my wishes out of the picture.

'I don't know.'

'Don't be so negative. At least give it some thought. You'll have your own airline. And he is good-looking. He looks Pakistani more than Arab.'

'What an intriguing definition of beauty you have,' I observed drily.

'Georgie,' he said impatiently, 'stop being flippant. This is no joke. It's a once-in-a-lifetime opportunity that will never be offered to more than a handful of girls all over the world. Think of the odds. Maybe five out of the billions of human beings on the face of this earth. Think. You can be a Queen.

You'll have palaces and ladies-in-waiting and servants galore. Money will never be a problem again, no matter how long you live.'

'Will I have to sleep with him?'

'Of course you will. But he has three other wives and all those Arabs have countless concubines.'

'But I won't be in love with him.'

'No, that you won't,' my friend, who knew how romantic I was, agreed.

'It's really prostitution on the most glorious scale, isn't it?'

'Don't go all soppy on me, please. This is a great honour and you know from your own family that that's how many marriages are arranged.'

'And if the marriage doesn't work?'

'He'll divorce you. You'll have the title of princess, your own house wherever you wish, and an income suitable to your rank. You could do worse.'

'What about religion?' I asked, certain no Muslim would want a Christian wife.

'You'll have to become a Muslim. And even if the marriage doesn't work out, you'll have to remain one. Recanting is a capital offence for Mohammedans.'

'I don't suppose you know it,' I said, 'but one of the Ziadies is the Archbishop of Beirut. I can see why your ruler doesn't mind my past: he has something much more significant as leverage. A member of one of the Middle East's best-known Christian families becoming a Muslim. God, wouldn't all the Muslims love that!'

I wish I could say the offer tempted me, but it did not. Giving up my religion was unthinkable. Moreover, the idea of being marooned in a strange land, surrounded by strange people, with a man I didn't love seemed too high a price to pay. My own airline I did not need, though it has always amused me that it was used as an inducement.

I still hankered after emotional fulfilment, and this yearning, of course, was not purely a matter of current emotional need. All my life I had felt that my father did not love me.

While I would later come to see that he did, this belief was not totally unfounded. His rejection of me far exceeded the aloofness he displayed with his other children, none of whom felt spurned the way I did, because they had not been. What I needed as an adult in a man was therefore more than just a sexual partner. I needed a new daddy, one who would wash away all the pain that my father's rejection had caused. Until that happened, I would always be saddled with this sense of loss.

In the meantime, there was no shortage of really nice, eligible men to wine and dine me. Some, such as Shane, Earl Alexander of Tunis, did not get further than the dinner table; with others, among them Oliver, Lord Henley, I formed rather closer associations. Oliver went on to become a conservative minister under Margaret Thatcher and John Major. I first met him before he succeeded to his father's title. We ran into each other again in April 1978, at Bennett, the Battersea nightclub which Liz Brewer, the society PR woman, launched to huge acclaim. It became the most fashionable club in Europe for all of about six months.

At the time, I thought of Oliver as nothing more than a friend. I often went out to dinner and parties with masculine innocents, and entertained them at the weekly dinner parties I had. But I would have had to have been blind not to notice how attractive he was. He was well over six feet tall and very handsome (the Edens are an exceptionally good-looking family – even his cousin, Sir Anthony Eden, Earl of Avon and prime minister during the Suez Crisis, was better known for his looks than for his political ability). But I did not view him as a potential lover any more than I did my other chums, who included Roddy Llewellyn (then Princess Margaret's boyfriend) and Ned Ryan (her greatest male friend) until one evening after a party, when, as we were sitting having a cup of coffee, Oliver changed gears. One thing led to another and we ended up in bed. He was a wonderfully tender lover, and I woke up feeling more relaxed than I had felt for a long time.

Shortly afterwards, Oliver and I were sitting in Bennett

having dinner when he suddenly said, 'You'd make a lovely Lady Henley. How about it?'

'Is this a proposal, Oliver?'

'If you want it to be,' said Oliver, who was a barrister, in true advocate's style.

I thought very quickly. Fond as I was of Oliver, I was not in love with him, nor would I ever be. Tender as he was, the chemical fireworks were simply not there. And I didn't believe that he was in love with me, either. I had to be careful how I conveyed my refusal, because I wanted our friendship to emerge unscathed. I decided that making light of the whole thing would be the best way of dealing with it. 'Oliver, you're not in love with me. You simply want a glamorous Lady Henley. Why don't you wait a bit till you find someone who's glamorous and whom you're in love with? Now, how about ordering me another glass of Cointreau?'

Having acknowledged that I did not want our relationship to progress beyond its present limits, I now felt I had to call a halt to the physical side. Having spent so many years living in limbo, I did not want to muddy the waters as far as other men were concerned, and I didn't want him falling in love with me when I liked him so much and wanted what was best for him. Besides, there was little point in continuing with a relationship that I knew could never lead anywhere. Fortunately, Oliver found his glamorous and charming wife within a few years, and I went to his wedding to see him safely married off.

While I was having my fling with Oliver, I was also seeing Eli Wallitt, the multimillionaire American businessman who was Bernie Cornfeld's partner in IOS. But Eli was only ever a friend because I simply wasn't physically attracted to him. Nothing he did could alter that. 'I'll get you to change your mind,' he said the second time we went out to dinner. 'I'm used to motivating people. I was responsible for motivating thousands. It might take time, but I'll find the way through to you.' I was thoroughly alarmed that he might undermine my free will. Eli was 'into' psychology, so he was forever finding reasons why no really meant yes. Much as I liked him, I would hardly have said we got along. In fact, he used to drive me crazy, and we were forever rowing. It bothered me more than it bothered him, for Eli's philosophy was that: any attention was better than none. Nevertheless, Eli and I saw each other regularly for three years. He even weathered Hurricane Larry, my intense and wonderful romance with the English actor Larry Lamb.

In the late 1970s, Larry stood on the threshold of stardom. Acclaimed first in Canadian repertory, where he had appeared with Dame Maggie Smith, and then in the English theatre, working with Joan Plowright (Lady Olivier), he was being hailed as one of the new generation of leading men. Tall, well built and ruggedly handsome, he was bright, entertaining and exquisitely mannered, like so many products of good working-class homes.

I first met Larry at the opening of the London Ritz Hotel's casino. I was gossiping with Robert Sedore of St Laurent and the interior designer John Siddley, Lord Kenilworth, when Edward Duke, the actor best known for his one-man show *Jeeves*, came up to say hello. With him was this mouth-watering hunk who zeroed in for the kill before I could even get out a greeting. Talk about taking your breath away. For the rest of the evening, Larry made sure he was the focus of my attention. Not that I was complaining: far from it. He exuded charm and humour and sex appeal and fun and laughter like no one else I'd ever met. Like Colin Campbell, he had an impressively strong personality, but unlike Colin, Larry was acutely attuned to the reactions of others. Just the way he scanned your face, looking for clues as to what lay behind your eyes, was a revelation.

The course of passion promised to run no more smoothly than true love, however. Even if I had been inclined to jump into bed with him straight away it would not have got this romance off the ground, for the following morning I was leaving to spend several weeks in Jamaica.

'I'll take you to the airport,' Larry said – just the right move.

On the evening of my return, Larry and I were due to

have dinner at La Poule au Pot, a fashionable restaurant in Belgravia. My cousin Enrique, who was staying with me, met him when he picked me up. Larry was an instant hit. 'He'll be so much better for you than that snooty racing-driver you used to go out with,' Enrique said. He hadn't taken to Richard Down, who I thought a real sweetie-pie, and who used to compete with Prince Michael of Kent.

Over dinner, I was able to see something of the man behind the good-looking face. Larry had a sparkling and original intellect. He was also a nice guy. Without a doubt I was drawn to him, though by now I was well into my 'Everest attitude': whoever wants to scale this peak had better get out his pickaxe and get down to the serious task of chipping away at the rockface. He therefore had to exercise a lot of patience and embark upon some heavy seduction before he was able to hoist his flag. When he did, though, the experience was as exciting as it was gratifying. Not only was Larry an accomplished lover with highly developed technical prowess, but he was also a healthy young man at his sexual peak. And he was even more entertaining in bed than out of it.

For several months Larry and I had an enchanted romance. He had been married twice before; he was also something of a ladies' man, which didn't bother me. We got along famously. My brother Mickey was as enthusiastic about him as Enrique had been, and my friends all adored him, the girls because he was so good-looking and attentive, and the men because he was so masculine and intelligent.

Unlike his British predecessor who had turned the difference in our backgrounds into a battlefield, Larry made it a source of interest. He was truly fascinated by some of the things people like us did. 'Even the way you drink soup has a logic I bet you've never figured out,' he observed, pointing out that ladling the spoon away from one was a way of preserving one's clothes by minimising the risk of spillage. For my part, I saw no reason why Larry's working-class roots should be an issue, and they never were. He didn't have a chip on his shoulder, so why should the circumstances of his birth matter? If anything, his background was a bonus, for he had a sensible handle on life that many an overprivileged wastrel did not – and having been married to one, I certainly knew what I was talking about. Besides, Larry was one of nature's aristocrats. In terms of intelligence, energy, height, looks, courtesy and just about any other human quality you could think of, he was out of the top drawer.

Once I got to know Larry well, it became apparent that he was ready to marry again, which indeed he did with his next girlfriend. Wonderful as he was, and enchanting as our romance was, I simply did not believe that we would be compatible in the long term. We were two artistic tempera-ments, with all the passion and emotionalism typical of our type – I simply didn't believe we'd survive five good rows without both of us licking our wounds to the detriment of the relationship – and even if I surmounted that in my tem-perament, I wanted a man who was calm instead of volatile. Once I had come to that conclusion, it was only a matter of time before the romantic side of things came to a halt. This they did, appropriately enough, over dinner after a birthday party hosted by Mary Archer Shee, whose great-uncle was the subject of the famous Terence Rattigan play *The Winslow Boy*. Larry's response could not have been more gentle-manly, and we have remained friends from that day to this.

I was now twenty-nine years old. I had left Colin Campbell four years before. Although I had not married, as I had expected to do, it was not through lack of opportunity. I knew my father especially was concerned, but fulfilment and development were my goals, and I had no doubt I was on the right track. It did not frighten me that I was following a rockier path than the one Daddy would have chosen for me. As long as life was good, what did it matter if it was also sometimes tough as well?

11

In 1980, Jamaica rid itself of its Cuba-loving prime minister, Michael Manley, after eight horrendous years which not only saw the imposition of democratic socialism (a euphemism, if ever there was one, for encroaching communism) but also the suppression of wealth, initiative, law, order, and the ostensible racial harmony that was responsible for the national motto: out of many, one people. Racial prejudice, which had been a feature of Jamaican life under British rule, had ceased to be a national problem in the decade since independence in 1962. Jamaica really had been on the way to becoming a colour-blind society until Michael Manley came to power in 1972. Jamaica's tragedy was that the suffering of the Manley years – and no one suffered more than the poor – proved to have been entirely unnecessary.

Prior to Manley's regime, most people recognised that the society had to change, that there had to be a narrowing of the chasm between the haves and the have-nots. The pie had to be divided more fairly, and even the rich were in favour of more equitable slices in the interests of national harmony. Because the country was now more prosperous than it had ever been since the eighteenth century, there was indeed a pie to carve up, and Manley was elected on the basis that he would take out his knife and give a fair portion to all.

Once he was in power, instead of fulfilling his election promises, the loquacious, egocentric prime minister began to preach Black Power and the dastardliness of the white oppressor, inciting racial hatred and class envy. In the process, he managed to destroy the tourist industry, one of Jamaica's prime sources of revenue, as well as the economy: the American government promptly embarked upon a policy of subversion geared to toppling the racist, anti-American politico on their doorstep.

Of course, Michael Manley's own English-born mother, Edna (a delightful woman and a fine sculptor) was white, which made for some ludicrous scenarios when her son's Black Power cohorts tried to explain her away. As the Trinidadian poet Wayne Brown recounted in his acclaimed biography, *Edna Manley – The Private Years, 1930–1938*, Edna laughed at their assertions that she could not be Michael Manley's mother because of her colour, and at the implication that she was a vicious white who had stolen a poor black woman's baby. I know from contemporaneous conversations with her that she didn't think the matter in the least funny, but she had her son's political position to protect and her own face to save.

Manley's rhetoric, beamed over the airwaves, was geared towards earning him a place upon the world stage as a leader of the Third World (making a triumvirate with Africa's Nyrere and Kaunda). So what if he alienated Jamaica's closest neighbour, the United States of America, and ruined the national economy? What did the poverty of the people matter compared with admiring column inches in Britain's *Guardian* newspaper? As the economy of the country faltered he thrashed around for scapegoats. Naturally, he chose the least sympathetic sector of the Jamaican population: the haves. So families like ours became the bogeymen responsible for all the nation's ills. The Jamaican government now encouraged the poor to take what was theirs 'by right of need'. Violent crime and murder became the order of the day, as the criminal element misinterpreted government rhetoric as permission to have an open session of lawlessness.

These criminal elements now divided their targets into three main groups. The first was any politically motivated person of any affiliation other than the government's People's National Party. These people were gunned down on a daily basis in busy streets in front of crowds of witnesses. Although the Gun Court, a detention camp for perpetrators of gun crimes located beside the Army's headquarters at Up-Park camp, was full of gunmen who were supporters of the opposition JLP, there was a dearth of gunmen who were supporters of the PNP confined within the concentration camp-like barbed wire fences. Of course such lawlessness provided an ideal cover for the gunmen of all political persuasions to settle personal scores, or merely to hold up anyone who had a gold chain or bangle worth stealing. The victims of crime now shifted to include the poor, who inadvertently became the second target group. As the government-sanctioned gunmen terrorised the people, the world's press reported that Jamaica had become one of the most dangerous and violent places on earth. Although the government had not intended the average voter to become a target of their henchmen, once the predicament arose, they did nothing to alleviate it, reasoning that it would destabilise their power base if they went after their own.

The third target group consisted of the established families, the haves, without whom, the more radical element in the government declared, Jamaica would be better off. We had oppressed the people and fleeced the country of its lifeblood, and we should leave. The democratic-socialists, as the communistic element in the government called itself, then sat back and watched the decimation – and cull the criminal element certainly did. Every one of the established families lost friends and relations in barbaric murders.

In 1978, an attempt was made on my father's life. He was held up by gunmen at work, and as they openly discussed executing him, Daddy, recognising that his one chance of survival lay in knocking the gun from the thug's hand at the moment the bullet was leaving the chamber, kept calm and struck out at the right moment. Although the bullet did hit him and at point-blank range, it passed beneath his heart, missing all his vital organs. He never got over this experience, however. He not only became a nervous wreck – thereafter we could never go out without an even lengthier diatribe from him than the one he had perfected after Grandpa's murder – at sixty-two, he was too old to recover physically. His back muscles had been irretrievably damaged, and he spent the last sixteen years of his life in varying degrees of infirmity.

Some of the so-called democratic-socialists' techniques aimed at ridding the country of families like ours were more direct, calculated to terrorise us into fleeing. The most successful ploy was the List of the Twenty-Two Families. This contained the names of generic families who were supposedly being considered for liquidation once the glorious declaration of communism was made, along with all their offshoots – cousins, in-laws, cousins of cousins – a neat way of getting rid of just about all of the establishment, the democratic-socialists' own establishment supporters excluded, of course. Even we had relatives in Manley's government: Delroy, J.W. Ziadie's son, and Mummy's first cousin Dan Williams, although of course they, and people like them within the government, frequently had no idea what the more radical wing was up to.

The circulation of the list created pandemonium among the established families and I personally know many people who fled as a direct result of it. I paid scant attention to it until just after the election in late 1980, because I viewed it as nothing but scare tactics. 'Delroy is a good boy,' Daddy said to me that Christmas while updating me on the political situation. 'Do you know what he did just before the election? He came and told all of us that we had three days to leave Jamaica if that bunch of rogues got in again. Can you imagine, they had taken a decision to arrest all of us and strip us of our citizenship! The government planned to go completely communist. You don't need much imagination to figure out what our fate would have been once the glorious revolution and show trials got underway.'

Fortunately, Michael Manley and his cronies were resoundingly voted out by the people after eight years. In came Eddie Seaga, son of Uncle Philip and Aunt Babs. Whereas Manley had talked about his love for the people while he continued to live at the elegant uptown Manley residence, Drumblair, Eddie, as a young man, had left the comforts of the Seaga family home to live in Trench Town, the worst slum in downtown Kingston, with his followers. Here was someone who really did put his money where his mouth was, and, as American aid reappeared, Jamaica returned to a semblance of normality.

It is fascinating to observe what an immediate and profound effect a change of leadership can have upon a whole nation. Almost overnight, the rhetoric of hatred yielded to a recognition that everyone, black, brown, yellow or white, rich, poor or in between, had a place within society. It was now OK once again to be white and rich, to be elegant and civilised, to be poor and black and a non-PNP supporter. The nightmare was over.

Once Eddie became PM the fawners were out in force – the average Jamaican seemed to think that the Ziadie and Seaga families were related, especially as Arthur Ziadie was a senator and a leading light in the Jamaica Labour Party. Security, expatriates and a measure of stability returned, though the financial battering that the nation as a whole and people like my father had taken could not be so easily remedied. Though by no means poor, my father was no longer as comfortable as he had once been.

Money no longer mattered to me. Having spent the latter part of my twenties living on very little aside from what I earned (and that was no fortune), I knew that one does not need a great deal of the green stuff to live well. So what if you could not afford to serve the finest wines? 'No one comes to my dinner parties for the food or the wine,' I often said. 'It's strictly for the company.' The hidden wealth – the human wealth, the wealth of shared experience, of fun and laughter, of good times and unexpected adventures – I had acquired as an independent woman of limited means far exceeded what I would have gained as a rich man's wife. And I learned far more about antiques, for example, from having to go and ferret them out from the dross in Portobello Road Market than I would have done swanning into some smart shop in Bond Street.

I was now thirty years old. Although I enjoyed my life and firmly believed, like Miss Jean Brodie, that I had entered my prime, it was not what I had envisaged it would be. Eli Wallitt often told me that I was too romantic and that I idealised sex too much. 'You should have a purely sexual relationship,' he used to advise (no Brownie points for guessing whom he wanted me to have it with). In 1980, as I headed off to spend Easter in Jamaica, I wondered if Eli might be right. Providence soon presented me with the prospect of finding out in the shape of J.E.

J.E. was an actor with the looks of the young Richard Burton, except that he was burlier and had good skin. He had been brought up in Latin America, where his family had extensive holdings, and Britain, where he was educated. Like me he was equally at home in the First and the Third World, and like me he was fun-loving. We met in the least likely of circumstances, when I almost tripped over his luggage at Heathrow Airport. We then coincidentally found ourselves in adjacent seats on a flight to Miami, or so I thought – he later confessed that he had swapped seats with someone else. I had a firm rule about never speaking to anyone on aeroplanes, but I made an exception for J.E. He radiated sexuality through every pore.

By the time we parted in Miami, I had no doubt that the first thing he would do when he returned to London was telephone me. The first evening I saw him again I decided that J.E. and I had no future. I was picking up strong alcoholic signals which were anathema to me for obvious reasons. Then and there I decided that he would be the perfect candidate for the sort of relationship Eli was constantly advocating.

Bed with J.E. was heaven on earth. Our bodies might have been designed for one another. As well as being an accomplished lover, he also provided me with unintentional pleasure simply because his physique so perfectly complemented mine. Nature had been generous to him, and his manhood was thick and lush and wonderfully formed. Even his alcoholism worked in my favour when the lights were out, for he took a welcome eternity to climax.

In time a strong bond of affection was formed between us for the most incredible of reasons. J.E.'s sister, whom he adored, had been born with a medical condition identical to mine. She was one of the lucky ones; she had been brought up as the girl she was, and had lived a normal life. We fought like cat and dog – he was a macho drinker much given to bursts of actorish temperament – but beneath the volatile surface, this bond became the basis for solid friendship.

J.E., though, was never going to be anything but a lover, and during the two years I lingered with him I was aware that the clock was ticking and I still had neither the relationship nor the job I truly wanted. I left Lloyd's in 1981 and went to work for my brother, who was setting up a law firm. A committed Christian, Mickey had switched from being a barrister to a solicitor so that he could start a law practice that would benefit the poor West Indian community in London. I took quite a cut in salary, but working with him seemed a good way of helping him out and at the same time doing something for society.

For the eight months I worked with Mickey, I discovered rather too much about British society for my own comfort. 'You know nothing about life as it's lived by most people,' he had always said, and he was right. Often the police were as crooked as the crooks, all of whom pleaded innocence even when they were palpably guilty. Fascinating though it was to visit murderers, rapists and fraudsters in prison, to provide comfort to families when the judicial system was 'stitching up' an innocent person, and to get to know the disadvantaged – who frequently displayed more generosity of spirit than the great and the grand – frankly, the pain and suffering were too taxing. I decided that if making a contribution to society were my motive, I might be better suited to raising funds for large groups of people whom I would never see or know, but who would benefit nevertheless, on a voluntary basis. It was a more effective way of reaching a larger mass of people, and, while it was less spiritually enriching, it was also less emotionally enervating. So I left Mickey's firm when he no longer needed me, in February 1982, and returned to writing, which was the best thing I could have done.

In July 1982, my grandmother died. It was a great blow: I adored her, and as longevity ran in her family, I had always expected her to live well beyond the seventy-nine years she managed. But her health was irreversibly ruined by a beating she sustained at the hands of two gunmen in Jamaica in 1979, who spared her life only when my step-grandfather placated them with a lavish display of humility. A great character as well as a lady of the old school, Grandma had had a profound influence upon me. She was broad-minded, vibrant and two generations ahead of her time. Independent in an age when women were meant to be docile, she loved earning her own money and became a successful businesswoman without surrendering either her femininity or the respect of her peers, most of whom would have preferred to kill than to work.

Grandma loved her only grandson, my brother Mickey, more than her three granddaughters, but of the girls she liked me the best, and chose to leave me her house in Grand Cayman.

Grandma's death provided the spur for two important decisions. I gave up smoking on the evening of her burial and went into therapy when I returned to London.

Ever since the debacle of my marriage, I had been carrying around an unbearable load of pain. There was no healthy way of getting rid of it, save talking it out of my system.

Friends and relations, however, really don't wish to be burdened with too much anguish, nor did I wish to burden them with it. 'Laugh and the whole world laughs with you. Cry, and you cry alone,' Mummy used to warn us when we were growing up, and, recognising the truth of that adage, I decided to pay a professional to listen while I relieved myself of this weight. Basil Panzer turned out to be the ideal therapist, cosmopolitan and sophisticated, elegant and polished, and wise and sensible as only the spiritually enlightened can be. He and I clicked from the outset. Once a week, every week for the next four years, I went to see him, although by the last year he was recommending, 'Don't waste your money. You don't need me any longer. We can have tea instead.'

Shortly after I began to see Basil, James Buchanan-Jardine returned to live in London after five years in Hong Kong. 'Do give him my number and ask him to bring his wife around for dinner, if he'd like that,' I said to Vanessa Hoare, a mutual friend, who relayed the message. When James telephoned and asked me for dinner, I fully expected him to show up with his German wife. Instead, he was on his own. 'She's in the south of France with the children,' he explained.

Over dinner, it became apparent that James had never got over me. He was too loyal a person to badmouth his wife, but I gathered, reading between the lines, that their marriage had seen better days. Although they had two little girls, the younger only a few months old, they were leading independent lives. Sitting there in L'Avenue de la Poissonerie, looking across the table at James, I was shocked to realise how fond of him I still was. He was no longer the beautiful young man I had met nearly six years before. His hair had thinned dramatically and he was well on the way to portly middle age. If anything, though, he was an even more attractive person than the Adonis I had known, for five years away from Britain had given his personality a breadth and scope it had previously lacked.

By the end of the evening, it was obvious to both of us, though neither of us said a word, that we had bitten off more than we could chew. Nevertheless, we both behaved with formal rectitude. I presented James with my cheek, and he pecked it gently, saying, 'I'll ring you tomorrow.'

When James rang, he asked if I could have dinner with him again that evening. 'There's something I have to tell you,' he said. I knew what it was even before James walked in through my door, swept me up in his arms, and declared that he still loved me.

'I do, too,' I replied, as we engulfed one another in a passionate embrace.

Thereafter, and for the next eight years, James and I were very much an item. Each morning we went running together; each evening he came by after work to see me. Sometimes, we went to dinner; sometimes we saw friends or went to the movies; sometimes we did nothing. Sometimes, too, we went our separate ways, for we were not an official couple and had our own lives to lead. Although the issue of marriage reared its head pretty early on, and I would definitely have married him if he had been free, James did not want to disrupt his family life with another divorce. He knew from bitter experience with the daughter of his first marriage what it was like to be a father to a child he seldom saw. He wanted to be a daily part of his two young daughters' lives, to occupy the same house as them, to have breakfast with them, to do all the things fathers cannot do when they are divorced and custody falls to the ex-wife.

Although I was not exactly thrilled that we would not be living together, I not only respected James's point of view but also supported it wholeheartedly. Like most Mediterraneans, I understood that children should come first, even if that priority complicates adults' lives.

Moreover, I already had a lot to be grateful for, and knew that I should count my blessings instead of demanding myself out of the happiness and fulfilment James brought into my life. If he had been a dream come true the first time around, this time he was everything a waking woman needs: a wonderful lover, a delightful companion, a warm, nurturing Daddy. He really cared whether I was happy or sad, well or sick, up or down. Gradually, I came to recognise that he was all I had ever wanted or needed. So what if I didn't have the sort of structure I wanted for the relationship? I had the relationship, and all its benefits. Marriage was not a necessity in the circles we moved in. Established liaisons were accepted as valid alternatives to matrimony, and were treated with equal respect. Friends of James' as well as mine frequently asked us out together as a couple. Some of his friends would even ask me to one party and his wife to another. Occasionally she and I even entertained one another, though I tried to keep such events to an absolute minimum. The restraint they called for was simply not conducive to relaxation, and frankly, who needed the tension?

Perhaps my attitude towards having a protracted relationship with a married man might have been less serene had I not had the benefit of a superb therapist like Basil. Recognising how special James was, however, and how good what we had between us was, he encouraged me to 'go for it' for as long as it made me happy.

After three years together, James presented me with a 'love-child', whose importance cannot be exaggerated. James and I were both dog-lovers, and Tum-Tum (named in honour of James' tum-tum, which was then a very sexy and inviting cushion) was the nine-week-old daughter of James' springer spaniel, Sooty. 'Why do you want the responsibility of a dog? It will tie you down,' my brother Mickey said, completely missing the point. I wanted to be tied down, I wanted responsibility, I wanted to be needed, I loved loving. Although I had come to terms with living alone, I had never regarded a solitary existence as being a desirable one, and Tum-Tum's presence cheered up that empty flat at West Eaton Place in a wholly unexpected way. Before her arrival, I had often been lonely; after it, I never was.

As my personal life went from one level of fulfilment to another, I decided to shift the focus of my writing to books. Paul Sidey, a close friend and successful editor (then at Century Hutchinson, now with Random House), suggested I capitalised upon my background and wrote a guide to being a modern lady. This idea had appeal, so I set about writing it before I even bothered to find an agent.

In the end, I did not need one. In winter 1985 I attended a dinner party given by Anne Hodson-Pressinger, the only daughter of Pamela, Lady Torphichen and met Graham Lea, who published the autobiography of Sara Keays, the mother of former Tory cabinet minister Cecil Parkinson's illegitimate baby, Flora. He asked me what I was working on, and said he'd like to see it. I sent him what I had written so far, he liked it, we signed a contract and I wrote like the furies to finish the book within the deadline. To my astonishment, Graham liked it so much that the only editing he did was to fuse the odd split infinitive.

In October 1986, *The Guide to Being a Modern Lady* was launched with a party at the Foreign Press Association. The photographers and gossip columnists were particularly excited to see my stepmother-in-law Margaret, Duchess of Argyll there. (Margaret and I had become great friends since meeting in 1975.) 'Duchess, hold up the book. Lady Colin, move in closer,' they instructed us as she gamely posed with me for picture after picture. The rollcall of prominent names – my friends Princess Katarina of Yugoslavia, Prince Philip's great-niece, Prince and Princess Lew Sapieha, Lord and Lady Pennock, Lady Delves Broughton, Sir James and Lady Mancham; my ex-boyfriend Larry Lamb; my cousins Peter Jonas (then managing director of the English National Opera) – had the journalists salivating. The launch party was a great success; it remained to be seen whether the book would be.

To my surprise, it sold well and got even better press coverage – the glossies, of course covered the launch party in depth, and even the broadsheets dedicated valuable column inches to the book. Graham Lea was even more pleased than I by the favourable reaction. I went on a book tour of Britain and had a delightful if taxing time giving interviews and receiving a positive response wherever I travelled.

Where British journalists are concerned, however, adulation is never universal. The gossip columnist Nigel

Dempster now decided to disparage the flavour of the month with the rancour which I, and other victims of his attention, have found so predominant. He not only sought to damage the book by dismissing it as 'commonplace', but he also dragged my relationship with James into his odious commentary. He also brought up my medical history in typically venomous fashion. I had reached the limits of my patience with that sub-species of journalist, and wanted to take action. Hadn't it occurred to Dempster that people might wonder why he had never once been able to write about me without mentioning the circumstances of my birth in as spiteful a manner as possible? Did he not realise it raised more questions about him than it did about me? By attacking me for a birth defect he was making a public admission about himself.

James, however, wanted the whole matter ignored. Out of respect for him, I let the innuendos pass. My relationship with James was not affected; nor was the public reaction to my book. James' wife Irma did not like having her nose publicly rubbed in it, and I sympathised wholeheartedly with her reaction. It was indeed cruel to hurt her by publishing the story of our relationship, but then, I have never met anyone who would attribute kindness to Nigel Dempster.

Once the dust settled, life returned to normal and I mused on what my next professional project should be. The difficulty with being a writer is that you can go for long stretches without an idea for a book, then suddenly come up with ideas for two or three. In the meantime I did occasional journalistic assignments for publications such as *You* Magazine or the *Sunday Express* magazine. I was under no illusion about the reason I was hired. I had access to people and places that real journalists did not. For instance, I was able to get *You* magazine into the gala held by Prince Alfred of Liechtenstein at the Schwartzenburg Palace in Vienna, with the president of Austria and his wife in attendance. And I was able to pull in people like Prince Charles' old confidante, Lady Tryon, or the Duchess of Norfolk for features on subjects as disparate as the Derby and charity work.

Working for newspapers took some adjustment. I had major misgivings about associating professionally with a class of people I did not always have respect for. I did enjoy the protection of a few honourable journalists, and sheltered behind them. Chief among these were Jonathan Dawson, a commissioning editor at *You* magazine, and Alan Frame, deputy editor of the *Daily Express*, who was introduced to me by my good friend Catherine Olsen, both of whom understood that I would only write about 'feelgood' subjects, and that I was not about to rubbish my friends in print or embarrass anyone who put their trust in me.

In 1988 my journalistic career took another turn when Baron Marc Burca, a friend of many years' standing, asked me to become the social columnist for *Boardroom* magazine, the glossy he owned which could be found in the reception area of the office of every chairman and managing director in the city of London. He assured me that I would not be writing a gossip column – this would be strictly reports of social functions. It was up to me to set the tone of the page, to be as witty or catty or anodyne as I wished. Did I want to give it a whirl? Yes, I did.

It certainly turned out to be an edifying experience. The power it afforded one in the social world was akin to that otherwise enjoyed only by major movie stars and royals. I had never lacked invitations beforehand, but I was now inundated with them by all sorts of PR firms, socialites, companies and charities. Some chased publicity like heroin-addicts chasing the dragon, while others maintained their dignity and kept things in proportion.

I'll start as I mean to go on was my motto, and from the beginning I wrote a column that I hope was witty and seldom bitchy. I never gossiped. If I knew that Mr This and Lady That were having an affair, I was always careful to separate their names when listing guests. I also included loads of people, as Betty Kenward did in 'Jennifer's Diary', for most people like to see their names mentioned. Society-addicts liked to figure out who was who in the pecking order, so I subtly indicated the different gradations of celebrity. Where I was less gentle was in the selection of events I covered. I attended only three sorts of functions: those organised by friends, actual or prospective worthy causes; and glamorous occasions such as the Queen's Cup or the Cartier polo match at Windsor.

At first, I never wrote about any event I had not personally attended, nor did I mention anyone I hadn't seen or spoken to, but after the fourth year, I changed my approach. 'Send in a list of the people and some photographs, and I'll write it up as if I'd been there,' I often said to friends or PRs.

When I wasn't partying or writing or with James and my friends, I dedicated myself to charity work. This I loved, not only because of the personal satisfaction it brought, but also because I was acknowledged as having a flair for fund-raising. I understood that no one wants to be taken for a ride and that everyone wants value for money, even when they're giving to charity, and I accepted that charities had become big business. People are ultimately selfish, no matter what they say to the contrary, and this was as true of the fund-raisers as it was of the ticket-purchasers and donors. Most of us raise funds because it makes us feel good or reflects well upon us, while those who give usually do so to receive some hidden benefit in return, whether material or spiritual. Neither I nor any of the other experienced fund-raisers had much patience with people who saw themselves as Lady Bountifuls. We were there to raise funds, not to stroke egos, unless those same egos were offering a fat cheque, in which case we oiled our fingers and started massaging.

I had a great deal of fun, but in the final analysis my colleagues and I were there to produce, and produce we did. A journalist from the *Express* once sat in on a meeting of the Red Cross committee. 'You ladies are so capable you could run companies,' she told me afterwards. It was refreshing to see how realistic the successful fund-raisers were. Charity work had evolved during the 1980s from a traditional occupation for ladies into a cut-throat business where positive elements like altruism were intermingled with bullshit, status-seeking and rampant social climbing. That, however, only made it more interesting for those of us who were not snobbish.

Another type whose motives were often mixed was the showbiz celebrity. Some of these people, of course, were genuinely altruistic, but most displayed nothing more than a profound desire for a photo opportunity to show the world how wonderful they were. One particular, and genuine, sport – in those days, anyway – was Joan Collins. I met her in 1979, when she and her third husband, Ron Kass, attended the premier of *Oklahoma* to help raise money for one of my charities, KIDS. Their daughter Katy was then in hospital with brain damage, having been run down by a car. The committee had delegated me as the committee member most suitable to tuck her under my wing, and I could not sing her praises highly enough. Throughout a long evening – pre-performance champagne reception, first half of the musical, royal interval reception, second half of the musical, post-performance royal party – she was the soul of co-operation. She charmed everyone she should have and a few she didn't need to. She even displayed a touching insecurity, getting me to rehearse her curtsy and mode of address before I presented her to Prince and Princess Michael of Kent.

Regrettably, La Collins' modesty did not outlast her change of status from national to international star. The next time I saw her was just about the time *Dynasty* was ending, when she attended a cocktail party given by my stepmother-in-law, Margaret, Duchess of Argyll, whose life story she was rumoured to be interested in bringing to the small screen. Margaret reintroduced us, and she was cordiality itself until Charles Beresford, a close friend of Margaret's, joined us. Now that she had an audience, she turned before my eyes into a more competitive and insufferable prima donna than I had hitherto had the experience of encountering socially. At first I could only stare in disbelief. I took in her beautifully preserved face; looked at the over-made up green eyes mirroring a soul I would much rather not have been glimpsing; shifted my gaze to the dark brown wig, bound by a white polyester headband that matched a ruched, figure-hugging dress of the same synthetic material; stared at the grotesque plastic hooped earrings as she continued in Alexis vein. Eventually something within me snapped. 'I've had quite enough of you,' I said, and stormed off, relieved to be rid of Mme Superstar's brand of charm.

For real personal enrichment, the charity work that proved the most rewarding was one that brought no recognition or spin-off benefits. This was my involvement with the International Organisation for a Just Peace in the Middle East, a pressure group which operated in strict secrecy. The organisation was started shortly after the Intifada began by a few like-minded people of Middle Eastern origin who believed that the cause of peace would be best served if we could convince both sides in the conflict that their ultimate interests lay in living together in harmony. That required, as a first step, the Israelis and Zionists to recognise the rights of the Palestinians, and the Palestinians to acknowledge the existence of the state of Israel. The second step was the one the peace process is now at, and the third will, one day, be the creation of a sovereign state of Palestine.

Our work required absolute discretion. Many people on either side of the divide who actually sympathised with the aspirations of the other side could not say so openly, for obvious reasons. Many diplomats and members of the governments we dealt with also had to play their cards close to their chests, as did many influential businessmen and other opinion-formers.

One of the initial hurdles we faced was the negative image the PLO had in the West. Unless we could help to wash off some of the mud which had stuck to what was effectively the Palestinian government-in-exile, there was no prospect of a peaceful solution. This we sought to accomplish in a variety of ways. Some were straightforward, like writing or meeting journalists who were in a position to write articles which might further the cause of peace; others were more meandering, like having publishers and writers to dinner and courting them over a glass of champagne and a leg of lamb.

Another barrier was the hostility of the Zionists, even moderate Zionists like the Chief Rabbi of Great Britain, to any settlement involving reconciliation with the Palestinians. I was appalled, having written to Lord Jakobovitz asking for his support, to receive a reply which I considered to be wildly inappropriate in view of the fact that he was a man of god, and that the Palestinians undeniably had rights which remained valid no matter how loudly the Zionists shouted. We did not lose heart, for we were already in touch with prominent Jews, Jewish lobbyists and people of Jewish ancestry who would reassure their fellows and, wherever possible, promote our cause. Moreover, the Zionists could remain militant only as long as the American government gave them unstinting support, and we were already in touch with that same government, as were other organisations involved in the peace process. It was only a matter of time before the US government forced the Zionists to acknowledge the aspirations and rights of the Palestinians.

In work of this kind, you cannot see the results of your labours as immediately as you can with fund-raising. There were times when I felt I was pushing against a mountain instead of an anthill, and wondered if it was unrealistic to expect my paltry efforts to make a difference. Ultimately, you have to have faith, to trust that your pressure will have a cumulative effect. And if it does not, at least you know you have done your best.

12

For some women, their thirtieth birthday is the milestone that precipitates an examination of their lives. This did not happen to me, because I regarded my thirties as my prime. Instead it was turning forty that prompted me to take stock.

I hated looking older. Between the ages of eighteen and thirty-nine I did not age at all; then one morning I woke up and saw that crow's feet were eroding the deep-set eyes and high cheekbones that are a characteristic of the Ziadie family, and that laughter lines had appeared from nowhere. But if I felt very lucky indeed to have got this far with what I regarded as a minimum of wear and tear, I realised that the time had come to think about what I wanted to change and to act on it, for soon the die would be cast and it would be too late to alter the course of my life.

Glamorous as my life was, being a socialite had never been compatible with anything but a tiny part of my personality. It was not satisfying my need for human interchange on a deeper level. What I really wanted – had always wanted – was my own family. It was unlikely that I would have my own husband, partly because I was having a relationship with someone else's, but largely because of my resistance to going back into the lion's den after the mauling

I had taken from Colin Campbell. However, the world had changed to such an extent that there was no reason why I could not become a single mother. I decided to adopt a child, beginning a process so arduous that only the most tenacious hang in there to a successful conclusion.

When I took my first steps towards motherhood I had no idea how completely perverse the system in Britain is. Each council has its own rules and regulations, so what is acceptable to one can be and often is anathema to another. Some councils, for instance, will not allow single women to adopt, while others positively encourage them to do. Some would sooner place a baby with a poor family than a rich one, on the politically correct premise that an 'ordinary' life is more desirable than a 'privileged' one. Most councils have rules governing age differences between parents and children, though some, sensibly, do not adhere to them. This is just as well, for few prospective adoptive parents fall within the guidelines: by the time most people realise they cannot have children of their own, they are too old to qualify. And the age requirements do not apply to foster parents, which can mean that councils which rigidly adhere to their age rules end up paying out vast sums of money to have children brought up by foster parents who are even older than the prospective adopters they have turned down.

Of course, I didn't know how mad the system was when I put out feelers to the adoption and fostering departments of several councils and various agencies, and I was optimistic that I would find a child from the massive pool I knew existed. Most of the councils I contacted wrote back with information and advice, and I thought them most helpful – until I embarked upon the next stage, which was applying for specific children.

Details with photographs of these children were to be found in the *Find a Family* newspaper, or in equivalent books published by adoption and fostering units. There were few babies available, and those that were went to married couples, so I knew there was no likelihood of me getting a baby. Although I would have preferred a baby, I was happy to take a child as long as it was not too old. There seemed to be a lot of children available who had passed the toddler stage, most of whom had been messed up by years of being shunted from foster home to foster home so that they would not become too attached to any one family. I applied for a few, but in only one instance was I even invited for an interview (the little boy was placed elsewhere and I have nothing but praise for the social worker at Ealing who dealt with me then). In practically every other case I was informed that a more suitable match had been made – and then I would see the children mentioned again, exposing that response as a complete lie.

Gradually, I realised that the children were being used to meet the employment needs of the social workers who were responsible for finding them parents. If too large a percentage of the children in care were adopted, the adoption and fostering units would be deemed overstaffed, and cuts would be called for. The social workers' job security therefore required that the majority of the children be deprived of the prospect of a permanent family and rotated from foster home to foster home until they were old enough to enhance the careers of other social workers: those who would be responsible for them in residential homes, or their probation officers, when they were older.

After two years of naïvely trying to bend myself into this insane system, I looked at adopting from abroad. Romania was then much in vogue, South and Central American countries such as Ecuador and Costa Rica were also possibilities, and there was the USA as well. A friend of mine, who provided invaluable help, had adopted her daughter in the US, and she kindly offered me access to the channels she had used.

Before deciding how to proceed, I needed a home study, which is an in-depth report from a social worker detailing the prospective adopter's lifestyle, her reasons for adopting and her suitability to be a parent. No adoption can proceed without this all-important document. When I got in touch with Westminster City Council, which had a duty to provide me with a home study as I was a taxpaying resident of the borough, I was informed that the charge was £2,750.

'This is an outrage,' I said to Bridget Ward, the social worker to whom I spoke. 'The fact that I can afford to pay such an extortionate sum in no way alters the gall the council has in pitching the cost so high that adoption is put beyond the reach of the average person. The message I'm getting is that Westminster has decreed that only the better off can adopt. That is a violation of the rights of the less well off, and it is inhumane to the children who need homes. How *dare* the Council condemn orphans in Romania to a lifetime of institutionalisation and deprivation when there are people out there who can give them a good and loving home but can't afford to cough up £2,750 for a document we should be getting for nothing?'

'We don't do the study ourselves,' Ms Ward explained. 'We get an outside agency to do it.'

'Well then *they* have a hell of a nerve, and so does the council for going along with them. What are we talking about here? Ten hours of work, maybe twenty at the most. Are you telling me any social worker's time is worth between £150 and £300 per hour? You're not models, for god's sake.'

'I don't know what to say,' she said.

'I do. It's a disgrace, and I shall be writing to Virginia Bottomley to register a strong protest.'

This I did, requesting that she not burden me with a reply, as it would be nothing but a self-serving catalogue of excuses, but instead used her time and energy to change the system in general and that aspect of it in particular. Needless to say, she did reply – with a self-serving catalogue of excuses. At present the government is looking into ways of improving the system so that the rights of adoptive parents and children will be better served, so who knows? Maybe those of us who protested were heard.

While all this was going on, I set the wheels in motion to put myself in a stronger financial position. It was one thing for me to live, as I had for the last several years, on a wing and a prayer, but quite another to bring a child into my life and then burden it with financial insecurity. I needed enough money to move to a larger home, to employ a nanny to take care of the child while I worked, and to spare my family from having to rescue me if the overdraft became too big.

As luck would have it, the ideal vehicle for providing me with my 'baby money' now hove into view. The year before, I had been having lunch with Kate Mancham and Alan Frame of the *Daily Express*, who loved to hear all the gossip about the royal family I picked up on my social rounds. I was obliging him with the latest story when he suddenly cut in: 'I've got the most fantastic idea. You shouldn't be buggering around writing books on etiquette. With your connections, what you should be doing is a biography of the Princess of Wales. It'd be a real money-spinner.'

Kate flashed me a smile. 'He's right,' she said.

'I don't know,' I replied. 'Writing about the royal family is always so difficult, and they're so boring. I might jeopardise myself socially, too.'

'You'd make so much money that wouldn't matter,' Alan said. 'I promise you, Georgie, you'd have an international bestseller on your hands.'

For months I turned the idea over in my head. Attractive as the potential earnings were, I was reluctant to put my social life on the line. Then one day, at a committee meeting of one of the charities I supported and of which the Princess of Wales was patron, I had a brainwave. Why couldn't I write an official biography that focused on her charity work and lightly touched upon other aspects of her life. I could direct most of the earnings to that charity and to others on which the Princess and I agreed, and that way, everyone would benefit. I would have a good steady income for the next few years, the charities would have handsome donations and Diana would have a biography that focused on her most positive accomplishments.

When dealing with the royal family, the first step is always to sound them out unofficially. I got in touch with a friend of mine who is a good friend of Diana's and asked him to approach her. I was told that she liked the idea and would give a positive response if I made an official approach. I wrote to her private secretary, Patrick Jephson, and received a reply from Dickie Arbiter, her press secretary, asking me to make an appointment with him to discuss the idea in more detail.

Some time between that letter and my arrival at Buckingham Palace in August 1989, Diana had a change of heart. The result was that Dickie Arbiter was no longer co-operative, and I was back to square one. What now? Should I take up Alan Frame's suggestion and create a comprehensive portrait of Diana? This book would bear no resemblance to the official biography I had envisaged. It would undoubtedly cause a stir, and sell better than the charity fund-raiser, but did I really want to jeopardise the serenity and structure of my life?

I knew that some of Diana's friends were prepared to impart a wealth of information to me about her private life, most of which was so sensational that I would have been staggered myself had I not known it already. Friends of the royal family do not co-operate with a controversial book unless they have the express permission of the royal in question to do so. This gave me a valuable insight into Diana's character, which I was rapidly discovering was more complex than I had hitherto thought. Certainly she did not play by the rules. This might have been bad for the royal family in general and Prince Charles in particular, but it was good for any writer who penned the first biography that showed her in her true colours.

It takes as much courage to accept the consequences of a courageous decision as it does to accept those of a cowardly one. And cowardly choices always compromise an individual's integrity. I had tried the smooth way; now I'd take the rough. 'Baby money', I called the biography which my English agent soon placed with Robert Smith of Smith Gryphon publishers. From the outset, there was no doubt in anyone's mind that we were dealing with dynamite and that the book was destined to be an international bestseller.

Before getting down to work I had to fulfil a commitment I had made in 1990 to the drug- and alcohol- addiction charity the Chemical Dependency Centre, to organise a large fund-raising ball at the Hippodrome nightclub in London's Leicester Square, which the Duchess of York had agreed to attend as guest of honour. No sooner had I begun the arrangements in earnest – it takes six months properly to plan something with over a thousand guests – than the Gulf War broke out. Charity after charity cancelled functions they had been planning for a year, but I decided that we would steam ahead with a two-pronged approach. The war might end before the date of the ball, 30 April; if it did not, we would approach one of the armed forces charities and offer to give them some of the funds raised. As the date loomed and the war continued, I contacted the Soldiers' Sailors' and Air Forces Association, and Colonel Pat Reger, who was in charge of their fund-raising, was happy to benefit from the event. Indeed, everyone at SSAFA was such a delight to work with that I was happy they were going to share the kitty, even though in the end the war was over before the ball came off.

The Maypole Ball took place to much acclaim and was hailed by the press as one of the social functions of the year, which pleased me no end, though not as much as the tens of thousands of pounds my committee, my assistant, Roger Day, and I raised for the two charities.

Between organising the ball and researching *Diana in Private*, as the biography was ultimately called, I was so busy that I seldom had time to see James. This turned out to be a propitious development. Time had been a corrosive factor in our relationship and James had been taking me for granted for at least a year. His attitude seemed to be: 'We've been together for so long, we'll always be together.' I tried time and again to warn him, but all my attempts fell on deaf ears. Then, in October 1990, he said one morning while we were running in Kensington Gardens, 'I have some good news. I've been asked to open an office in Hong Kong. I'll be going at the end of the year.'

I was stunned. 'That's good news? What about me?'

'Nothing will change between us. I'll be over several times a year. I'll also go to Switzerland. You can join me there, or come to Hong Kong and visit.'

I was so staggered that I went home and headed straight for bed. The idea of living my day-to-day life without James being readily accessible was distressing in the extreme until I actually faced the prospect. Then I realised that although I was still in the habit of loving him, I was no longer in love with him. He was no longer necessary to my life. It was not because our relationship had ceased to be good, but because he had fulfilled me so effectively for so many years that he had freed me from needing any man ever again. He had replaced the emotional void created by my father with a solid serenity, and the irony was I would never have noticed it had he not made the two simple mistakes he did: taking me for granted, and forcing me to become aware of the independence with which he himself had endowed me.

'I never want to be in love again,' I told Mickey. 'I've channelled too much energy into my relationships with men. From now on, I'm going to use that energy to plump up my own life. I'm going to write the Diana biography, and I'm going to get the baby.'

In December 1990 providence put me to the test. Massimo Gargia, the publisher of *Best* magazine, a French glossy, hosted a magnificent reception in Paris at La Conciergerie, the fortress abutting the River Seine where Marie Antoinette was imprisoned until her execution, to announce their awards for the most elegant men and women in the world. As I walked up to my table to take my seat, I was introduced to a tall, blond, handsome Frenchman sitting three seats away from me. I didn't catch his name, which I thought was Luc something or other, but what was unmissable was his reaction. He literally shook upon meeting me, as if he had grabbed a live electric wire. Moreover, it was a two-way street.

Throughout dinner this Luc and I seemed powerless to avert our gazes from one another. I was mortified for his date until the man beside me told me that they were just friends. As soon as dinner was finished, Luc swapped seats with the man on my right and the flirting began in earnest. So intimate were some of the things we both said that I cannot repeat them. Suffice it to say that neither of us left the other in any doubt that we were already a bit in love. I was completely captivated. Luc had charm in spades, was relaxed in a way no British male ever is, and had such a wonderful sense of humour that he had me in stitches. Even when I was not laughing I was gently amused by his wit.

At some point it became apparent that he was actually named Elzear, and was none other than the Duc de Sabran-Pontèves. 'I met a Sabran in London the other day,' I said. 'Gersande de Sabran. She came over with her husband [the Duc d'Orléans, the French equivalent of the Prince of Wales] and the Comtesse de Paris [wife of the pretender to the French throne, Gersande's mother-in-law]. She played at a charity recital organised by the Norfolks. She was very sweet, and pretty too.'

'That's my sister,' Elzear said.

Oh dear, I thought. How cruel fate is. It throws me this divine man just when I've decided that I never want to be in love again, and to make matters worse, he turns out to be one of the most eligible men in Europe. It was the worst qualification he could have. Someone of his standing, as handsome and attractive and seductive and eligible – and unmarried – would undoubtedly be major trouble some-where down the line. Grand men and rich men are always spoiled, and I was too old to be training brats of fortysome-thing when I wanted my own, aged a few months or years. So when Elzear offered to take me back to the Royal Monceau, where I was staying, I declined, though I did promise to give him my number in London when he tele-phoned the following morning.

Nothing came of my evening with Elzear, for I made things impossible for him from the moment we met, through innu-merable conversations and an encounter at a later date in Paris, to our final conversation. I was all the things I loathe in spoiled men: capricious, moody, difficult, and, a first for me, unreliable. I would say I was going to do something, then not do it, either deliberately or unconsciously. Timing, of course, is all-important, and the timing was rotten, but I cannot in all truth say I regret the choice I made. While I was sabotaging my potential relationship with Elzear, things fell into place so effortlessly with both the baby and the book that I had no doubt I was fulfilling my destiny.

In June 1991 I went to Russia with Enzo D'Agostino for the confirmation of my godson, Alexander Trofaier. His mother, Maria Theresa, was an old friend of Enzo's and mine, and his father, Brigadier General Maximilien Trofaier, was the Austrian defence attaché in Moscow. To make me feel at home, Max and Maria Theresa asked the Jamaican Ambassador Arthur Thompson and his wife Eleanor to the reception following the ceremony. I hit it off with Eleanor Thompson immediately. When she heard that I was interested in adopting a baby, and that I was now considering a Russian child, she encouraged me. Arthur promised practical help through the embassy, and he delivered magnificently. Even after he was posted as ambassador to the European Union, Miss Dias, his former secretary, kept me up to date with the ever-changing rules and regulations governing Russian adoptions.

Because Enzo and I were in Russia for only a week, and our trip, organised through Intourist, left us with precious little free time, I was unable to initiate anything concrete then, but I sensed I had found the right place. Russia and its people impressed me mightily. They could not have been warmer, friendlier or more generous-spirited. They seemed to enjoy a higher standard of education than we in the West did. They were good-looking too, and I reflected that one would be hard put to find a better gene pool.

Resolving to return to Russia as soon as I had finished the Diana biography, I returned to London and worked like a slave every day from early morning until late at night. For a writer, there is usually a gap between handing in the manuscript to the publisher and beginning work with the libel lawyer and editor. Smith Gryphon wanted to release *Diana in Private* in the spring, so I had to make myself available early in the new year.

I had planned what I regarded as a well-deserved break in Jamaica just before Christmas. Just after I had delivered my manuscript, Mickey telephoned me to say that our adored Auntie, Mummy's only sister, had been diagnosed as having Hodgkin's disease. While this form of cancer is usually responsive to modern chemotherapy, it was now so advanced that her chances were not promising. Auntie and her husband, Stanley Panton, flew to New York to Sloane Kettering, the world's finest cancer hospital, where a course of treatment was devised which she opted to have administered in Florida.

Meanwhile Smith Gryphon were selling the British serialisation rights to *Diana in Private*. Competition was fierce, but in the end Eve Pollard, the editor of the *Sunday Express*, won the rights by offering what was then the highest sum ever paid for a royal book: £100,000. Naturally, I was ecstatic about this coup.

I told my publisher that my aunt might be dying, and that I had to extend my trip to spend some time with her. 'Do what you have to,' he said. 'We'll work around you.' I was deeply appreciative of his understanding, and agreed to be back by the middle of January.

As I flew to Miami to see Auntie, I reflected upon the vagaries of life. Here I was on the threshold of an exciting success, yet I might be losing one of the people I loved most. Would life be giving with one hand and taking with the other? Or would I be lucky, and have two strikes?

13

Few books can have reached the bookshop in the face of so concerted an attempt behind the scenes to sabotage them as *Diana in Private*.

The royal family had of course known of the book for some time, not only because I had been entirely open in seeking official co-operation, but also because some of the people to whom I spoke were passing them information. The royal family is one thing; their advisers are quite another. In February 1992 Richard Aylard, the Prince of Wales' private secretary, had an early-morning meeting with Nicholas Lloyd, editor of the *Daily Express* and husband of the *Sunday Express*'s editor, Eve Pollard. In the course of that meeting he assured Lloyd that there was no truth whatsoever in the rumour that the Prince and Princess of Wales' marriage was in difficulties.

Within days, Dickie Arbiter had rung Smith Gryphon demanding sight of my manuscript. When Robert Smith told me of Arbiter's call, I rang him. 'Just who do you think you are, demanding a copy of something to which you have no entitlement? Just because you work in Buckingham Palace, it doesn't give you the right to throw your weight around. You might be very impressed with yourself, but you don't impress anyone who isn't a title-hunter. If you can't speak to my publishers politely, don't speak to them at all. Do I make myself clear? Good. Goodbye.'

Some days later, the *Express's* office requested a copy of the manuscript from Smith Gryphon. We were then working with the editor, having already had it read for libel by Mishcon de Reya, now Diana's law firm. Because of the highly explosive nature of the contents, Robert was reluctant to send it over to the *Sunday Express* until he had received an undertaking that it would be returned the same day. The *Express* gave the undertaking, but never returned the manuscript.

Days later, the Palace Press Office initiated a whispering campaign against me. One royal correspondent told me, 'They went to each of us saying you were nothing but a Jamaican transsexual, and what could you know about what was going on?' Royal correspondents, regrettably, are working journalists who have no real access to the upper reaches of society. They therefore never know who's who or what's what. They probably wouldn't have known for instance, that being Jamaican certainly does not preclude one having an ear to the ground at Buckingham Palace. As for being a transsexual, most royal correspondents only come into contact with members of the royal household and the staff at the palaces (they're notorious for buying secrets from servants), a hefty proportion of whom are gay. Indeed, the Queen Mother once quipped, 'Will you queens down there stop what you're doing and get the queen up here a drink?'

There is no doubt that a significant proportion of the population has sexual prejudices, and James Whitaker, the *Daily Mirror's* corpulent, red-faced royal correspondent, duly obliged his readers with a poisonous front-page story dismissing me as a 'Jamaican transsexual'. I immediately sued for libel, but the wheels of justice grind exceedingly slow, and it was three years before the case was settled and the *Daily Mirror* had to cough up damages, my legal costs, an apology and a retraction.

While Whitaker was doing his worst, the behaviour of

Eve Pollard of the *Sunday Express* made me wonder whether
she was interested in outshining her competitors by publishing the scoop of the century. This, after all, was the first
book ever written to reveal that the Waleses' marriage was
over and catalogue their confidantes (his, Camilla Parker-
Bowles; hers, private detective Barry Mannakee, the King
of Spain, Princess Alexandra's godson Philip Dunne, and
the man she would later confirm she had been in love with,
James Hewitt). It also broke the news that Diana was deeply
unhappy; that she had bulimia and a history of making hysterical scenes; that she used alternative therapists and
astrologers – and that she had stated that she wanted a separation.

I knew that Eve Pollard had cold feet when journalists at
her newspaper started infringing the confidentiality agreement between itself and the publisher in a way that was
likely to undermine the credibility of the book. This they
did by ringing up people I had quoted and saying things
like, 'Do you know you're quoted as saying such and such in
a highly controversial book which is going to cause a scandal
and get everyone concerned bad publicity?' Most eminent or
respectable people did not wish to be dragged into a press
mess, and this was nothing but a crude attempt to get them
to recant. It was hardly conducive to the success of a serialisation, especially one with the potential to be as newsworthy
as *Diana in Private*. I telephoned Henry McCrory, the managing editor of the *Sunday Express*, and demanded they
desist from damaging the book and my reputation, and that
he abide by the confidentiality agreement. He agreed to do
so. Nevertheless the following day a reporter and photographer turned up to check out yet another person whom I had
interviewed for the book.

The constituent parts of the *Express* now began to pull in
opposing directions. 'The book is inaccurate,' they said, and
asked for a meeting, which was held at my flat in February. In
attendance were Henry McCrory, deputy editor, Craig
McKenzie, Justin Walford, the *Express* in-house lawyer, my
publisher and myself. I tape-recorded the whole meeting,

making sure that I got Justin Walford to annotate each tape.

The inaccuracies they had come up with were inconsequential, preposterous things like one misspelled proper name in 434 pages of typescript. The *Express* was in any case working from an unedited manuscript, so they had no valid reason for objecting.

When they saw that they were not getting very far, Craig McKenzie tried to turn the screws on us. He brazenly told Robert Smith and me that the *Express* would damage the book unless we played ball. Playing ball involved taking the £50,000 they had already paid us upon signature of the serialisation contract and forgoing the £50,000 that was due on publication. In return, the *Sunday Express* would serialise the chapters covering Diana's childhood and marriage. They would be skipping some of the sensational bits, but keeping the juiciest – driving down the price and currying favour with Buckingham Palace at the same time.

Thereafter negotiations between Smith Gryphon and the *Sunday Express* rumbled on in ever-increasing bitterness. Every time the publisher thought he'd struck a new agreement the *Express* sabotaged it. For instance, they substituted the word 'worldwide' for 'British' in the clauses governing the territory covered in the revised contract. Book serialisations are customarily sold separately to newspapers in each territory so we would have been losing a great deal of money had we gone along with that 'revision'. Finally, on 5 March, the negotiations broke down altogether. The *Sunday Express* then sued us for breach of contract, even though they were the ones who had initiated the breach. We promptly counter-sued, filing a claim that grew from the relatively modest amount of £50,000 to £5.5 million in damages, lost earnings and other monies owed by the *Sunday Express* to us.

Within days, the *Sun*, the popular Murdoch-owned tabloid, had bought the serialisation rights. The newspaper's editor, incidentally, was Kelvin McKenzie, brother of Craig at the *Express*. A third McKenzie brother, Drew, worked as a stringer for the American tabloid, *Star*, which bought the

American serial rights from the American publishers, St Martin's Press. The extracts reproduced by this newspaper revealed that they were based on the original manuscript supplied to the *Sunday Express*.

As the book's publication date, 27 March 1992, approached, the media frenzy intensified. Newspapers and television companies from places as disparate as the United States, France, Japan, Australia, Turkey, Spain and Argentina were clamouring for interviews. Those whose requests were not fulfilled sometimes followed me around or 'doorstepped' me. 'It shows people are interested. This is great,' my publisher and my agent said when I complained about being hounded.

They changed their tune, however, when the newspapers resorted to the oldest scam in journalism to do an author out of a serialisation's earnings. It works like this. A British journalist leaks the contents of the book to an American publication, which reproduces some juicy bits. Another British newspaper then picks up enough of the material published in the US to jeopardise the serialisation deal, which is nullified by pre-publication in Britain of the material in question.

The *Star* in America now published a story, in the same week as the British serialisation was running, revealing that my book detailed Diana's relationships with other men during her marriage and identifying them. This was picked up by the *News of the World*, which ran a huge piece on the men named in the book. Although Kelvin McKenzie still went ahead with the serialisation in the *Sun*, he refused to pay us the £35,000 he had bought it for. This necessitated another lawsuit, and this too dragged on for two years before they were obliged to pay us the amount in full, as well as our legal costs.

Meanwhile, Peter McKay of the London *Evening Standard* got in on the act with an article demanding that Diana sue me. Although I had known McKay for years – he had even offered me my own column in the mid-1980s, when he was the editor of the Sunday edition of *Today* – he now tried to stir up an old hornet's nest by accusing me of being a man. Again, I sued, this time for libel.

What made me all the angrier was that Associated Newspapers, which now owned the *Evening Standard*, had known since 1975 that I had never been male. This had not stopped their gossip columnist, Nigel Dempster, from making insinuations to the contrary, with the result that in 1979, the editor, David English, had been obliged to provide an undertaking, a legally binding document, never again to repeat the libel. My libel lawyer now issued a writ not only demanding an apology, a retraction and substantial damages, but also aggravated damages arising out of their breach of their own undertaking.

Associated Newspapers then made a mistake which would cost them dear. They confused the woman of 1992 with the girl of 1975. Stringing me along for three years, openly co-operating with Express Newspapers in an attempt to batter me into submission, they resorted to every trick in the book, and a few of their own invention. Their ploy was simple: to exhaust me financially and to undermine me morally. They bumped up the costs at every turn, filing needless motions and appeals, all of which they lost; they sought all my medical records, which the judge Sir Michael Davies and the court of appeal denied them, threatening to make the trial so sensational that I would be psychologically destroyed. Unfortunately for them, I was older, wiser, richer and tougher than I had been when we had first crossed swords. Of course, they did not see things quite the way I saw them. From their point of view, they had a duty to defend the action as vigorously and fulsomely as possible. While I respected that stance I was nevertheless going to show them that the sweet and naïve little Georgie who had once approached Vere Harmondsworth for a lady's and gentleman's agreement no longer existed. She had been killed, largely by press abuse, and in her place had arisen someone who was being forced to be a finely honed though reluctant warrior.

Eve Pollard, in the meantime, was throwing around every

ounce of her not inconsiderable weight. In an apparent contravention of the confidentiality agreement, she gave an
interview to Mark Llewelyn of the Murdoch-owned Channel
7 in Australia, in which she accused me of plagiarism,
among other unwarranted assertions. Quite how I could
have been guilty of this when most of the material had never
been printed anywhere she didn't explain. When Llewelyn
tried to repeat Pollard's allegations in an interview with me,
I retorted trenchantly. 'I am not prepared to sit here and take
rubbish from a puppy like you,' I declared. And I rose from
my seat and called over the security guards to chuck him
out. To my consternation, but to the delight of the book's
publicity agents, that moment was beamed throughout the
world. Which just goes to show that it pays to have integrity.

I had reached the stage of utter disgust with both toady-
ing journalists and the Machiavellian palace. It is one thing
to discredit an author who is trying to damage the monarchy
with false claims, but quite another to vilify one who is
merely recounting facts in a measured and fair-minded way.
Once *Diana in Private* was released, the book just jumped off
the shelves, shooting straight into the bestseller list. Thrilled
though I was about this, it gave me no satisfaction that the
palace had undermined not only my own credibility but also
other long-term interests of the future king. For I knew that
Diana had got another author, Andrew Morton, to write the
damning and distorted tale which I had been fed, but been
too even-handed to purvey, and that it would be published
within a matter of months. By damaging the one writer
whose version of events gave a balanced picture of the sorry
state of the Prince and Princess of Wales' marriage, and of
both their characters, they had put Charles on the defensive.
And as the whole world now knows, he has never recovered
from being manoeuvred into that invidious position.

I was never happier to leave Britain and the machinations
of the press and the palace behind than when I flew to New
York in May to launch the American edition of the book. St
Martin's Press, the American publishers, put me up in a
suite at the Intercontinental Hotel on East Forty-Eighth

Street in Manhattan. This was my old stamping ground, from the days when Bill Swain had his nightclub above Kenny's Steak Pub in the Beverly Hotel. It brought back many memories of a more pleasant and gentle time.

I snapped out of my reverie when Cindy Adams, the famous American columnist with whom I had an interview scheduled, called. She was everything most British journalists were not: correct, decent, fair and honourable. She had only one thing in common with them: she was incisive. Cindy understood that there were certain things I could not say, and worked her way around those lacunae with consummate skill. The result of her professional approach was a front-page story in the following day's *New York Post* with the witty headline 'THE KING AND DI'.

From the moment the *Post* hit the streets until I left North America I was run ragged, giving interview after interview to the newspapers or television. Everyone wanted to hear about Diana. And Cindy Adams was not unique – I could not help being struck by how much more professional the standards of journalism were in the US and Canada than in Britain. Whether it was Dini Petty or Katie Kouric or Joan Rivers or someone less famous, interviewers never seemed to have an axe to grind. They were after a story, and they got it within the confines of accepted journalistic ethics. They did not seek to embarrass their interviewees on television with offensive questions delivered in an aggressive manner. Nor did print journalists do what the British do, which is to make up quotes and generally twist or ignore the facts in accordance with the storyline they have conceived beforehand, and which they then print despite what you have said to them.

It is said that the British loathe success while the Americans love it. I had often heard that in America anyone seeing a man driving a Rolls-Royce would say, 'Good for him. I hope I'll be able to work hard and get one for myself one day,' whereas in Britain people said, 'Look at that rich bastard in his Rolls-Royce,' and then took a nail to its paintwork and scratched it. This, I now discovered, was true.

Everywhere I went in North America I was given a fair audience and treated with respect. If people did not like what I had to say, they picked me up on the points, not on the colour of my eyes or the structure of my body. I have no doubt that some of the malicious personal attacks on me in Britain had an element of envy. There the unstated question emanating from each journalist was: 'Why should you, who are not even a professional journalist, have written a world-wide bestseller with information I would never have had access to? Why couldn't I have had your connections? And since I don't, why shouldn't I pillory you for having the success I wanted for myself?' Can you imagine American writers abusing Louis Auchincloss because he had written a book about a world they did not have access to? Or lambasting Jackie Onassis for using her name and connections to acquire a book out of everyone else's reach? Americans simply have too much pride and dignity to indulge in the backbiting envy which proliferates in class-conscious Britain.

Time, of course, is a wonderful thing to have on your side. It not only heals all wounds; it also wounds all heels. While I was in New York, my publisher faxed me through a copy of the front page of the *Sunday Express*. Eve Pollard seemed to me to be actively promoting the forthcoming Morton book on Princess Diana, which was due to be serialised by the rival *Sunday Times*. In my opinion, she was enhancing a competitor's acquisition with free publicity right after she had deprived her own publication of the opportunity to profit from a similar product. Coming from a mercantile background as I do, I thought this was little short of commercial self-mutilation. It is hardly surprising that, under Pollard's stewardship, the *Sunday Express*'s circulation plummeted. The consequences to her career were fitting: within two years she had departed, not to edit another newspaper, but for something akin to an editor's version of oblivion. She bobs up every now and then on British television at three o'clock in the morning. So much for throwing out a bonny baby and trying to pass off dirty bathwater as eau de Cologne.

The case against the *Sunday Express* quickly became Fleet Street's largest damages action. Pollard, I am pleased to say, was not the only one to come a cropper. As costs on both sides escalated into the hundreds of thousands, the board of directors of Express Newspapers became aware that they stood to lose several million pounds if the case went against them. Meanwhile, Henry McCrory and Craig McKenzie were reaping the harvest of failure: both men left the *Sunday Express*. Indeed Justin Walford is the only central character of this fiasco still employed by the *Sunday Express*. They were forced to settle the action in August 1996 to avoid an even greater disaster in court.

I had written *Diana in Private* purely for 'baby money', and although in 1992 I was embroiled in expensive litigation, I still had enough to buy a nice place in the country. My flat in London was too small to be a permanent home for a baby, a nanny and my three dogs. Tum-Tum, the dog James Buchanan-Jardine had given me, had presented me with Popsie Miranda in 1987, and she in turn had recently given birth to Maisie Carlotta, among four other puppies. However, if I made our main home in the country, the London flat would serve as an adequate pied à terre.

As soon as I returned from America to Britain, I turned my attention to acquiring a suitable place, and within four weeks I had bought it: a four-bedroomed flat in a converted Jacobean Grade 2 listed manor house in the heart of the picturesque Gloucestershire countryside. I chose a flat within a house to get the best of both worlds. Large houses always have large rooms, and if you have neighbours you have better security, which was an important consideration given that the flat would often be unoccupied. It had superb features which I knew a child would love: long, wide passages for riding bikes; our own inner courtyard where kids could safely play or catch the sun. The grounds, some seven acres, were also ideal for children. There was a long driveway and a wonderful ancient oak tree for climbing. The flat itself had appeal for adults, too. The drawing room was particularly beautiful, with panelling and a huge stone fireplace. The

bedrooms were large, and in bed, looking out on the adjoining fields where cows grazed, you felt quite like Marie
Antoinette at Le Hameau. And as a management company
was responsible for the maintenance, I wouldn't have to do
a thing except write the occasional cheque.

As summer passed and I shopped for antiques for the
new flat, the worm began to turn. The Morton book was
published, Diana's co-operation became evident and
Buckingham Palace went into overdrive to protect the interests of the monarchy. Suddenly, I found myself inundated
with requests for interviews from the foreign media, all of
whom said, 'Buckingham Palace gave us your number. They
said if we want to know what's really going on between the
Prince and Princess of Wales, you're the person to talk to.
You're the one who really knows.'

So, I thought with malicious delight, the very courtiers
who had been pulling strings behind the scenes since
February to discredit me and the veracity of *Diana in Private*
now appreciated the value of a balanced and authoritative
account of the marriage and the characters of the royal
couple. Although I was still angry about the way I had been
treated, I knew how useful the publicity would be for *Diana
in Private*. So I jumped on the bandwagon. Any benefit that
accrued to anyone at the palace was purely coincidental, I
can assure you.

I was both amused and annoyed by the courtiers'
attempts to use me to protect the Prince of Wales' interests. If
they thought I was gong to give countless interviews standing up for Charles against Diana, they were wrong. I gave
only those interviews which would add to the success of
my own book. 'The prince can fend for himself,' I told one
courtier. 'He has a whole organisation behind him. Where
the royals are concerned, my only interest beyond adhering
to the truth and fair play is my own self. While I wish the
royals well, and I do think their existence lifts Britain out of
its real insignificance into a more special, undeserved cate-
gory, whether they live or die, reign or are deposed, makes
very little difference to the true essentials of my life. I don't

owe my social position to them; I don't owe what I will inherit to them. If they had never existed, I'd have lost out on a nice little earner like *Diana in Private*, but doubtless I'd have found someone else to write about.'

I would be a liar if I denied that it was gratifying to see the palace crew eat humble pie, but I had more important things on my mind. As soon as I returned in August from Japan, where I went for the launch of the book there, I was off to Russia to see about adopting the baby that was the reason I had written *Diana in Private* in the first place.

This trip was really a shot in the dark. I had no idea whether I would be coming back with a baby, or whether I would merely be taking the first steps. So I made Moscow my first stop, staying with Max and Maria Theresa Trofaier at their magnificent apartment near the Kremlin. We went to see a British woman Maria Theresa knew who had adopted a Russian baby. She said her Russian lawyer had handled everything, and although she made it clear that adoptions were possible, she did not seem keen to give me his name. I did not mind, for I understood how protective people can be in such circumstances. In any case, I had already met Nikolai Kassyan, an eminent Russian jurist, through my Moscow guide, and he had agreed to act as my lawyer if I needed one. He seemed confident that he could devise a successful formula.

From Moscow I went by overnight train to St Petersburg, a romantic journey reminiscent of the days of the Czars. At the end of each carriage, little old ladies sat heating up tea which they served to us in glass cups with silver holders. I was to stay with my guide from my previous trip, Eugenie Visharenko, and I was going to see Russia as the Russians view it, not through the eyes of a tourist or diplomat. Life, I discovered, was tough, but the Russians are a warm, generous and resourceful people. They are cultivated and educated to a standard rare in the West. Whatever its ills, communism had provided everyone with a knowledge of literature, music and philosophy as well as the more practical specialised education required by their careers.

As a guide with Intourist, Eugenie had occupied a privileged position under the communists and knew her way around the system. She was confident that she could act successfully as my representative in an adoption, and, realising that she was indeed capable and intelligent, I gave her power of attorney. Thereafter I went from palace to palace, ballet to ballet and opera to opera while Eugenie made contact with various members of the Nomenclatura and learned the ropes. After a week, there was still no sign of a baby to adopt, but I had not expected mountains to be moved in moments. I returned to London optimistic that he or she would come in the not-too-distant future.

I came home to find that some unpleasant ghosts from the past had reappeared to haunt me. The two newspaper groups which I was already suing, Associated and Express Newspapers, had been put up to rubbishing me anew, and I knew exactly who was responsible: Colin Campbell and Ian Argyll had been up to their old tricks again. This did not come as a complete bolt from the blue, for I had received a telephone call from Ian earlier in the summer. 'I feel it's only right that you should compensate my brother by settling an annuity of $20,000 on him. You owe your success to his name.'

'I rather thought I owed my success to my literary talent, and to the people I know as a result of having been born the daughter of Michael and Gloria Ziadie,' I replied.

'If you hadn't married my brother, no one would be interested in anything you have to say,' Little Ian said.

'I dare say the name Campbell explains why Andrew Morton's book is doing so well.'

'Colin can make life very awkward for you.'

I had told him exactly what I thought of him, his brother and his proposal.

Now Little Ian had made contact with Associated Newspapers, who had set up an interview in New York with Colin and a tabloid journalist named Geordie Greig. For good measure, a *Daily Express* journalist was included in the act.

Argyll later gave a signed statement (starting: 'We, the most noble Colin Campbell' letting slip his twenty present and previous titles) which was a hatchet job and inaccurate to boot.

The result was two big interviews with Colin Campbell, first in the *Evening Standard*, and then the next morning another in the *Daily Express*. Both stories alleged that I was a hermaphrodite. Apart from anything else, this was inconsistent: the very first report about my medical history ever published in any newspaper anywhere in the world began with the damning words: 'Lord Colin Campbell last night disclosed that his wife of nine months was once a man.' Both interviews were as illogical as they were mendacious and vituperative. Campbell and I had neither seen nor spoken to one another since October 1975, and we had no friends in common who could run news back and forth – I had severed contact with everyone I had met through him – yet he set himself up as an authority on my current social life. Stating that I did not know nor had I spoken to any of the people mentioned in my book, he decreed that its contents were a tissue of lies. He was not specific, of course, but then, he couldn't be, for he had never met or mixed with any member of the royal family, and was as personally ignorant about them as a mechanic from the Adirondacks.

I was amused at the newspapers' attempt to present Campbell as a successful art-dealer and someone worth listening to, and not as a dissolute ne'er-do-well. This apparent success I took with a pinch of salt. When we were married he claimed to have been a deep-sea diver for black coral in Fiji, yet he had not one stick of it to show for his efforts. And you will remember that he also called himself a travel writer on the strength of six handwritten pages. The interviews might have concealed the stench of failure which emanated from the tiny, rent-controlled apartment where he has been holed up since returning to New York to live in the late 1970s, but the accompanying photographs showed a face distorted by a lifetime of substance abuse. So many of his teeth were missing that I quipped to my brother, 'Colin's teeth and his stories seem to have entered a race to see which have the most gaps.'

My lawyer was holding up the newspaper as he read out the piece to me. 'You know,' I said to him, 'I never felt glad or grateful that my marriage came to an end until now, seeing what Colin Campbell looks like today. At twenty-seven he had the face God gave him; now he has the face he deserves. He's like Dorian Gray's picture. Every thought, every feeling, every failing, every sin is etched there, for all the world to see. Please turn the picture away from me. The mere sight of him is making me feel like being sick.' I was not simply being catty. Had my lawyer not turned the page, I would have heaved all over my sitting-room floor.

Neither Associated Newspapers nor Express Newspapers could have been in any doubt that I would institute proceedings against them. Of course, I sued them for defamation and asked for an apology, a retraction, damages and aggravated damages. They played the same old game, stirring up as much trouble for me as they could in the hope that they would overload me with financial obligations and break my bank account or my spirit. Doubtless they thought they were only fulfilling their obligations by vigorously pursuing their quarry, but I was determined to hit them where it hurt – in their pockets. Nothing else would satisfy me, for nothing else would keep them in check.

Of course, I recognised that there were forces here that had nothing to do with me personally. Associated Newspapers and Express Newspapers were both spearheads of a segment of the press which represented the Establishment point of view. While I might qualify as an Establishment figure when it suited them to write about me as such, the newspapers had no compunction about downgrading me when it suited them to do so. The fact is, some segments of the British Establishment have a strict scale of values. Few women are the equals of men, and an ex-wife is seldom rated on a par with an ex-husband when he is a lord, and certainly never when he or his brother is a duke.

To those of us who know the true as well as the relative

value of dukes and lords, such an attitude is antiquated, anachronistic, indeed naïve. It also perpetuates a myth, about the power, position and influence of a group of people who have become increasingly marginalised as the century has worn on. The result is that the mighty dukes and lords one reads about are frequently only mighty within the confines of Establishment newspapers. Everywhere else, they are pretty much judged according to their worth or merit, which is often rather less than their public image implies.

Because of this inclination towards anachronistic reportage, the Establishment newspapers chose to ally themselves with Lord Colin Campbell and the Duke of Argyll. Which meant that I had to be presented adversely, and the two men complimentarily.

14

As the falling of the leaves and the dropping of the temperature signalled the arrival of autumn 1992, I turned my attention to my next book. *The Royal Marriages* was an examination of the marriages of the Queen, her children and her parents. The idea had been my publisher's and it made me uneasy, chiefly because of the rumours about the legitimacy of the Queen's second son. I was painfully aware that I had a readership in the United States to whom I owed a duty, and that many of the people who read my book, or interviewed me about it, would have read Christopher Hitchen's article of May 12 1991 in the *New York Times* in which he quoted Nigel Dempster asserting that Prince Andrew was not Prince Philip's son.

How best to deal with the issue of Prince Andrew's paternity niggled me throughout the writing of the book. Although I had no reason to believe that the rumours were true, and I had no desire to do the Queen an injustice, I recognised that I would have to confront them headlong. This was principally because Dempster himself was also writing a book on the royal family and I was not prepared to allow him to peddle his whispers without comment.

I had learned from my previous book that no royal writer

can be too careful in closing gaps. I had been the first author to be fed the suicide stories which Andrew Morton had reproduced wholesale as fact, when he ought to have known they were nothing of the kind. In *Diana in Private*, I had avoided mentioning the tales Diana herself was spreading, partly out of a sense of compassion for her, but mainly because reason clearly dictated that these 'suicide attempts' were no more than hysterical tantrums thrown by a young woman at the end of her emotional tether. After the Morton book was published, I saw that I had made a mistake in not defusing such an explosive issue with the dampener of truth. I should have raised the matter and dismissed it as insignificant. Instead I left the field open for Morton's sensational claims, which press and public alike then endowed with a seriousness they did not deserve.

So in *The Royal Marriages* I mentioned the question of Prince Andrew's paternity, emphasising that the stories were only rumours. With hindsight I can see that I was right to do this. By airing the whispers I destroyed the potential they held to be twisted. And when Sarah Bradford came to publish her acclaimed biography of the Queen in 1996, she too dealt with them in the same way, helping to put them into their proper perspective and thereby taking the sting out of them.

People might wonder why I cared at all, especially given the way Buckingham Palace had behaved over *Diana in Private*. But I did not blame the Queen for the conduct of her underlings. Indeed, I both admire and like the Queen. Not only has she been a conscientious Sovereign, but in person she is unstuffy, with dancing eyes and a lack of pretentiousness that her stiff public image decries.

To give an example: one of her ladies-in-waiting used to live above me when I resided at Lochmore House. From time to time, HM would drop in for drinks. One evening she was departing with her hostess giving a deep farewell curtsy and Commander Osborne King holding open the inner swing doors by leaning against them, when I opened up my ground floor flat front door to let my dogs out for a walk. Of course, they couldn't care less whether someone is a queen or a dosser. They promptly bolted for the open doors. The Queen, being sharp and a dog-lover, made a quick judgement call, springing into action to open the outer door which she was afraid the dogs, who run like furies, would slam into. The only problem was that the police cars which protect the Secretaries of State resident in the flats always drive around the circular inner courtyard so fast that you dare not let out the dogs until you've checked that the coast is clear. More worried about my dogs' well-being than ceremony, I screamed out their names as I dashed past the Queen, nearly knocking her over in the process. Did she mind? Did she feel insulted? Decidedly not. She fully understood the situation and was even complimentary about my 'girls'!

Moreover, anyone who has been the subject of rumour and speculation herself identifies with others in the same boat, whether it is the Queen and her two younger sons or someone in much humbler circumstances. If I had shown no consideration, I would have been no better than the prejudiced people who seem to think I can't possibly have feelings just because I have had more advantages than they.

Apart from that awkwardness, and the unpleasantness generated by the break-up of the marriage of the Prince and Princess of Wales, *The Royal Marriages* was fun to work on. I love doing research, and I happily took loads of documents and books down to the country, spread them out in the drawing room and my bedroom, and read away to my heart's content. The juiciest morsels, however, came, as ever, through friends. And after the Morton book, I was flavour of the month with certain courtiers to such an extent that they approached me when they heard that I was writing a new royal book, and provided me with damning information about their *bête noire*, the newly separated Princess of Wales. Diana's camp, of course, continued to funnel through dirt about Charles. I treated all of this with scepticism. Proof, proof, proof, I demanded, and I was careful only to use what could be substantiated.

I was sickened by the game being played as the Waleses' marriage unravelled publicly. There was no way of writing about what was going on without feeling defiled by it, but I had little choice in the matter unless I was prepared to return the advance. I needed the money, for I would soon have an extra mouth to feed. Aside, of course, from his worst characteristics, I felt there were some similarities between Diana and Colin, such as a troubled family background riven with strife and recrimination. Diana, I was told by a close mutual friend, was doing everything in her power to destroy Charles' life. The popular belief was that she was seeking to deprive him of his reputation and his throne. Female solidarity alone made me want to sympathise with Diana, but my own experience of a vengeful spouse left me in no doubt that Charles was the person to be pitied.

I had such a tight deadline that again I had to work from early in the morning till late at night, seven days a week. I would just about finish on time if I had no interruptions. I took no breaks for anything except preparing my papers for the adoption. Eugenie had sent me a list of the many documents I needed: health and police checks, character references, proof of earnings, and, of course, a home study. The last document was the most time-consuming to organise. While the social worker attended to the report at a measured pace, I continued writing the book, grateful to have this time free to work. If I got the baby, I would never again have such freedom.

In November 1992, out of the blue, Eugenie telephoned me to say, 'Come next week. There's a baby for you.'

Oh my God, I thought. I was torn by a multitude of conflicting emotions: joy, nervousness, crunch-time disbelief, anxiety about how I could possibly finish writing the book if I had to care for a newborn child. Well, I rationalised, life is about rising to occasions, and the baby takes precedence over any inconvenience or difficulty caused by its sudden arrival.

Visas for Russia are not obtained at the drop of a hat, but I had met Vladimir Voronoff of the Russian embassy in

London through the Russian Princess Helena Gagarin-Moutafian. 'Can you please help?' I asked him. He put me on to the consul, who could not have been more kind, and I got the visa without delay.

Next I got in touch with the social worker preparing my home study. 'Can you please have it finished as soon as possible?' She couldn't complete it in time, but what she could do was prepare an interim report, which would have to do until the final draft was ready. That necessitated her rushing down to the country to see what the place was like. I groaned, wondering how I would ever be able to make up the lost day.

No sooner did I have my visa and interim home study than Eugenie rang again. 'Don't come. The baby was born in Ukraine, near Chernobyl. The doctors say they won't let you have him. He most likely has radiation sickness. Wait.'

The feeling of relief that I would be able to finish the book before embarking on a monumental new role as a mother was supreme. There were ten other books on the royal family coming out at the same time. The others were written mostly by, in my opinion, dull uninspired writers like James Whittaker and Nigel Dempster, who hoped to muscle in on the success Andrew Morton and I had achieved with our Diana books, both of which had sat on the bestseller lists in the London and New York *Times* for months, reputedly earning us millions. This was an exaggeration, but I must say that I didn't do badly. My new book, therefore, could not be delivered one day later than the deadline of 28 February, for if it were not published on time, it would enter a market that had already been cleared of readers.

In February, just as I was nearing the home stretch, Eugenie called. 'Come as soon as you can. We've got your son for you. I've seen him. He's a beautiful boy with brown eyes and blond hair.'

Once again I applied for a visa, and once again Eugenie telephoned to delay my departure just as I was ready to leave. This time the hitch was that I needed to have all my papers legalised. 'But they're perfectly legal,' I said.

'"Legalised" is a specific term which the Hague Convention covers. Get in touch with the embassy and ask them if they can authorise the papers,' she advised.

I contacted Vladimir Voronoff again, explaining the situation. It was only after the papers had sat for three weeks in the Russian embassy, been couriered back to Russia and handed over to the authorities that I discovered I had made a mistake. The Russian powers that be took one look at the papers and said, 'They have been verified by the embassy in London. That's not the same as being legalised. They must be legalised by the British Foreign Office.'

Every cloud has a silver lining. By this time, I had finished writing the book and was in the middle of the libel-checking and editing processes, so in a way I was grateful that this new hiccup had saved me a second time from being torn between the baby and meeting my professional obligations.

Once the papers had finally been given their individual apostils, they went back to Russia while I awaited the call that would tell me I was a mother at last. Eugenie telephoned. 'You're not getting the boy born in January,' she said. 'There's been a change. You're getting a beautiful, blue-eyed blond boy who was born on 1 March. I've seen him himself. He's lovely.'

No mother who gives birth naturally has a choice about her baby. 'Eugenie, I'm happy to have either baby,' I told her. 'I only hope this change won't delay the process.'

'No,' she said.

This was a relief. Moreover, it would be in the baby's interest if he were two months younger when I adopted him, for he would have spent less time in the orphanage, suffering less damage from the traumas of institutionalisation. 'I'm coming over as soon as I can,' I told Eugenie. 'Whether the papers are ready or not.' Nothing hastens progress like the presence of the most interested party, and the time had come to make mine felt.

First I had obligations to fulfil in Britain. The serialisation rights to *The Royal Marriages* were bought by the *Sunday*

Mirror, whose decent and talented royal correspondent at the time, Tim Willcox, was one of the few journalists in his field. An author has to collaborate with the journalist who converts his or her book into a serial, and I can say without hesitation that it was a real treat to be able to entrust the serialisation to someone as capable as Tim.

Naturally, publication in Britain caused another sensation, but it was less traumatic and less intense than the last. The novelty value of *Diana in Private* and the Morton book was a thing of the past, for everyone now knew that the private lives of the Windsors were a mess. Only those people who loved reading in detail about the royal family felt the need to supplement the wealth of information – and misinformation – published by the papers on a daily basis with a book on the same subject, and consequently sales of the book were lower. The response in America was almost identical, with one notable exception. Nigel Dempster had arrived in the US a few days before me to plug his own book. At the same time, he was busy telling everyone that I was a man, and everywhere I went, journalists asked me about it.

I recognised, of course, that the subject of the British royal family was large enough to accommodate more than one fairy at the top of the Christmas tree. Dempster, however, obviously felt it necessary to sabotage the competition by giving his favourite hobby horse yet another airing. When a journalist from San Francisco telephoned me in New York and asked for my comments, I explained that Dempster had an obsession with my crotch going back nearly two decades. I still have no idea why – I've only ever met the man on maybe five occasions, on three of them for no more than twenty seconds. Enough was enough. I decided to retaliate by furnishing the journalist with a few truths about Dempster.

It was with relish that I later read, in various American and British newspapers including *The Sunday Times*, that the Greatest Living Englishman, as his colleagues at *Private Eye* had dubbed him, was in fact an Anglo-Indian from Calcutta.

Of course, I do not despise Dempster for his Indian origins. India has one of the oldest cultures in the world, and anyone who hails from the subcontinent should be proud of his heritage. I do despise him for what I perceive as a lack of pride by him about the Indian part of his heritage, and for his behaviour towards me, and what it tells me about him as a person. I had always nicknamed him the Calcutta Creep.

Having made my response, I mentally flicked Dempster off the lapels of my consciousness the way you would a dying fly. I knew he was rattling around the world implying that he was so mighty I didn't dare sue him, but as long as he stayed within his own boundaries, I proposed to ignore him. I had far more important things to deal with.

As soon as I arrived back in the UK, I organised my mission to Russia, and at the end of June 1993, I boarded an Aeroflot flight for St Petersburg. I was met by my driver, a biochemist on a sabbatical from his job so that he could supplement his tiny income to the tune of US$20 a day, a not inconsiderable sum in Russia then. I nicknamed him Volodia Helicopter, for I was always asking him to fly, and he somehow managed to do so through the streams of traffic that were now clogging the roads of that beautiful Baltic city.

When Volodia took me to Eugenie's flat in Peter's District, I had not one stitch of baby clothes, nor had I bought a cot or any other equipment before leaving London. Although not superstitious by nature, I was nervous about 'setting a goal mouth', as the Jamaicans would put it, on the enterprise. I had left bottles, disposable nappies and baby food, which I had brought over from England, with Maria Theresa in Moscow the last time I had been there. Having left empty-handed then, I didn't want to buy anything for the baby until I had him safely in my arms.

When I arrived, Eugenie said, 'If you'd like, we can go and look at your son at the orphanage tomorrow.'

'Will they allow me to?' I said, concerned not to put a foot wrong with the unknown personages who had such power over the future of me and my baby. No British or Jamaican citizen had ever tried to adopt a child from St Petersburg, and in breaking new ground I could not be assured of a successful outcome until the process was completed.

'The doctors in charge of the orphanage are looking forward to meeting you,' Eugenie said. The positive note pleased me no end.

On the last Sunday afternoon of June 1993, Eugenie and I piled into Volodia Helicopter's lovingly tended Lada and headed across town, over the Neva River and up past the Tauride Palace, home of Catherine the Great's lover Prince Potemkin, to the other side of town, where the orphanage was situated. It was in a stark, well-tended two-storey building near a subway station, wings shooting off wings in a reflection of necessary expansion rather than architectural purpose.

As Eugenie pressed the bell and waited for what seemed like an eternity for a nurse to open the front door, my heart was beating fiercely. This was the moment of truth. A hundred thoughts passed through my mind, an equal number of emotions through my heart. My greatest hope was that I would like the baby; my greatest dread that I would not. I knew of mothers who had not taken even to their natural children – an antipathy that in some lasted a lifetime. What if that happened to me? My innate optimism quickly shoved that fear aside as ever-increasing waves of anticipation engulfed me.

By the time the nurse opened the door, I was like a horse at the starting gate. Fortunately, Eugenie is a fast walker. I followed her down the corridor to the doctors' office, where they greeted us and we exchanged pleasantries for about five minutes while I quelled my desire to bolt off and see my baby. 'We're sure you'd like to see the baby,' said the two doctors at last. 'Would you follow us, please?'

Eugenie and I followed Valentina and Yelena to one of the infants' wards. They opened the door to reveal a spacious, airy room with a huge, brightly coloured playpen and two nurses in attendance. On one of the two nappy-changing tables lay a baby, naked except for a yellow bonnet.

'Come,' Yelena said and Eugenie translated, 'come and look at your son. He's a beautiful little boy.'

The baby on the table had huge blue eyes. He was kicking

his feet in pleasure.

'Would you like me to be your Mummy?' I asked him.

The baby looked me straight in the eye, which is very unusual for three-month-olds, as all mothers will know. He gurgled delightedly, broke into a big smile, and said, 'Gaa.' I was gobsmacked, and so was everyone else. From that moment on, Misha, as I named him, had my heart.

'He likes you,' Valentina said delightedly through Eugenie.

'You see?' Eugenie added. 'I told you he was a beauty.'

'Go on, pick him up,' Yelena encouraged, seeing that I wanted to hold him.

For an hour I held my little bundle of joy in my arms. Eugenie and I took him for a walk in the grounds of the orphanage. Already I loved him as only a mother can love her child, though intermingled with my joy was the knowledge that someone had had to give up this magnificent, adorable little boy.

When it was time to return Misha to his cot, I steeled myself and handed him over to the nurse with a minimum of fuss. I understood that the nurses and doctors did not have time to tend to more than children's basic needs, but I wanted for Misha what every mother wants for her baby: to see him surrounded by unlimited love and care.

I was also curious to see the baby that had been earmarked for me before Misha. Eugenie asked the nurse to show him to me. I followed her into one of the rooms off the central ward where there were fourteen babies asleep in individual cots. 'There he is,' said Eugenie, who had already seen him. 'He's sweet, isn't he?'

I looked down at an angelic bundle asleep in his cot over-looking the window. He was far less Western European-looking than Misha with the broad face and slanting eyes of a Russian with Tartar blood. I bent down, kissed his forehead and said, 'Have a good life, darling boy. I'm sorry I'm not going to be your Mummy, but I understand you're due to get one soon.'

The following afternoon, Eugenie and I went to see the official at the Ministry of Education without whose approval the adoption could not proceed. The Russian system of dropping in on officials without an appointment, and being seen by them if they were available or coming back if they were not, was novel, to say the least, but I was not about to tell Romans how to behave in Rome, or Russians in St Petersburg. When we were finally called in to this official's 'study room', I was encouraged by the hospitable way she greeted us. Everything was going swimmingly until she learned the identity of the baby selected for me. 'You can't adopt him until November next year,' she said through Eugenie. 'I can understand why no one has picked this up for his papers don't make it clear unless you're familiar with the minutiae of the law. But the law is definite on this point. He can't be adopted till then.'

I nearly passed out from the shock. I could hardly grasp what I was hearing, though of course I understood the ramifications immediately. 'Have another baby,' the official suggested. 'There are so many lovely babies you could have.'

'But I love him,' I said, nearly breaking down at the thought of leaving my little Misha in an orphanage for another seventeen months. What would happen to him in the interval? What effects would the deprivation of a mother's love have upon him, in both the short and long term? Both Eugenie and the official did what they could to console me, but to no avail. Already Misha was my baby, if only in my heart.

'Have the baby originally earmarked for you,' the official suggested. 'He's a beautiful little boy, and his name means gift of God in Russian. Maybe he's God's gift to you, and this is God's way of bringing you together.'

This was absolutely the right thing to say to me. Believing in God as strongly as I do, I saw exactly what she meant, and, having seen him the day before and found him adorable, I said, 'OK, I'll take him. But can't you find some way of letting me have Misha as well? It will break my heart to leave him in the orphanage.'

She picked up the telephone and made a series of calls. Eugenie later told me that she had telephoned the doctors at the orphanage and an important medical official. While she did this I prayed harder than I have ever prayed in my life that God would give her a way to get me Misha as well.

'What we can do for you,' she eventually said through Eugenie, 'is allow you to take the baby out of the country for medical treatment. Then you can keep him with you until next November, when we will process the adoption. Would you like that?'

'Thank you. Thank you from the bottom of my heart.'

The following day, when I went to the orphanage to see the children, I understood how desirable it was for Misha to receive medical treatment in London. Although the Russians love children and the authorities do everything in their power to ensure that the orphans receive as high a standard of care as possible, the state's finances are such that specialised medical treatment is not readily available to every child who needs it.

When I took off Misha's bonnet, which I had not done the first time I had seen him, I noticed that his head and one side of his face were covered in carbuncles. 'He has an allergy,' the doctors said, but I wondered whether it might not be something more serious. AIDS did cross my mind as a possibility, but I resolved to have him no matter what was or was not wrong with him. Fortunately, when I did get him back to England I discovered that his condition was non-infectious, though more serious than an ordinary allergy. It was eminently treatable, however, and he is now cured.

Back in St Petersburg, I spent three weeks in a haze of meetings. Volodia Helicopter ferried us between the various 'study rooms' of a plethora of officials, to whom we had to extend the courtesy of punctuality, but who invariably seemed to reside on opposite sides of the city. In the evenings, I sometimes went to the ballet, to concerts and to the opera, but often I was so wrung out that I curled up in bed with a book. It was a fraught period, as I knew I must not count my chickens before they were hatched. So I could not breathe easily until the adoption papers for the first baby were on their way to the Smolny Palace, where the official concerned signs the decree to authorise the adoption certificate to be issued.

The decree was due to be signed on Friday 9 July 1993. 'Pick it up at five o'clock,' the official's assistant advised Eugenie.

'Nothing can go wrong now,' Eugenie said. 'The baby is yours.'

Only then did I allow her to take me to GKN, the massive department store off the Nevsky Prospect, to buy blankets and all the baby clothes I could lay my hands on. Afterwards we headed for the Smolny Palace to pick up the adoption decree. When we got there, we were informed that it had not been signed yet. The official who was obliged by law to sign all adoption decrees had been abroad and had not had time to sign it since his return. 'He will sign it on Monday,' the assistant solemnly promised us after Eugenie explained that I had irrevocable travel plans for the following Monday evening.

That Monday, 12 July, Volodia certainly put his helicoptering skills to use as we zipped from one part of town to another, picking up the adoption decree and taking it to obtain an adoption certificate and a birth certificate for my son. I named him Dmitri in honour of the land of his birth, Jonathan because it means gift of God in English, Victor after his godfather Sheikh Victor el Khazen, and Jesús for his godfather Jesús Mora. His surnames were my maiden name, Ziadie, and Campbell, to connect him with the name by which I am known. Eugenie and I then headed across town to pick up Dima's Russian passport, which was stamped with an exit visa stating that he was leaving the country permanently. Afterwards, we returned to her flat for my clothes and grabbed a sandwich which we ate in the car as we hurtled across town to the orphanage to collect the kids. I already had Misha's passport and papers, which had been prepared the week before.

We were now horribly late and in danger of missing the

overnight train to Moscow. This I had to catch, as I had to be there the following day to get Misha's visa for England and Dima's Jamaican passport, without which he would not be granted entry into Britain. I had planned to take photographs of the orphanage for the children to see when they are older, but when push came to shove there simply wasn't time. We made it without a second to spare. I thanked Volodia for his help and kissed Eugenie. I was a Mummy at last.

When I returned home to England, the first person I telephoned was my brother. He had not been in favour of me adopting, asking, as he had done when I had first got Tum-Tum, 'Why do you want to tie yourself down with so much responsibility?'

'How did it go?' he asked.

'Rather better than I thought it would. I've got two beautiful little boys.'

'You what?' he said.

'Well, they more or less gave me the option of taking one or two, and since I wasn't about to leave either, I took both.'

'Only you could go for one baby which you don't need, and come back with two,' he said, ever the big brother. 'I'll come and see you on my way from work.'

The rest of my family had been as fretful as Mickey before the adoption in case I saddled myself with a 'lemon', and reacted with equal consternation afterwards. 'Can you believe what Georgie has gone and done?' Daddy asked my oldest friend, Judy Ann MacMillan. 'She goes to Russia for one baby and comes back with two.'

'I know,' Judy Ann said. 'Isn't it wonderful?'

'I don't know about that,' my father retorted, 'but at least it shows she has a big heart.'

My family's worries did not perturb me in the least. Life offers no guarantees, however you come by your children. Is adoption actually any more of a shot in the dark than birth by more conventional means? Does one really have any more control over the destiny of one's progeny if one produces them oneself? Of course not. You only had to look at me to see that I was hardly the sort of child my own father would have wished for. Because of the accident of birth which had so affected my life, I took a very relaxed view of what is and isn't acceptable where children are concerned. So what if the babies turned out to be flawed in some way? Why should that make me love them less?

Every mother knows how tiring infants are, and mine were no exception. Although Misha gave no more trouble than the average good baby, Dima had discovered in Moscow, thanks to the attentions of the four Trofaier children, Maria Theresa and me, that if he cried he got a response. For the next six months he did little else unless he was snuggled firmly in my bosom. There were times when I wanted to tear my hair out, but never once did I regret having taken him. He was my baby, and I was prepared to endure the process of deinstitutionalising him, no matter how long it took.

I did not mind getting up in the middle of the night, nor did I feel that I was missing out on anything by being tied down by two babies. I had been to all the parties I needed for this lifetime; I had slept with enough men to know the glories and limitations of passion. I had had my great love, romantic fulfilment, and a life that had sometimes been rather too fascinating for my own comfort. The virtue of coming to motherhood so late was that I knew exactly what I was missing, and I couldn't have cared less.

I still needed a nanny, for tiredness has never held any attraction for me, and I would need to resume working at some stage. This I had actually organised as far back as December 1991: the nanny, a country woman aged about forty, with several children of her own, had been hovering in readiness. I telephoned her and told her to pack her bags – her airline ticket was on its way.

As if I did not have enough on my plate, I returned to London to discover that the Calcutta Creep had taken advantage of my absence to stir up more trouble. According to him, the trip to Russia had been arranged to conceal the fact that I had not been asked to the opening of a social event. Not only did I have my invitation to hand, but I had also declined it prior to leaving for Russia. Going to fetch a baby was rather more important than attending a social occasion. I fired off a writ for libel to stop him in his tracks. Bored though I was with lawsuits, I had to keep fighting if I was ever going to stop the press harassment. It did not prevent Dempster's rats scurrying over my babies' cots. On the very afternoon of my return to London, I was sitting in my kitchen having a cup of tea and recounting my experiences in Russia to Anna, Lady Brocklebank, a close friend who is also a doctor and had acted as a referee for the adoption, when the doorbell rang. 'Who is it?' I asked over the intercom.

'The *Daily Mail*,' a woman's voice replied.

'What do you want?'

'Can you please let us in, Lady Colin? I'd like to talk to you about the two babies you've brought back from Russia today.'

Someone from one of the other flats let the woman and her photographer into the lobby, so I cracked open the front door of my flat to speak to them. 'I am terribly sorry to tell you that you've wasted your time coming here. I have nothing to say to you.'

I slammed the door shut and walked back into the kitchen. 'Can you believe that?' I said to Anna. 'Two babies. Two babies, indeed. You know who's tipped them off, don't you?' I mentioned the name of a mutual soon to be ex-friend. 'She phoned me shortly after I got in from the airport. She, you and my brother Mickey are the only people who know I'm back in the country and that there are two babies.' Anna herself had been in such a hurry to get over to see us that she hadn't known I had both Dima and Misha until she arrived. 'As my brother would never even think of speaking to the press, that leaves only you-know-who.'

'It could be a coincidence,' said Anna, kindness itself.

'I doubt it. Either she's currying favour with Dempster in the hope of getting a mention for herself, or she's supplementing her paltry income with a few pieces of silver, Judas like.'

I was certain I was right, but just to make sure I set a trap. I gave each person to whom I spoke about the boys different variations of their names, and kept a record of what I had called them to whom. Less than twenty-four hours later, the trap was sprung. I had been to see the doctor with the babies. As I took the first baby out of the car outside the house, I was accosted by a photographer who loomed out of nowhere.

The paper would have no story if there was no picture, so I hunched my back and shielded Dima, running between the cars in the courtyard with the photographer in hot pursuit. 'You do not have the right to photograph me on my home ground without my permission,' I screamed from behind the cars. 'Get off this property before I have you arrested.'

Much shouting went back and forth, as I demanded he withdrew and he and a woman begged me to come out. After a minute or so, the woman declared in a cultivated voice, 'It's OK, Lady Colin, you can come out now. He's gone. I've sent him back to the car and he won't take any photos of you without your permission.'

I straightened up, so angry I could have shredded him alive with my bare hands.

'My name is Hilary Douglas and I am the royal correspondent of the *Sun*,' said the young, dark-haired, rather attractive woman. 'I've come to interview about the two babies you've adopted.'

'Forget it,' I said curtly. 'This is private property. You're in contravention of the Press Complaints Commission's rules. Please get off my property.'

'Are these the babies?' she said, looking into the Jaguar XJ6 at one and back to my arms at the other.

'I am not answering one question,' I snapped.

'Can you at least confirm their names? Our informant has told us they're called Dmitri and Misha.' These were the versions of their names I had given to the treacherous social climber.

'You obviously didn't hear what I said,' I told her

furiously. 'I will not answer one question. I suggest you get off this property before I have you thrown off.'

Realising that I meant business, Miss Douglas apologised for inconveniencing me and left. Once she had reached the gate, I walked across the porch to the building's front door, my back shielding the baby from view. I noticed that the photographer was snapping us from the street. This was also a clear violation of the Press Complaints Commission's rule concerning invasion of privacy, and even though I was pretty sure he would have nothing he could use, I was not about to leave anything to chance. Any photograph was better than none. I put the baby back into the car and ran across to the gate.

'Give me that film,' I demanded.

'You've got to be joking,' he sneered.

'I'm not,' I said solemnly. 'I want that film and I will get it, on that you can depend. Please hand over the film and save us both a lot of trouble.' I stretched my hand out.

'Fuck off, lady,' he said, and got into his car.

I positioned myself right in front of the vehicle.

The photographer started the engine.

I stood my ground.

He edged towards me.

I still stood my ground.

He had to stop when his bumper was about to touch my shin.

'You're going nowhere until you turn that film and any other photographs you've taken over to me,' I shouted.

He revved the motor.

'Mr MacDonald!' I screamed, calling the porter, whose office was nearby. 'Mr MacDonald, please call the police. Call the police!'

Hilary Douglas reached over, picked up the camera, and handed it to the photographer. He removed the film. She got out and handed it to me. 'I'm really sorry,' she said. 'You must think we're the lowest of the low. I had no idea it would be like this. I only started on this job last week, you see. I'm the new royal correspondent, and they asked me to cover this story. I can't apologise enough.'

Over the next few months, press interest in the children remained constant, though word soon spread that I considered no publicity worth the expense of my children's privacy. When invasiveness failed, they tried money – I was offered tens of thousands of pounds.

Two weeks after my return from Russia, my step-mother-in-law, Margaret, Duchess of Argyll, died. Margaret and I had been great friends for nearly twenty years. When I was married, ever one for reconciliation, I had even brought Colin, whom she had not seen since the age of twelve, back into her life. That was a big mistake: within weeks he was threatening to smash her face in. As she knew what he had done to mine, she thereafter refused to see him. In the last five years of her life, Margaret and I had become particularly close. Twice a week, every week I was in London, I went to see her and took her adored poodle, Louis, for a run in the park with my dogs. Her glory days now over, she was often at a loose end, so until she became housebound, I frequently asked her to small supper parties at my flat, or we would go to the cinema together. Margaret and I had had a unique bond: our husbands, father and son, had both committed themselves to our destruction.

If ever there was a dire warning on the destructiveness of publicity, it was the latter part of Margaret's life. Born in 1912, the only child of George Whigham, the founder of the British, American and Canadian Celanese Corporations, Margaret was the greatest debutante of all time in an age when debutantes were as famous as rock stars are today. By the age of twenty-five she was so celebrated on both sides of the Atlantic that Cole Porter included her in his hit song, 'You're the Top'.

Margaret would undoubtedly have lived out the remainder of her life as an ultra-respectable, stylish and beautiful heiress and a pillar of society, had she not made the cardinal error of marrying Ian Campbell, 11th Duke of Argyll. He was penniless, a chronic alcoholic and shunned in good company as an unscrupulous reprobate. His second wife, Louise Clews, who was the mother of his two sons, warned Margaret's first husband, Charlie Sweeny, that he was a wife-beating opportunist who was marrying Margaret solely for her money.

By her own admission, Margaret was always a sucker for a good-looking face and a glib line in chatter, and Big Ian, as he was known, had both. Margaret did not believe Charlie's warning and went ahead with the marriage, which was not a happy one from the outset. Big Ian's cruelty towards Margaret has been recounted by many of their friends, and was surpassed in scale only by the voraciousness with which he worked his way through a large chunk of the Whigham millions.

Inevitably, the marriage collapsed, in 1959. As I have recounted elsewhere, Big Ian tried to blackmail Margaret into making a settlement of £250,000 upon him, and when she refused, he dragged her through the courts in a sensational divorce. The attitude of the judge, Lord Wheatley, was symptomatic of the prejudices rampant in Britain in 1963 and which still exist, to a lesser degree, to this day. He could not believe that any gentleman, much less a duke, could be as dishonourable and disreputable as Margaret testified. Big Ian's peers knew otherwise, however, and he lived out the remaining ten years of his life in exile in Paris, shunned by all but a handful of stalwarts.

Margaret survived for another twenty years. The court case had made her undoubtedly the most notorious woman in British society, and she was deeply traumatised by the loss of her respectability. She was one of my most avid supporters, telling all who would listen that Colin Campbell was doing to me what his father had done to her. 'Character assassination', she called it, and would not stand for one word against me. Our shared trauma was not the only reason why I was so fond of Margaret. She could be tremendously good company and had the courage of her convictions. While strangers did not see beyond the haughty duchess, those of us who knew her well recognised her as a witty, amusing, loyal woman who always stood up for what she believed.

Although I felt Margaret's loss, I appreciated that death had been a release for her. The last few years of her life had been a torment, largely because of financial problems. After she was forced to leave the Grosvenor House Hotel, where she had had a flat since the sale of her Georgian townhouse in Mayfair in 1976, she often said, 'I should have died while I was still at Grosvenor House.'

Margaret's death was the media event in Britain in the summer of 1993. Even at her funeral the press blocked my way into the church and hassled me for a comment until I snapped, 'For God's sake, can't you leave people alone? This is a funeral, you know, and while her death might not matter to you, it does to some of us. No, she was not the godawful creature you've made her out to be ever since my father-in-law divorced her. The obituaries and articles that have been printed in the last few days are a disgrace, and I wish you'd just leave us all alone.'

'Why did he do it, then?' a reporter asked, thrusting a microphone under my nose as the flashbulbs popped and the television cameras whirred.

What the hell, I thought. It's about time someone stood up and was counted. 'Because he was a dirty, rotten stinker who tried to blackmail her, and when she wouldn't succumb, made money in a different way. By selling stories about her,' I said. 'Now, if you'll excuse me, I'd like to go into the church and say my goodbyes.'

No one gets Brownie points for guessing whose comment featured on the television news that evening, or whose picture was published large as life in all the newspapers, along with a word-perfect quote. Was I sorry? Not a bit. Margaret deserved to be stood up for, and I was glad that amid all the sensational obituaries and salacious articles there was at least one fair remark.

After Margaret's funeral, I returned to motherhood and a quiet life. In October, the boys were christened at the Brompton Oratory by Father Harrison, to a resounding public silence which I had worked hard to achieve. The occasion was magical. After the babies were received into the Church at 2.30 p.m., my closest friends and I returned to my London flat for a champagne tea party. It was wonderful to be surrounded only by people who wished us well, and when it was over I had cause to reflect upon how lucky I was to have so many good and loving friends. I planned to dedicate myself totally to the children until the new year, when I would start work on my next book, and I looked forward to the future with optimism.

15

As 1993 drew to a close, looking for a house in London for my expanded family became the number-one priority. Now that I had two sons as opposed to the one baby I had anticipated, we needed somewhere bigger. In some ways, it was the ideal time to look. The market was depressed and prices were lower than they had been for a generation. However, I was still funding my lawsuits at this stage, and consequently much of the capital I would otherwise have used had to be kept available for legal expenses. I would have to be incredibly lucky to find the sort of place I wanted, for I was not prepared to move out of the Belgravia–Pimlico–Chelsea–Kensington grid.

'You'll never find what you want,' my brother used to say. 'You're going to have to move to Clapham or Battersea or Fulham.'

'In that case, I'll stay at Lochmore House,' I'd respond.

Lochmore House was one of the four blocks of Deco-esque flats which comprised the Cundy Street Flats. Situated on the corner of Eaton Terrace and Ebury Street in Belgravia, the smartest area in London, they were, like my previous flat, owned by the Duke of Westminster's Grosvenor Estate and housed the highest concentration of aristocrats and pukka establishment figures in the land. Among them were the former prime minister Lord Home of the Hirsel; arts ministers Richard Luce and David Mellor (whose flat was actually the property of his girlfriend, Viscountess Cobham); the Queen's former private secretary, Lord Charteris and her Master of the Horse, Lord Westmoreland and his Countess; and the Princess of Wales' great-aunt, the Dowager Duchess of Abercorn.

I was fortunate in having a brother who was a solicitor. Although he refused to get involved in the actions lest something go wrong and cause trouble between us, he used to warn me of the pitfalls of the legal system. My solicitor, did the same, and usually agreed with Mickey. It was reassuring to have such a close and knowledgeable sounding board in the background.

Mickey and I had always had what Richard Adeney described as a 'close but antagonistic' relationship. It was a closeness based on mutual respect for one another's characters rather than on similarity of personality. We were so radically different that, aside from a love of people, music and art, we had nothing in common. Indeed, we were so opposed in some respects that I used to say, 'I'm going to check that I'm doing the right thing. If Mickey disagrees with it, I'll know I should do it.' This did not stop me loving him, however, and I confidently expected my only brother to continue to bug and bless my life for many years to come.

On Christmas morning 1993, I awoke bright and early and prepared the children for mass at Westminster Cathedral. This was going to be a quiet Christmas. Unusually, neither Mickey nor I was having a large luncheon party. This year I was going to the El Khazens and he to Daksheenie Abeywardene, his partner. Later, he would call in at Lochmore House on his way home and we would exchange presents.

Six o'clock came and went, and there was no sign of Mickey. Six-thirty came and went. Still no Mickey. At seven o'clock, I stomped to the telephone in high dudgeon and called Abbey. 'He didn't come,' she said. 'He said he wasn't feeling well.'

This was most unusual. Mickey was never ill. He was a powerhouse of such energy that even going for a walk with him was an experience few survived unscathed.

I telephoned my brother, straight away. 'I was sleeping. I'll come and see you in an hour,' he said.

Two hours later, by now very worried, I called Mickey again. 'I'm sorry, I fell asleep again. I'm just so exhausted all I can do is sleep.'

Suddenly, a host of little observations I had made in the last few months fused before my eyes in one horrid moment of recognition. The time in August I had gone to his office and asked him, as he rose from behind his desk, 'How come you have a tan and you haven't been abroad?' The pasty but somehow even more tanned look he had had in October at the children's christening, which prompted me to repeat the question. How the indefatigable Mickey had fallen asleep at Richard Adeney's dinner to celebrate his birthday in November.

'Is there something wrong with you? Do you know what it is? And if so, what is it?' I asked, my tone grave.

'Come round tomorrow. We'll speak then,' he said.

From his evasive answer, I knew that Mickey had a life-threatening condition. Of course, I said nothing, and we rang off with the normal civilities. Without even replacing the receiver, I telephoned Jesús Mora. 'I just had the most extraordinary telephone conversation with Mickey. I'm sure he's going to tell me tomorrow that he's dying.'

'You might be wrong,' said Jesús, trying to console me as I broke down in floods of tears. The truth, however, has a sound as clear as a clarion to the ears of those who listen to it. I hoped against hope, but I was prepared for the worst when I turned up at Mickey's the following morning.

He took a seat on a chair beneath the picture window in his drawing room and I took one diagonally opposite him. He looked at me. I looked at him. I couldn't read his expression, and I was pretty sure he couldn't read mine either.

'I've got cancer,' he said. 'It's in the right side of my mouth and the sinuses.'

I didn't even blink lest I convey what I was thinking.

'Do you remember how I told you the other day that I was having trouble with one of my teeth, that it was wobbling? Well, I went to the dentist and he said, "You'd better go and see a doctor. There's no bone beneath this tooth." I went to the doctor. She referred me to an oncologist. They did some tests and it turns out I have lymphoma – that's a form of cancer of the lymphatic system.'

Our maternal Aunt Majorie, now happily in remission against all the odds, and paternal cousin, Peter Jonas, had both had another form of cancer of the lymphatic system, Hodgkin's disease. I calculated that the genetic odds were not in his favour. 'What's the prognosis?' I asked.

'I don't suppose I'll die in the next week or two, but the odds are I'm not going to live as long as we all expected.'

'I take it you'll start treatment immediately and cancel your trip to Jamaica?' He was due to leave in three days' time.

'No, no, no. The ticket's booked and paid for, and I'm not changing my plans. I'm going, and I'm going to see everyone I planned to see.'

He's going in case it's goodbye, I interpreted.

'The oncologist says I can go,' he went on. 'A few weeks one way or the other won't make any difference.'

'Does he know how long you've had this growth?'

'I didn't ask him that.'

Typical. Mickey never delved. I made a mental note to speak to the doctors as soon as I could engineer a meeting. Someone had to know exactly what was really going on.

Two days later, Mickey left as planned for Jamaica. Catherine Graham was writing a biography of Camilla Parker-Bowles, which I had assisted with. Catherine suggested that I wrote a series of articles on Diana for her employers, the *Sun*. Never was a commission more welcome. I was haunted by the possibility that Mickey might die at forty-six, and having something to do straight away took my mind off the appalling images which flickered through it. As the days stretched into weeks, it was easy to put the issue on the back-burner and think, where there's life, there's hope.

Mickey returned from Jamaica at the end of January and promptly went into St Mary's Hospital for his first course of chemotherapy. It was difficult to get a measure of how worried or hopeful one should be, and I was keen to waylay a doctor to get a more accurate prognosis. There was never a doctor around when I was, however, so I had to judge by the dramatic improvement the chemotherapy wrought. Within days, Mickey looked so much more like his old self, and had so much more energy, that I dared to hope that he would be as lucky as Auntie and Peter had been.

The second time Mickey was in hospital for his chemotherapy, I made sure that I arranged for one of his doctors to see me. 'I know from my brother-in-law, who is also a doctor, that you doctors don't like giving firm prognoses or making estimates with time,' I said. 'But the rest of our family is relying on me to keep them informed about what is really going on with my brother. What I need to know is, is he dying and if so, how much time does he have?'

'The prognosis for a cure is not good,' the doctor said. 'But I'd be very surprised if he doesn't last at least another two years.'

Two years, that was good. Anything could happen in two years. Medical science was making such strides that what was not curable today might be in six months, or eighteen. I was even more encouraged when Mickey was released from the hospital and returned to his old routine of working till eight o'clock every evening. On two occasions I deliberately dropped into his office unexpectedly so that I could judge his progress. He was back to being the old, energetic Mickey.

The Sunday before he was due to return to St Mary's for his third course of chemotherapy, Mickey spent the afternoon with me after church. I can still see him, sitting on the sofa beneath the window overlooking the garden on Ebury

Street. He looked so healthy, so vibrant, that, for the first time since Christmas, I thought, he's going to make it.

Two days later he phoned me. 'Don't bother coming to take me to the hospital. The oncologist says he wants to see me in his office.'

Bad sign, I thought.

Bad sign indeed. 'The chemotherapy isn't working as well as it ought to,' Mickey said on the telephone when he got home. 'It's not containing the growth effectively. It shrinks after each course, but then begins to grow rapidly after the drugs wear off. They're switching me to radiotherapy.'

It was at the moment that I knew that my brother was going to die, and that it would be sooner rather than later. Radiotherapy was just a palliative, something to ease his last few weeks or months.

'I have to go to the Hammersmith five days a week for six weeks, once they fit my face mask. The laser is so specific and the rays so strong they have to mark your mask and strap you down to the machine.'

Mickey expected to be able to drive himself to the hospital, but his condition deteriorated so rapidly during the week before his first fitting that I took over. The lassitude from which he had been suffering prior to the infusion of steroids which are a part of the chemotherapy cocktail returned in force. Worse, the weight just dropped off him. I encouraged him to eat; I even cooked a variety of meals he liked and took them up to his flat to freeze. The cancer, however, was now growing at such a rate that it was uncomfortable for him to eat and, of course, the less he ate, the less he felt able to, and the more lethargic he become.

'You'll die of starvation if you don't watch out,' I said.

He opened his mouth to show me an upper back molar on the right side of his mouth dangling from a ball which was about the size of a dime.

'Um,' was all I could say.

'If you stop to consider that that's the tip of the iceberg, and that the rest is also expanding in my sinuses, you can imagine how I feel.'

'Does it hurt?'

'No, it's more of a pressure than a pain.'

'Then you'll have just have to liquidise your food, Mickey. You must have nourishment.'

A few days later I took Mickey for a fitting and he discussed the problem with the doctors, who put him on liquid food. When we got back to his flat, I looked in his mouth again and nearly passed out from terror. In five days, the visible part of the growth had increased from the size of a dime to that of a quarter.

It made me frantic with worry. Everything I saw told me that Mickey was dying right before my eyes. I was now so unsettled that I could not write. Nor did there seem much point in looking for a house. The last thing I needed to do was move at a time like this. I put my life on hold. The feedback I was getting from the family also discomfited me. Every time I spoke to my parents, Aunt Majorie or my sisters, I could almost hear them thinking, 'Georgie's being alarmist. We saw Mickey at Christmas, and he wasn't anywhere near as bad as she's making out.' Tut, tut, tut.

A month after the chemotherapy had been aborted, I took Mickey to the Hammersmith Hospital for the final fitting of his face mask and a meeting with the oncologist. I made up my mind that I was going to speak to him on my own, by hook or by crook. When Mickey was called away, I bolted to the nurse and told her that I had to speak to the specialist before my brother returned. She responded to the urgency in my voice. 'Of course,' she said gently.

What a pleasure it is to be with people who have some humanity, I thought. I was so used, in public life, to being regarded as an inanimate object. The kindness of the nurses and the doctors was a spiritually enhancing aspect of the whole nightmare.

The nurse ushered me into the professor's consulting room. 'I'll be brief,' I said, once we had greeted each other. 'I know you're very busy, and I want to be out of here before my brother returns. I need the truth, not only to deal with what's happening realistically, but also to inform my family, who are depending on me to provide them with accurate information.'

The professor, who was devastatingly handsome, looked at me and said in a tone that conveyed both compassion and agreement, 'What would you like to know?'

I wanted to ask, 'Is he dying, and if so, how quickly?' This time, however, the words, would not come out, and had I tried to force them, I would have broken down. Knowing that doctors do not like tears, I said instead, 'It doesn't look good, does it?' and smiled to conceal the tears that welled up anyway.

'No, it doesn't,' he said, returning my smile with an understanding look. 'Michael's cancer has turned out to be far more virulent than we expected. If he's lucky, he could last two or three months, but he could go within a matter of days if anything happens.'

I was so devastated by this news that I did not think to ask what 'anything' might be. In fact, I couldn't think at all. Before I knew it Mickey was back, and the three of us were having a chat about politics.

It is astonishing how people in extraordinary situations hang on to the ordinary fabric of life. This was the first time I had seen this phenomenon at first hand. As Mickey's life ebbed away, I noticed how we all continually overlaid the awfulness of what was happening with mundane conversations and pleasures. Mickey's friends invariably took their cue from him and the family, and when Mickey was around, the atmosphere was often so jolly that we might all have been at a cocktail party. When he was not there, however, the masks fell away and the grief was painfully visible.

In Jamaica, Mickey had formulated the plan that Sharman and Margaret would come over in June and the four of us would tour Scotland by car, staying in bed-and-breakfasts. A sort of 'us four' tour to celebrate his recovery – or to celebrate what was left of our relationship if he did not make it. It was now mid-April.

When I had dropped Mickey off, I telephoned both my sisters. 'You have to come right now – you can't wait till

June,' I said, and told them what the oncologist had said.

They both came over as soon as they could, at the beginning of May. Margaret was only able to stay for two weeks because of work commitments. During that fortnight, the three of us laughed or comforted or understood in Mickey's presence and cried when he was out of sight. Like our father, he had never been one for displays of emotion, so we respected his wishes and covered up madly.

Mickey, as I have said, was a born-again Christian, and he was firmly convinced that God was going to cure him. We all hoped against hope that he was right. Nevertheless he had an estate of some significance, and he knew he would have to make arrangements for its disposal if God deemed otherwise. He had always said that he would leave his collection of Jamaican art to the National Gallery, whose curator was his best friend and schoolmate, David Boxer. I was therefore pleased when he asked me one day on the way back from the Hammersmith if I wanted his pictures. 'Yes,' I said. 'But you plan to include Sharman and Margaret as well, don't you?'

'Of course I do,' he replied. 'If the radiotherapy doesn't work, the three of you can choose what you want among yourselves.'

The next hurdle to overcome was what Mickey planned to do with the bulk of his worth. He owned real estate and other holdings of some value, and the family's fear was that he would do in death what he had done in life. For years, he had been giving away 90 per cent of his income to a few worthy Christians and a string of no-good leeches who had the lingo off pat and pressed his buttons with glib talk about callings from God. 'If the needy ask, they must be given,' was Mickey's motto, and while we in the family felt that it was one thing to be a Christian, and quite another to allow yourself to be exploited the way Mickey did, we had never been able to reason with him.

Fortunately, family feeling asserted itself. Mickey spoke about his wishes to each of us separately, and made a will leaving everything, bar a few outside bequests to true friends, to his three sisters, his maternal aunt and his mother.

So far, the radiotherapy seemed to be keeping the cancer at bay. Although by no means well, he was holding his own. While there was no hope of a recovery, we all began to wonder if he might not last longer than anticipated. This was a reassuring thought, especially as Daddy could not come over to see him. He was suffering from advanced Parkinson's disease, and could not travel. Mummy was afraid to leave him alone with only his nurses for company, for he was so distressed at the prospect of losing Mickey that he was now saying, 'I don't want to live without my son.'

Our world seemed to have turned upside down. Who would have thought, only a few short years before, that our robust father would now be a bedridden shambles, or that Mickey would be dying in his prime? 'Health really is the most important thing in life,' Mickey observed to me one afternoon as he was shuffling down the corridor on the way from the car park to the radiotherapy department at Hammersmith Hospital. 'God is teaching me compassion. You know, I never used to have any sympathy for people when they were ill. Because I was always so healthy and energetic, I despised sickness as a weakness of character. I'm certainly learning my lesson,' he said, without bitterness.

By now, life had assumed a recognisable pattern. Four afternoons a week, I took Mickey for his radiotherapy, after which I took him home and sat with Sharman and Margaret. Often, he was so drained by the palaver of waiting for his treatment that he would rest while we talked. Friday was Nanny's day off, so I would stay at home with the children while Richard Adeney took Mickey to the hospital. Later on, I might take the boys to visit him, but only if he were in a good mood, for he had very Victorian attitudes about children and believed that they should be seen and not heard.

When the day came for Margaret to leave, she was in a terrible state, knowing that she might never see Mickey again. He was his normal, stoical self. One could only guess at what was going on beneath the surface. Aunt Marjorie and her husband, Stanley Panton, now arrived from Grand Cayman. Auntie was a second mother to the four of us, but she had always adored Mickey most of all. 'I don't know how I'm going to survive his death,' she said, voicing the worry of everyone in the family. Her own cancer had only recently gone into remission, and we all knew what stress could do. (Fortunately, it has remained in remission.)

Mickey still couldn't eat. Although the growth was shrinking with the radiotherapy, the inside of his mouth was now burned from the rays, as if someone had applied a hot iron to it. His hair had fallen out from the chemotherapy, and now he was losing the beard on the right side of his face and the few wisps of hair that remained at the back of his head, the follicles destroyed by the radiation. 'I look like Daddy,' he had joked with Sharman, Margaret and me, but to Auntie his condition was no laughing matter. She took one look at him and began praying for him to die quickly. 'I can't stand to see my son suffer,' she said. 'If he's going to die, he may as well go sooner and be spared more suffering.'

Sharman now returned to her family, arranging to return before Auntie's departure, and her leaving, too, was extremely distressing.

From Mickey's point of view, it was the indignity of illness that was bothersome. We had all been brought up from the cradle to be dignified, and he loathed shuffling around like an old man, and cared intensely about the loss of his looks, his health and his vigour.

Suddenly, he took a turn for the worse. First he developed searing pains in his neck and shoulder, which indicated that the cancer was spreading to his spine, and possibly his brain. He was put on liquid morphine, which created such an aura of wellbeing that he put on some Mozart for the first time in months. Then he developed blood poisoning from something to do with the radiotherapy and death became an imminent possibility. I shall never forget the way he looked around him as he was walking downstairs to the ambulance. Auntie noticed it, too. 'He's looking around in case he never comes back,' she said. 'Oh, how I hope God takes him quickly.'

For a few days things were touch and go, but the doctors and nurses at St Mary's stabilised him. This gave us an opportunity to see the National Health Service at its finest. They were fantastic, everything doctors and nurses should be: dedicated, humane, compassionate. They were also extraordinarily jolly, full of life's best qualities in the midst of so much pain and suffering. I remembered the Duchess of Norfolk once saying to me of her work for Help the Hospices, 'I was surprised to see how much joy there can be when people are dying.' Now I could see exactly what she had meant.

Having Mickey in hospital made life easier for family and friends alike. Auntie and I did not have to worry that something might happen with which we could not cope medically. His friends continued to drop in at all hours of the day and night, but when he grew too tired it was easier to propel them homewards from the hospital than it was from his flat.

One afternoon Auntie and I were sitting with Mickey, chatting, when his oncologist arrived with a team of other doctors. 'I've been feeling lumps in my side,' Mickey told him.

'I'm afraid the cancer is spreading,' the professor said.

'I thought as much,' said Mickey, without a shade of a tremor.

'As you know, we've more or less contained the growth in your mouth and sinuses. We can send you for radiotherapy to the Hammersmith for the metastases in your gut.'

'What's the point? I have no quality of life. I'll have the inconvenience of being taken there by ambulance, of having to wait in some godforsaken corridor till my turn comes, of returning here hours later, for it all to be repeated the following day. You can't cure it, can you?'

'I'm afraid not.'

'I'm not afraid of where I'm going. If it's inevitable, let's stop treatment,' Mickey declared.

Auntie and I shot one another a look. The crunch time had come. When the professor and the other doctors left,

Mickey said, 'There are details we must speak about.'

Auntie and I promptly burst into tears.

'I'm sorry,' I said. It was the first time I had broken down in front of him.

'It's OK,' he replied, as Auntie struggled to contain herself.

'I need to tell you what to do when I'm gone,' he said. Then he broke down himself for the first and only time.

Auntie and I sprang across to the bed, where we stood over him and held him while he cried.

As suddenly as he had started, he stopped. We sat down and he said, 'I want you to cremate the body. The burial should be at home. Mummy can choose the spot.'

Fighting back the tears, I asked, 'Do you have any favourite hymns you'd like?'

'I leave that up to you.' He turned to Auntie. 'When you've gone I'll speak to Georgie about business matters. As my executor, she'll have the thankless task of winding up the estate, and I suppose selling the flat and disposing of its contents.'

Sharman flew back a few days later. She, Auntie and I sat around Mickey's bed, reminiscing about old times. Whatever each of us had to say to Mickey, and vice versa, we said then. Poignant as those conversations were, they also contained a great deal of joy, and some comical moments, too.

I was not seeing nearly enough of the children. Although I took them and the dogs to the park every morning, I left home for the hospital as soon as they had had their lunch and seldom returned before their supper time. My social life no longer existed, though from my social column in *Boardroom* magazine it would have appeared otherwise. By June, I felt the need for a change of scenery, so when I received an invitation from Ivana Trump to attend her party at the Mayfair Hotel to celebrate the television movie of her autobiographical novel, I jumped at the chance to attend a joyous instead of a sad occasion. And I must admit that I had a wonderful time.

For the same reason, I accepted an invitation from Sally Jesse Raphael to appear on her television programme. During the two days I spent in New York O.J. Simpson's wife was murdered, and I watched events unfold on television, as transfixed as any American. It did me a world of good: a change can truly be as good as a rest.

Auntie and Uncle Stanley had to return to the United States for her check-ups, and that was another heart-rending goodbye. Although no one knew exactly how much longer Mickey had, it was apparent that the end was near. The hospital was happy to keep him, but he wanted to go home to die. So, in the middle of July, an ambulance took him back to Elgin Mansions.

What was especially upsetting was the fact that although Mickey was dying with confidence, it was without cheer. Despite being a committed Christian, he was angry with God. 'I feel he's cheating me out of the last thirty years of my life. He promised me he'd cure me,' he said, referring to 'visions' from other born-again Christians who had doubtless only been trying to keep up his spirits.

By Friday 22 July, it was apparent that death was imminent. The cancer had spread into Mickey's throat and consumed his voice box, and he could no longer swallow or speak. Trying to console him, I said, 'I know you don't want to die, but look at it this way. If each of us has a purpose on this earth, and you've fulfilled yours, God is giving you a compliment by saying you've finished your work early. I know it's a backhanded compliment, because you don't want it, but it is a compliment nevertheless.'

He looked at me and blinked, his huge pale green eyes trying to say something.

'Everyone you love is going to be with you thirty or so years from now. If life is truly eternal, thirty years isn't very long to wait. It will most likely seem like the blink of an eye to you. And in the meantime, you'll have Grandma and Grandpa and a host of other friends and relations for company.'

He smiled. He was now on a morphine drip and free of

pain. Was he humouring me, or did he agree with what I was saying? I hoped it was the latter.

By the next morning he was semi-comatose. 'Mickey, I have a few messages for you to take for me. When you see Grandma, tell her I'm fine. Say hi to Grandpa and to Dickie Ziadie. Give Granny Ziadie my love as well, and tell Grandpa Ziadie I'm looking forward to meeting him one day. Gosh, just think: soon you'll be meeting Beethoven and Mozart and Tchaikovsky and Schumann and Schubert. You sure are going to have one heck of time.' I kissed him on the forehead and smiled. He gave me a flicker. Did he understand? Was he going anywhere, except into his coffin? Suppose this existence was all there was? You lived, you died, finito. Suppose faith in the afterlife was nothing but a panacea against the terror of nothingness?

For the first time since my teenage years I found myself grappling to hang on to my faith. What rattled me was the reluctance with which Mickey and his Bible-bashing cronies were facing his death. Sharman had observed the week before, while two of Mickey's ministers were praying for God to come and rescue His servant from death, 'How is it that these born-again Christians profess to love the Lord so much, and preach endlessly about wanting to go to His bosom, yet when one of them is actually in danger of doing so, the one thing they want is to keep him on this earth? Doesn't that strike you as inconsistent?' It certainly did. There was little I could actually do to force myself to have faith. Time, and mulling over what needed to be examined, would either restore it or destroy it.

By Sunday, Mickey was completely comatose. He spent the whole day thrashing, thrashing, thrashing. The nurse, who was fantastic, said, 'People are often restless before they die.' At 8.55 p.m. that evening, 24 July 1994, he gave up the fight.

Hard as it was for my sisters and myself, for our parents the death of their only son was a catastrophe. Mummy has still not got over it, and Daddy, who was disconsolate, kept on saying, 'It's my turn next.' The one positive thing to come out of all that pain was that each of us started to appreciate the others even more than we had before. We now understood how finite one's time on earth is, and by the time Daddy died on 7 December, no one had left anything unsaid or undone that needed saying or doing.

This was especially poignant where Daddy and I were concerned. He had been making an effort for years to show that he was as satisfied with me as he was with his other three children, but now he was intent on leaving no room for doubt. He explained that any mistakes that had been made had been honest ones, intended to spare me pain, not to inflict it, and started telling me that he loved me. It was such a comfort, not only to know before he died, that my father really had loved me, but to hear him say it.

The last time I saw my father was when I was leaving Jamaica after Mickey's funeral. 'I'll bring the children to see you in February,' I said.

'Please,' he said.

'What did you say?' I asked. It was difficult to understand him as the Parkinson's made his speech slurred.

'Please,' he repeated clearly, a smile lighting up his face.

Had I been asked to choose the last words in a relationship that had been so troubled for so many years, I could not have come up with anything better.

16

My faith in God was restored through unhurried reflection followed by a bizarre incident that could have come straight out of a bad novel or a movie, but which was nevertheless instrumental in reinforcing many of my basic beliefs about good and evil. I have always been a great exponent of the 'Lord helps those who help themselves', and that God gives us the means to fight evil with good, destruction with construction. What I was about to face would show me how very right I was. Contrary as that view was to my brother's brand of Christianity, once I began practising in earnest its usefulness cleared up many of the doubts Mickey's death had triggered off.

The first inkling I had that something was afoot came when I returned to England in August 1994, looking forward to picking up the pieces of my daily life. The nanny had been quite happy when I left, and I had asked Rosebud, a black West Indian who had befriended me a few years before, to look out for her and the children while I was away. Jesús Mora, Kari Lai and my cousin Enrique Ziadie, who had recently returned from the United States to live in London, were also keeping an eye on things.

Now the nanny was in a state of surly rebellion. No

matter what I asked her to do, she had some smart-alecy riposte. I ignored her behaviour for a few weeks, thinking that she needed a period of adjustment now that the boss had returned, in both spirit and body. I was only too aware that she had been 'manning the fort' while Mickey had been so ill, and doubtless this had suited her better than playing second fiddle to me, for she was a dominant personality. I certainly wasn't about to engage in a power struggle with any employee.

Soon I noticed that the nanny had taken to speaking to the children in an unnecessarily harsh manner, and that she was constantly on their backs, controlling the life out of them. 'They need to explore,' I said to her. 'They're only a year and a half. This whole world is a fascinating new adventure for them. Let them touch and feel, as long as they're not breaking things or endangering themselves.'

'You mus' wan' me to spoil them,' she snapped, her lower lip jutting out.

'Just do as I ask.'

'Who you think you is?'

'I know who I am. I also know who you are. They are my children, and they will be brought up according to my precepts, not yours.'

'If you don't like the way I take care of them, I can leave.'

'That's fine by me. I'd sooner you went than stayed and ruined them.'

For a while things improved. Then, early in October, my mother telephoned to say, 'Your father's been taken to Medical Associates. He's in intensive care. The doctors don't expect him to live, but he's not dying just yet.'

There had been previous false alarms over the years. 'Please keep me posted and give me enough notice so I can come and say goodbye to him,' I told Mummy.

That same day, Eugenie and I spoke about formalising Misha's adoption. I made no attempt to keep my voice down – I had nothing to hide, so it never entered my head that the nanny might overhear anything I was saying, let alone that it would matter if she did. Within days of those two telephone conversations, the nanny was back to her defiant self. Finally, I said to her, 'This is ludicrous. I'm not paying you to be rude to me. You will either do as you're asked, without further lip, or I'll be putting you back on a plane to the West Indies as soon as the crisis with my father is over. I've had quite enough of your nonsense.'

That initiated a round of abuse the like of which I had not heard since I'd lived in Jamaica. 'I hate you. You white people are all the same. Black is beautiful and white is corrupting,' she said. She repeated this like a mantra, day in, day out, for the next month.

Rosebud's behaviour also seemed odd, but I did not connect that with what was happening to the nanny – only a paranoiac could have suspected what was really going on behind the scenes. Rosebud had stoked up the nanny's latent prejudice against 'white oppressors'. This was easy enough to do, for Rosebud was a highly intelligent woman, while the nanny was an uneducated country woman. All Rosebud needed to do was to play upon the nanny's prejudices and hopes, attitudes with which Rosebud was only too familiar, since her own background was only one cut above the nanny's. Rosebud promised the nanny a job in America when she, Rosebud, moved there, which she has never done. This was a masterly touch, for every West Indian of no education or sophistication knows with the certainty of scientific fact that the streets of America are paved with gold, and that a lot of it will rub off on the soles of their feet as soon as they land at JFK Airport.

Blissfully ignorant of the intrigue taking place behind my back, I turned my attention to doing up the house in the country. the nanny's behaviour became so intolerable that I contacted the Spanish Convent in Kensington and got them to send me an au pair, whom I hired from Sunday 27 November. 'You will be going back to the West Indies on Sunday 27 November,' I informed the nanny, taking care not to tell her that I had replaced her. 'I have never been so disappointed in any employee in my life. I have always managed to have good relations with anyone who worked for me.'

Her response was to walk out on Friday 18 November. I would subsequently learn that she went straight to Rosebud's studio flat, where she remained until Rosebud made the mistake of taking the nanny to the cinema with friends she had met through me. Of course, they spilled the beans as soon as they discovered the full extent of her double dealing.

All this, however, lay in the future, and I was completely in the dark about Rosebud's relationship with the nanny. Stunned by the nanny's behaviour, I expressed my outrage to Rosebud, who made a point of inviting herself to dinner even as she was harbouring the nanny.

'If you're worried about who'll take care of the boys if you have to go to Jamaica, I will,' she said.

'Thanks,' I replied, so annoyed with the situation that I did not tell her that I had already employed someone else. 'That's very thoughtful of you.'

As I would subsequently learn from Rosebud, her plan was to seize my children once I was out of the country, and, by orchestrating a campaign to have the children taken away from me, to keep Dima, with whom she had fallen in love as soon as she saw him, for herself, and to give Misha to her childless sister. This seems extraordinary but bizarre things do tend to happen to me.

The first warning I had that whatever was going on was serious, came on Tuesday 6 December when I received a letter from Westminster Social Services stating that they had received a complaint relating to the children, and that they were therefore coming to see me the next day. I contacted my solicitor immediately. 'This is preposterous,' I told him. 'Someone is again using the children to pressurise me, doubtless into dropping one of my lawsuits. The question is, which case is it?'

It was not the first time something like this had happened. The year before, someone connected with the *Sunday Express* lawsuit had asked a neighbour who was a local councillor on Westminster City Council to express doubts to the social services about my ability to parent children on the dubious grounds that I had no qualifications in parenting skills. Westminster Social Services had not taken the complaint seriously, accepting the word of the health visitor that the children were well cared for and that I was a good and loving mother.

Four times that day I telephoned to speak to the social services. Important people seldom fail to return calls, but minor bureaucrats, it seems, lack either the will or the courtesy to do so.

The following morning, my mother phoned to say that Daddy had died. This was unexpected, as he had been making such a good recovery that he had been out of intensive care for over a week, and there had even been talk of sending him home. Alas, he had suddenly taken a turn for the worse two days before.

I telephoned to cancel the council's visit. 'My father died this morning.'

'How unfortunate,' the girl said. 'We can reschedule for next week. I'll write and give you a date.'

'That will not be possible. I shall be away.'

'We have a statutory right to see you to discuss the children,' she said.

'There's no way that anyone has a valid complaint about my children and I'll be at my father's funeral in Jamaica. I don't suppose you have a statutory right to follow me there, do you?'

'No. That we don't,' she said.

'Good, because it is my and my solicitor's belief that you are being used as an instrument of harassment in the same way as you were last year.'

'That is not so. That I can confirm,' she said.

'I don't see how you can confirm that, unless you know all the facts, which, obviously, you can't.'

'But I know the informant,' she said. 'There's no doubt in my mind that she's a sensible, fair-minded person and that she's speaking the truth.'

'Your ability to arrive at just decisions strikes me as severely impaired,' I said. 'You have just told someone you do not know, and have not had a conversation with for more than ninety seconds, that you had made up your mind about her before you had met or even spoken to her. My understanding of arriving at fair decisions is that one keeps an open mind until all the evidence is in. If you're as biased as you've just indicated, you can bet your bottom dollar I won't be letting you within a hundred yards of any child of mine.'

'We can force you to see us. I'll be in touch again after I've spoken to our lawyers,' she said.

'I have said all I intend to say to you, now or ever. If you wish to get in touch with me again, you may do so through my lawyers.' I gave her the details.

I took off for Jamaica a few days later to attend Daddy's funeral. So peeved was I with the way Rosebud had been behaving that I did not let her know Daddy had died or that I was leaving. My every instinct told me to distance myself from her, and I can only say I am deeply grateful that I listened to my inner voice. But for that, I would have found myself in an even bigger mess than I did, and one which was not so retrievable.

I returned from Jamaica the week before Christmas to discover that letters were passing back and forth between my lawyer and Westminster City Council's legal department. They refused to tell my lawyer what the complaints were or who had made them, showing a shocking disregard for my human rights and the very principles of the law they were seeking to hide behind. My lawyer asked them, 'How can anyone defend herself if she is not told what she is defending herself against?'

The Social Services continued to write to me directly despite having been requested not to by my lawyer and myself, and trying to make appointments in London when they knew I was in the country. My lawyer and I were surprised by the Council's tactics and attitude, which were unprofessional, discourteous, recalcitrant and intimidatory, to say the least.

I cannot say I was worried, for they didn't have one thing to pin on me. I was therefore rather surprised in January when my lawyer rang me in the country to say, 'They've applied to the family court for an assessment order. They are also disputing the adoptions. The informant claims you didn't adopt the children in Russia, but smuggled them out illegally after buying them. I told them I've never heard anything so ridiculous, but they're adamant.'

I was flabbergasted. Everything was above board, and by this time, Misha's adoption had been processed. The children were not even British, so the British courts had no jurisdiction over the adoptions, which were matters purely for the Russian and Jamaican authorities, both of which recognised them.

'There's nothing to worry about,' my lawyer said. 'As long as you don't allow Westminster Social Services across your threshold you'll be fine. We'll have to oppose the assessment order, for that grants them access, and if their behaviour so far is anything to go by, they'll twist, turn and fabricate nothing into something once they have you and the children in their clutches. I don't know what's going on, Georgie, but I can tell you, I don't like it one bit. Something is seriously amiss here, and my advice to you is to speak to no one about this, no one at all. I wouldn't believe the people I've been dealing with if they told me the time of day, but one thing I am sure of, and that is that they're telling the truth when they say that a friend of yours is behind this.'

But which 'friend'?

'Did you ever see *Gaslight*, that movie with Ingrid Bergman, where her husband tries to send her mad by psychological warfare?' he asked. 'This reminds me of it. Someone who knows you well is playing the most monstrous game. They're not only trying to destroy you in the eyes of Westminster Social Services, they're also trying to destroy you psychologically.'

I battened down the hatches. The only friends who then knew anything at all about what was going on were Jesús Mora, Anna, Lady Brocklebank, Patricia Harris and

Geraldine de Sancha. Jesús provided moral support, while the three ladies supported me not only morally but practically, by swearing affidavits. Anna and Patricia provided a comprehensive picture of me as a mother and of how happy and well cared for the children were. Geraldine also attested to how one of the parties to one of my lawsuits had once before asked her to lie about me to the social services before we had even met.

My lawyer is not a specialist in child law, so he turned the case over to Charles Buss, a capable, intelligent, charming and decent lawyer in his firm. From the word go Charles handled the matter, and me, with expertise. By this time I was frantic with anxiety lest anyone make a mistake and aid the opposition's case. Shortly before Christmas, Rosebud rang to arrange an exchange of presents. Isabel, the au pair, answered the telephone.

'You have a new nanny,' Rosebud said to me accusingly.

'Yes, of course.'

'I hope she has good references and you aren't jeopardising the boys' safety.'

'Thanks for your concern.' Her desire to control really had been overstepping the boundaries of acceptable behaviour lately. 'I will remind you I'm not some little airhead and you are not my husband.'

'How's your father?' she asked.

'He died.'

'So when's the funeral?'

'It's come and gone. I just got back from Jamaica last week.

'You went to Jamaica without telling me?' she said, so angrily that my ears pricked up. 'I had plans for you, I mean for them, when you were in Jamaica. Why did you do that?'

'You haven't been yourself lately, and I felt it would have been inappropriate to contact you,' I said enigmatically. Although I couldn't put my finger on it, there was something going on with her that was making me very uncomfortable. I resolved to see as little of her as possible until she had sorted herself out. And indeed, from then until my lawyer received notice that Westminster had initiated court proceedings, I saw virtually nothing of Rosebud and spoke to her only when she telephoned me. We did exchange presents, and she did grill me about when Isabel, the new nanny, was leaving for Spain and when she would be returning. I gave her the date of Isabel's departure, though not of her return, and this was what trapped Rosebud and led to her unmasking as the culprit.

Rosebud's attempt to gain custody of my children had required careful planning, and she is nothing if not a shrewd calculator. Before the old nanny walked out, Rosebud had come round, tipped off by the nanny, when I was away from home, messed up the flat and taken photographs of her handiwork. She had sent the photographs to Westminster City Council as proof that the children were living in 'squalid conditions'. But providence worked in my ultimate favour by presenting her with a second opportunity to take misleading photographs of the flat. She had offered to babysit on 22 November while I went to a funeral. This time, however, there was no nanny there for me to blame when I returned home and saw that things had moved, including some papers on top of my desk. 'I don't understand how you could have allowed the children to climb all over the place and play on top of my desk and in the drawers,' I said, irritated. If I had known what she had really been doing at the desk – rifling through my papers and photocopying material such as Dima's Jamaican travel document and any-thing else relating to the boys she thought might be useful for a future date – she might not have emerged alive.

Mistakenly believing that her tainted evidence was enough to hang me, Rosebud then wrote a letter, dated 22 November, to Westminster City Council, in which she stated that she was a good friend with intimate knowledge of me and the household I ran. She claimed that the children were dressed in rags and lived in squalor. She said that I had an excellent nanny who was about to leave, and that once she did the children's health and welfare would be in jeopardy, since I knew nothing about caring for myself, a house or children. She claimed I loved my dogs more than the children, and that I allowed the dogs to bite the children, whom I would then reprimand for having annoyed the dogs. She alleged that as a result the children were covered in deep bite marks. There were other allegations of a more puerile nature, all calculated to shore up her request that Westminster City Council embark upon an urgent investigation of me.

Rosebud had previously got Westminster City Council to take the freeholder of her flat to court. She had told me then that she had a friend in their legal department who would 'do anything' for her. As matters developed, I had cause to remember that remark though I am casting no stones at anyone there. Rosebud turned out to be so manipulative and calculating that she could easily have convinced someone that they were embarked upon the Christian equivalent of a *jihad*, when all the while she had them sacking a lone mother's family.

Prior to the first court hearing, which was held at the Marylebone Family Court on 11 February 1995, Westminster had to give us discovery of the documents they were relying upon to make their case. They handed over Rosebud's letter, in which she had used the agreed alias of 'Mrs Forbes', and the photographs she had taken in my flat. When I finally got sight of the letter, what struck me most was how much this woman hated me. Not only did she want to strip me of my children, she was also asking them to take away my dogs! That aside, I still had no idea who the informant was. As Charles Buss said, 'It's easy to find out the identity of someone who is speaking the truth. You recognise what they're saying and you place them accordingly. But it's virtually impossible to discover who's behind a series of fantasies, for none of what they describe happened, and so you can't match up scenario with identity.'

Meanwhile, Charles was trying to get the lawyers for Westminster to see that they had nothing to lose by divulging the identity of the informant, which was known to them. 'If it turns out that she's speaking the truth, she has nothing to fear,' he reasoned. 'And if she's not been telling the truth, you should *want* to unmask her, for she's not only been saying the most diabolical things about an innocent woman, but she's wasted your time and public funds. In those circumstances, surely you would not want to protect someone who has made a fool of you?'

Sound though Charles's rationale was, Westminster did indeed want to protect Rosebud, for reasons we did not then understand. We had no way of knowing that Rosebud and her friend at the council had fired up everyone else at Westminster to believe that orange was pink. It was the social worker who inadvertently led me to Rosebud. In her statement, she revealed the complaints made by the phoney Mrs Forbes and one pertinent fact: the date I had given Rosebud for Isabel's departure at Christmas.

Although I had another culprit in mind, as soon as I saw that detail, I strongly suspected Rosebud. To confirm my suspicions, I needed to get her to show her hand. On 2 February, the court had appointed a guardian ad litem, a social worker who was supposed to act as a protector of the children's interests. She was also in touch with 'Mrs Forbes'. I telephoned Rosebud, as if nothing were wrong, and had a friendly conversation with her, telling her a few lies about our intended movements in the hope that these would get back to the guardian ad litem and she would ask me about them. The social worker, however, was too cautious to reveal specifics.

Meanwhile, even though Rosebud's plan to get hold of the children had failed, she kept in touch with Westminster Social services, keeping the fires burning with further untruths about me and the children. Whether her objective was to try a new formula now that I had wrecked her old one, or whether it was merely the malicious actions of someone who had been thwarted, I shall never know. But the social worker accepted these complaints as gospel, even when she knew that I was down in the country, so Rosebud could not possibly have seen me and the children in town. By now, of course, the court case was semi-public knowledge, but I did not discuss it in detail with Rosebud and she had no idea that I suspected her. I was careful, on the rare occasions we were in contact, to remain as cordial as possible. It was the only way of smoking her out. Pleased that we seemed to be back on good terms, she tried to exploit the situation. On 13 February, the day of the first hearing, she telephoned. 'Can I drop in tomorrow for two minutes? I want to drop off the boys' belts. I won't keep you long.'

'You don't have to limit yourself to two minutes,' I said pleasantly. 'After all, we're friends and we haven't been seeing enough of each other for the last few months.'

That evening I telephoned the other person I suspected of being the informant. This was the social-climbing opportunist who had misrepresented my mission in Russia to Nigel Dempster.

'Oh, Georgie, darling girl, I'm so glad you've phoned. I'm thrilled that you've finally forgiven me. You have forgiven me, haven't you?'

'That depends,' I said.

'What can I do? I'll do anything, anything at all. You tell me and I'll walk over hot coals for you.' I hoped the friend who was listening in on the extension as a witness wouldn't laugh out loud.

'I only phoned to tell you that I might consider dropping my action against Nigel Dempster if you sign the affidavit stating that neither you nor any friend of yours has been in touch with the social services about me and my children.'

'Anything, anything, anything, Georgie dear. As long as you don't flash it around London and forgive me and we can be friends again.'

Clearly she wasn't the mysterious Mrs Forbes. 'That, I fear, is an impossibility. Nothing will ever induce me to be friends with you again.'

The following morning, Rosebud arrived just as I was dressing to go to Sandown Park races, where I was due to present a trophy to the winner of the Libel and Slander Stakes. Before she even had time to catch her breath, I said,

'You know, some people have told me in all seriousness that they believe you're the informant.'

'Me? I'm your good friend. I've always tried to protect you.' Against what I wondered. 'Only a monster could betray a friend like that.' She went on and on about how hurt she was that I might even begin to suspect her, fulminating so convincingly that I began to doubt my instincts. But the following morning, she made her big mistake. At the crack of dawn, she telephoned me. 'Don't say a word over the phone. Come and see me later. At my flat. I've got news for you.'

As soon as I arrived the affair took an even more ridiculous turn. Rosebud launched into a long diatribe about how she had been protecting me from the powers that be, whom I had offended by writing *Diana in Private* and *The Royal Marriages*. She tried to get me to believe that she knew through her contacts at the palace that MI5 was behind the plot to deprive me of the children. 'Your phone is bugged, you know. You've made a lot of powerful enemies,' she said. 'But I've asked friends from my days at the palace to intercede on your behalf.'

'Really, Rosebud,' I said. 'If you think MI5 would invent such a plot you're living on Mars.'

'It's true,' she said. 'Wait. I'll show you some documents they passed to me.' With that, she went and fetched the papers from my desk she had photocopied herself when she was babysitting on 22 November. As well as Dima's Jamaican travel document, there were copies of letters of instruction which Judy Ann MacMillan and I had written to the nanny before she left the West Indies to make her first plane journey easy for her.

As soon as I saw those letters, I knew that the nanny and Rosebud had been in cahoots and that Rosebud was, beyond all shadow of a doubt, the informant. 'If Immigration gets hold of these documents, they'll prosecute you for bringing the nanny into the country illegally,' she said. 'I've asked my friends to block the prosecution.'

'The nanny wasn't in this country illegally, Rosebud,' I

said patiently. Now intent on getting as much information out of her as I could, I was careful not to betray my new-found knowledge of her complicity.

'I thought she was?'

'If so, it's news to me. As a Jamaican citizen, I'm allowed to have Jamaican domestic servants here.'

'She was a nanny, not a domestic servant,' she said bristling.

'The papers I filled out for her at the British high commission categorised her as a domestic servant. If you have an objection, take it up with them, not me,' I replied silkily, pleased that I was dancing on a sore spot. 'But I don't see what all of this has to do with the children.'

'Do you remember the photographs?' she asked.

'I most certainly do,' I said, delighted that she was bringing up a subject I had never mentioned to her. That meant only one thing: she had supplied them.

'You think they were all taken at the same time, but they weren't. You go back and look at them, and you'll see that some were taken in the daytime and others at night.'

This was interesting. I had mentioned this supposition to the guardian ad litem. I played Rosebud along a little longer, then thanked her for all the helpful information she had given me. We kissed goodbye and I promptly telephoned my lawyer. 'Rosebud is the informant. She's familiar with the photographs and has information to which only the guardian ad litem is privy ,' I said, recounting the conversation.

'I'll give her a ring,' my lawyer said.

'You do that. Let her know her cover's blown.'

I still did not know what Rosebud's motive was. I presumed she was trying to protect herself against exposure as a source for *Diana in Private*. Although her information had been limited, and I had offered her anonymity, I had in my possession hours of tapes of her singing like a bird about Oliver Everett, Diana's first private secretary; Michael Colborne, Assistant private secretary to the Prince of Wales; Edward Adeane, Charles' private secretary; Diana; her mother, Frances Shand-Kydd; and Charles himself, for whom she had open contempt. She had signed the Official Secrets Act when she worked as a junior in one of the corridors of power and was in danger of prosecution, and possibly imprisonment, if her identity became known during the pursuit of my *Sunday Express* breach-of-contract action.

My lawyer now had a lengthy conversation with her, at the start of which he made it clear that I was going to sue her for libel. When she saw that denial was pointless, she tried to find a way out of the hole she'd dug for herself.

To say that I was stunned by Rosebud's conduct would not begin to describe the way I felt. I had genuinely believed us to be friends. Of course, I was aware that she had used me socially, to mix in a world to which she would otherwise not have had access, and to try to peddle a mini-series about Margaret Argyll's life. But Margaret had wanted it made, so I had not minded being of use. After all, if you don't want to help your friends who do you want to help?

I was reading the papers in the sitting room early that evening when Rosebud rang me. I could hardly believe that she had the temerity to contact me now that she was unmasked. 'Georgie, it's Rosebud,' she said. 'Don't hang up until you've heard what I have to say.'

'What possessed you to do it?' I asked.

'Why should you have everything?' she snapped.

'But I don't see what the purpose was.'

'You'd've seen it soon enough if you'd let me know you were going to Jamaica for your father's funeral,' she said.

Now I made the connection instantaneously. Had she seized the children while I was away, she would simply have retained them while Westminster City Council pursued their case against me.

I was staggered by Rosebud's cunning. Westminster City Council had an absolute right to determine with whom the children could stay throughout the duration of a legal battle to establish whether they should remain in my care, and because she was a family friend she could exploit what the

council would acknowledge as a valid and existing relationship with him. The process might have dragged on for so
long that they could have said to the courts, 'Even though it
emerges that Lady Colin Campbell was a good and concerned parent, the children have been out of her custody for
so long that we regard it in their best interests to remain
where they are. With Rosebud and her sister.' And the courts
would most likely have agreed.

Thank God I had not allowed the children to fall into her
clutches while I'd been away. I prepared a hole for Rosebud
to drop into. 'I'm afraid the connection eludes, me,' I said.
She wouldn't be able to resist the temptation of letting me
know how clever she'd been.

'No responsible person permits a mother under investigation to keep children that might be in danger. It would've
been my duty to keep them safely away from you. And once
we had them, how would you've got them back?'

'We?' I queried.

'Dima is the only one who interests me. My sister
could've kept Misha, for all I care.'

'Are you telling me you cooked this up with your sister?'

'She doesn't know anything about it.'

'So this wasn't about you protecting yourself in the
Sunday Express action?'

'No. I knew you'd never violate my confidentiality.'

'So you were prepared to disrupt the lives of two children
who have never done you any harm, and have already had
a difficult start to life, just so that you could get your hands
on Dima? Whatever made you think you'd get away with it?
Everyone knows the adoption policy in this country is to
match children with parents of the same race. They're white
and you're black.'

'If I had a baby with a white man it would be white,' she
said defensively.

'That's hardly the criterion. It is the colour of your skin,
the texture of your hair, the quality of your features.'

'What makes you think you're the only person in the
world with connections? It's never occurred to you that I

might have connections of my own,' she boasted.

'Ah. You have friends who are involved with this, do you?'

'You can't prove that.'

'No, I can't. But the mere fact that you didn't deny it shows me that you do. You know, Rosebud, whether you're aware of it or not, you must realise you are insane. Do you have any idea of the enormity of what you've tried to do? We were supposed to be friends. All I can say is, you are one of the most awful human beings it has been my displeasure to come across. Make sure you never get in touch with me again. If you try to, I'll get an injunction restraining you. And if you ever so much as go near my children again, I'll use the full force of the law to keep them well away from you. Do I make myself clear? Good. Goodbye.'

Although I had exposed Rosebud I still had to deal with the lawsuit she had instigated. The case against me was pretty pathetic. Rosebud's story was easily disprovable. Two separate GPs could attest to the fact that Dima and Misha were healthy and hearty. The children had no deep bite marks from the dogs; indeed, no scars at all. The 'huge, fierce hounds' she claimed were savaging the children through jealousy were springer spaniels: notoriously soppy and medium-sized at their biggest. Besides, Tum-Tum, Popsie Miranda and Maisie Carlotta were so affectionate that the only danger they posed to anyone was loving them to death.

Of course, in Rosebud's original plan, it would not have mattered whether her first allegations stood up or not, for their purpose was merely to instigate the investigation. A flat in the smartest part of town, with one of the most prestigious addresses in the United Kingdom, stuffed with antiques and works of art and featured in glossy magazines as the quintessence of elegance, could hardly be called squalid. Moreover, it was cleaned by a cleaning lady and there was a full-time nanny in residence described by Rosebud as 'excellent'. That being the case, in Rosebud's photographs, why were the children's clothes strewn all about their room? Why was the Nanny's room untidy? Why hadn't she put the plates in the dishwasher?

That hearing was adjourned after agreement from the legal representatives of the three sides: mine, the guardian ad litem's and Westminster Social Services'. They would drop the case if I would provide copies of the children's adoption certificates and confirmation that the Jamaican authorities recognised the adoptions, and allow Professor Donald Barlthrop, an eminent paediatrician, to examine Dima and Misha to confirm that they were in good health.

After discovering Rosebud's part in the plot and the degree of Westminster's complicity, I told the guardian ad litem that I intended at the end of the case to seek an inquiry into Westminster's conduct. I also said that if I did not get satisfaction in Britain, I would take the matter to the Court of Human Rights.

When her report, which was now extraneous to the proceedings because of the agreement reached by the lawyers, was complete, it was apparent to me that she was treading a fine line. She could find no fault with me, but that did not stop her from trying to protect the Westminster Social Services. Of course, she could hardly come clean and say that the whole thing had been a put-up job, although we had furnished her with sufficient evidence to that end. But even though she could find no evidence to support any of Rosebud's allegations, she failed to include much that was favourable to me in her report to the court. She even threw the other side a bone by commenting that she was concerned because I was angry with the behaviour of the other side – as if that were a fault. She seemed keen to protect Rosebud. Although she knew I was aware that Rosebud was the informant, in her report she stated that Rosebud denied it. This was absolutely crucial from Westminster's point of view, for if I went ahead with my libel suit against Rosebud, I would discover who had been co-operating with her at the council.

The Thursday before the next hearing, which was scheduled for Monday 27 February, the guardian ad litem came round for a visit. 'My lawyer wants more information about the adoptions,' she said, pulling out a long sheet of paper and listing a lengthy catalogue of documents I was meant to supply from Russia and Jamaica before the hearing.

Of course, it would have been impossible to have got these documents from abroad in what was effectively one day, all government departments being closed at weekends. It struck me as no more than a crude tactic either to present me to the court as unco-operative, or to prolong the case. It was contrary to what had been agreed between the lawyers.

Immediately, I jumped up from the sofa. 'I'm very sorry, but from here on in I'll have to tape this meeting,' I said.

'Why would you want to do that?'

'Because you have just furnished me with reason to believe that you have compromised your impartiality at my expense and in favour of Westminster.'

'My lawyer has a right to demand anything she wants,' she said churlishly.

'That she most singularly does not,' I said firmly, snapping on the tape-recorder. 'The three sets of legal representatives reached an agreement and *no one* will be deviating from it. Not me, not your lawyer, not Westminster Social Services' legal team, not you.'

'Why are you so upset about a simple little request?'

'Don't play the innocent with me. You know as well as I do that this is an attempt to drag this matter out or to sully my image before the court. Well, I won't be allowing it. You do not have a right of sight to any of the adoption documents, and if you people mess with me, I'll simply refuse to show you anything.'

'If you do that, I'll have to recommend to the court that they grant the assessment order.'

'You're not frightening me, so don't waste your breath. The court has no right to assess the validity of an adoption between two foreign powers, and if they try to usurp jurisdiction, they'll find themselves in the middle of a diplomatic row. My advice to you is, settle for what was agreed and stop trying to drag this out.'

The meeting, naturally enough, ended soon afterwards. The following afternoon I took the boys and Joyce, their nurse, to see Professor Donald Barlthrop at the Westminster & Chelsea Hospital on the Fulham Road. Not surprisingly, he found the children well cared for, well adjusted, and not only well loved by their mother, but loving towards her.

Once the report had been presented to all three sides, the court hearing was just a formality. The Westminster legal team had to explain to the court that there was no reason for pursuing their request for an assessment order, and ask for it to be withdrawn. My counsel then stood up and stated how distressing the matter had been for me, after which it was dismissed. *Gaslight* had drawn to a close – but not before Westminster's Social Services and the guardian ad litem sent their legal representatives over to say to Charles Buss. 'This is not the end. We intend to pursue the issue of the adoptions.'

'On what basis?' he asked.

'Because we want to,' they said.

I was not worried in the slightest. If you have a clear conscience, a good lawyer and an active mind allied to a quick tongue, intimidation will not budge you. But intimidation it was nonetheless. On three separate occasions Charles wrote to these lawyers requesting that they confirm whether or not they intended to pursue their threat. They simply did not bother to answer his letters.

For awhile, I was so incensed by the behaviour of the social workers and lawyers from the other sides that I toyed with the idea of reporting them to the Law society, the Lord Chancellor's department and Westminster City Council. However, I finally decided that I would spare myself the onerous task of dragging the matter out with inquiries and all the rest. On the theory that the pen is mightier than the sword, and in the knowledge that I was due to write this book, I decided that revealing what had happened would be an appropriate remedy.

As for Rosebud, I thought at first of teaching her a lesson by suing her for libel and wiping her out financially. Then I decided that I had better uses for the money it would cost me to pursue her. Instead, I blew the whistle on her to the people to whom I had introduced her. All the years of culti-vation she embarked upon, my friends and myself, has amounted to nought. Knowing that she is now freezing in social Siberia without a baby – especially *my* baby – to warm her hearth is all the revenge I need.

I will say this though. This episode above all has taught me that life really can be stranger than fiction. While I cer-tainly do not thank Rosebud for giving me a central role in a real-life version of a very bad B-grade movie, I am aware that many positive benefits flowed from the experience, not the lest of which was the restoration of my faith in God. And that is no small thing.

17

Victory is a comforting experience and, before life returned to normal, I had a few more wins to tuck under my belt.

Westminster Social Services were the first of my adversaries to collapse in the months to come. Shortly after their ignominious retreat, the *Daily Mirror* settled my libel action against them, instituted when I was writing *Diana in Private*. Because they had not sought to justify their behaviour, had conducted their defence civilly and were prepared to make a clean settlement, we allowed them moderate terms.

The next newspaper company to crumple did not get off so lightly. Associated Newspapers had defended the three libel actions I had brought against them as nastily, in my opinion, and vigorously in theirs, as it is possible to do, in the futile hope that I would throw in the towel. They had even had the gall to seek through the courts all my medical records. This request, Sir Michael Davies, the judge, threw out, making it clear that they had no right to any of my medical records, and to request all of them was a flagrant abuse of my right to privacy. Content to bump up my costs, Associated Newspapers appealed against the judgement, but the court of appeal threw out their claim and showed its displeasure by relisting the first of my libel actions back to back, instead of in June and October as previously ordered.

This was a disaster for Associated Newspapers. It meant that when I won the first action – and there was never any doubt in anyone's mind that I would if it went to court – the second would be heard either by the same jury, or by a new jury which had read all about the first case in the papers the week before. No jury likes to witness an individual being hounded by a mighty organisation, especially a tabloid newspaper company, so Associated Newspapers were in danger of losing a seven-figure sum in damages, punitive damages and legal costs.

The degree of success they had had with their legal tactics also carried over to their witnesses. In the first action, Peter McKay, the writer whom I was suing for saying twice in his column that I was a man born, raised and actual, tried to wriggle out of the hole he had dug for himself by claiming that Michael Thornton, and not he, was to blame for the information that had led to this libel. Michael Thornton was in fact my stepmother-in-law Margaret Argyll's biographer, and at the time a cordial acquaintance, though not a close friend. So inflamed was he by this treachery that he offered to be a witness for our side, and turned up for the hearing.

I should never have found myself in Court 13 of the High Courts of Justice at the beginning of the second week of June 1995. But Associated Newspapers still hoped that I would turn tail and run, even at this late stage. They had mucked about with a derisory settlement for weeks, so we steamed ahead and I arrived at the court in the Strand to find a solid phalanx of photographers and reporters massed outside.

No sooner had the court been declared to be sitting than Patrick Milmo, my QC, stood up and requested that it be cleared of all journalists. He had legal arguments, interlocutories, to make. The gist of our request was that the first action, against Associated Newspapers, the editor of the *Evening Standard* and the writer Peter McKay, be fused with the second. The second action was also against

Associated Newspapers and the editor of the *Evening Standard*, but had my jerk of an ex-husband as a co-defendant as well. As the first action was based on Peter McKay's assertion that I was a man, and the second on Colin Campbell's claim that I had been born a hermaphrodite with male and female organs and now possessed only of the latter, the quandary facing Associated Newspapers if we succeeded was obvious.

And they could not even rely upon Colin Campbell to appear as a witness. He was ensconced in New York, safely outside the jurisdiction of the British courts. To my side, this was a great pity – within five minutes, Patrick Milmo would have had him bleeding all over the court floor, his lies seeping into every aged crack and crevice. Campbell's witness statement, which was the basis of what he could say in court, was a travesty. He claimed that my mother had told him I had been born with male and female organs. Naturally, Mummy had provided us with an absolute denial in the form of a witness statement, and I had medical reports proving that I am, always was and always will be female. There was therefore no possibility that I could ever have had male organs.

Moreover, he now claimed, ludicrously, that he had known nothing about my gender problem until he read about it in the newspapers. This, of course, was easily disproven. Not only had he connived with his brother to capitalise upon that very problem – and I had the contract he had signed with the *Sunday People* to prove it – but the very first mention of the issue in any newspaper had started with the words 'Lord Colin Campbell last night disclosed . . .'

To cover up for his dishonourable conduct in 1974, Campbell stated that my friend Lady Sarah Spencer-Churchill had sold the article which he and Ian Argyll had placed. This was typical of him: commit the terrible deed and then blame it on someone else. But to choose Sarah was an act of folly. Sarah was the least likely person to need to sell out anyone, enemy or friend, to a gutter-press publication. She had been the main beneficiary of her grandmother,

Consuelo Balsan, who, as Consuelo Vanderbilt, had been the greatest heiress of the *fin de siècle*. I would dearly have loved to have seen Colin Campbell squirm on the stand as he explained why a Vanderbilt heiress would need to sell a lie about a friend of hers to a tabloid newspaper with which the Argyll family had been in cahoots for two generations.

Sadly, it was not to be. After a day of interlocutories, during which Sir Michael Davies ruled in our favour on every point, he adjourned the case for a week. This was because Associated Newspapers claimed that they needed time to dig out of their files their copies of the papers relating to the previous lawsuit I had settled with them in 1977. For three years we had been advising them that we would be including that action, the subsequent settlement and their repeated undertakings not to repeat the libel, as a part of our action, in order to increase the aggravated damages which the jury would award.

By the time we left the court, I was so disgusted by Associated Newspapers' conduct that I would sooner have supped with Stalin than said hello to anyone linked with them. By now they realised they were on a ticket to nowhere, so the following day Harvey Kass, their in-house lawyer, telephoned my lawyer bright and early. His hands were up in the air. Soon my lawyer had him digging them deeply into his pockets. When they were facing damages and costs of well over six figures, and waving around a fulsome and abject apology which would be published in a place of some prominence in the newspaper, along with an accompanying photograph of my choice, I decided to accept their offer of a settlement. This I did with some reluctance, for it entailed dispensing with all my litigation, which meant that my action against Nigel Dempster would never now reach a court.

To be enriched by one's enemies is some compensation for their existence; to have to deal with them is a bore. I was therefore happy to leave my lawyer to settle, with a minimum of reference to me, the last libel action. This was against Express Newspapers, the editor of the *Daily Express*,

Eve Pollard's husband, Nicholas Lloyd, and Colin Campbell. In many respects, the case was similar to the second action against Associated Newspapers. Both articles were virtually identical; both quoted Colin Campbell in full flow. I had also sued the *Daily Express* before, in 1975, and they too had given an undertaking never to repeat the libel. So much for the word of the untrustworthy. Recognising that his company too was facing a massive bill if the case went to trial, Justin Walford, their in-house lawyer, advised them to cough up a sum equally as massive as that spat out by Harvey Kass, and to publish a grovelling apology as well.

Now that justice was finally done, I hoped to settle down to a normal life free of the intrusions and abuses which I had had to endure since the publication of *Diana in Private*. Then Colin Campbell struck again.

Within days of the *Daily Express* settlement, he reported me to the New York Police for having made threatening calls to him over a two-year period – despite having given a statement to Associated Newspapers late in May which made it clear that we had not been in touch with each other for twenty years. 'I thought of the most damaging thing I could do to her, and did it,' he told Michael Thornton, who interviewed him about the report he'd made. 'I want to destroy her. I will not stop until I see her dead.' He then convinced George Rush, a tabloid gossip columnist with the *New York Daily News*, to run the story. The British papers, at long last, knew better than to touch it.

Sick to death though I was of Campbell's never-ending abusiveness, I kept a sense of proportion. This latest claim was only one of a list he had made up about me since the publication of my Diana book. Some allegations were so bizarre that they bordered on the insane. For instance, he had asserted in the Page 6 column of the *New York Post* that I was an agent of Colonel Gaddafi and had been paid by the Libyan dictator to bring down the British monarchy! Later, he would state, also on Page 6 of the *New York Post*, that the Duchess of York had sued me for libel and won $200,000 damages against me! (That one was calculated to stop

American television companies inviting me to appear on talk shows.) Both these stories, which were syndicated throughout the US, were doubtless believed by many readers simply because the source was a British lord (and it was thereafter repeated on American national television news and CNN). Of course, I could have sued, but suing in America is even more expensive than in Britain, especially if you live across the Atlantic, as I do. For that reason, I decided to rise above his ludicrous claims. Nevertheless, I was gratified, when Sarah York wrote her autobiography, to see that she quoted me more frequently and lengthily than any other writer, and that I was the only author she used as an authoritative source for some of the points she wished to make. So much for us being on the outs, or for her suing me.

Within days of the *Daily Express* statement, Campbell telephoned me. 'I've taken out a contract on your life,' he said. 'If you make it difficult for us to reach you, we'll get one of your dogs or those bastards you adopted first.'

'You don't frighten me, you miserable jerk,' I replied, incensed that anyone would ever threaten to kill a child or a dog. 'You want to kill me, come and try it. Just leave my children and dogs out of your sick equation. You really are depraved.'

I hung up and immediately telephoned the police, who filed a report, more as a precaution than anything else. But the odds are that he would never try to carry out his threats – he has no money to hire hitmen; no guts to do it himself. Indeed, I specifically requested that the police took no further action. Otherwise taxpayers' money would have been wasted in initiating proceedings to bring Colin Campbell back to Britain to face the courts, and who needed that fuss?

I had to face the fact that I would never be rid of the malevolent presence of my ex-husband. I had always hoped that he would mellow, or experience a spiritual rebirth; now I can see that he can't help himself. I would either have to endure his continuing abuse or unmask him as the monster he is, and I have opted for the latter course even though doing so means that I am having to violate my privacy in the process. However, as any parent knows, you have a different scale of values once you have children. My children come first, before my privacy, my peace of mind, and certainly my comfort. I will not allow Colin Campbell to taint their lives the way he has done my life. I will not permit him to make them the objects of ridicule and speculation, by cultivating the climate for their friends and schoolmates to ask them embarrassing questions about their mother. I will not allow him to deprive me of the means to earn a decent livelihood, so that they can live in the comfort and security that they deserve.

Unless I clear up the lies and misconceptions with which Colin Campbell has warped my life in his quest for my destruction, I will never be free of the aura of doubt or the salacious speculation which he has so diligently worked to create around me. And if I don't clear it up, my children will suffer. I live in hope that once the public's curiosity is satisfied, I will be allowed to lead my life in peace, free from the invasiveness that has characterised so much of it.

There is no doubt that the perimeter of my life has been invaded by the presence of such destructive elements as Colin Campbell, the tabloids and the odd opportunist posing as a friend. Those Nemeses aside, the core is sound, and it really is a good life. I have two wonderful children, four lovely dogs, a large and loyal family, good friends. I have a lovely home in the country; a charming house with a sweet garden in town. This I spent nearly a year doing up from top to bottom, and we moved into it recently. I am only sorry that my brother Mickey is not here to see that I finally found a house round the corner from where I have lived for years. But I confidently expect to have the satisfaction of being able to tell him one day.

Standing back to write about my life, I have enough objectivity to see that it has been an extraordinary one by any standards. It has taught me how lucky I am to have been born into a sound and sensible family, to have been born with a happy and loving nature, to have been blessed with a good mind. No matter what privileges each of us has, life throws us brickbats. I am supremely grateful that I learned so young that one of the secrets is to turn each negative into a positive, each destructive experience into a constructive lesson. This world is full of wonderful people, but it also has its fair share of venomous creatures who derive satisfaction from destroying the lives, chances, personalities or reputations of others. Experience has taught me that the rules of the animal kingdom prevail as much in the world of *homo sapiens* as they do in the jungle. Some animals help those in trouble, others ignore or devour them. As I look back, I can see many instances when people offered me a helping hand. I can also see the many sharks that circled, thinking there was blood in the water when all it was was a bottle of red ink.

However, these people have not succeeded in impoverishing my life, nuisance though they can be. One of our greatest gifts is knowledge, and any experience that does not end in death, any person who does not destroy you, can enrich your life. By that yardstick, I am a very wealthy woman indeed, for I have not only had adversaries who sought to devour me by confusing a source of strength with a sign of weakness, but also friends and relations who have supported me with love, compassion, kindness, understanding and companionship. I have undoubtedly had my fair share of pleasure, privilege, pain and poignancy, but as I look back on the rich tapestry of a life that was, in many ways, foisted upon me because of both the advantages and the disadvantages of my birth, I can only say that I am grateful for all of it. It has not always been easy, but everything has worked out for my ultimate good.